First World War
and Army of Occupation
War Diary
France, Belgium and Germany

60 DIVISION
181 Infantry Brigade
Headquarters
14 June 1916 - 30 November 1916

WO95/3032/2

Published by

The Naval & Military Press Ltd

Unit 10 Ridgewood Industrial Park,

Uckfield, East Sussex,

TN22 5QE England

Tel: +44 (0) 1825 749494

www.naval-military-press.com

www.nmarchive.com

This diary has been reprinted in facsimile from the original. Any imperfections are inevitably reproduced and the quality may fall short of modern type and cartographic standards.

© **Crown Copyright**
Images reproduced by permission of The National Archives, London, England, 2015.

Contents

Document type	Place/Title	Date From	Date To
Heading	WO95/3032/2		
Heading	60th Division 181st Infy Bde Bde Headquarters Jun-Nov 1916		
Heading	War Diary of 181st Infantry Brigade June 1916 Vol. 1 No.1		
War Diary	Sutton Veny	14/06/1916	24/06/1916
War Diary	Havre France	25/06/1916	25/06/1916
War Diary	Havre & Train	26/06/1916	26/06/1916
War Diary	Buneville	27/06/1916	27/06/1916
War Diary	Chelers	28/06/1916	30/06/1916
Heading	Appendix I to War Diary of 181st Infantry Brigade June 1916		
Miscellaneous	Brigade Notes For Entrainment	16/06/1916	16/06/1916
Miscellaneous	Railway Time-Table		
Miscellaneous	Table For Arrival Of Units At Station	24/06/1916	24/06/1916
Miscellaneous	Instructions Re Entraining for H.Q. 181st Infantry Bde. No. 4 Section 60th Div. Sig Coy and 520th Coy Divisional Train	23/06/1916	23/06/1916
Miscellaneous	Overseas Move Loading Time Table And Grouping-Tuesday June 20th Saturday June 24th Inclusive-Fresh Rations	20/06/1916	20/06/1916
Miscellaneous	Overseas Rations		
Miscellaneous	Order Of Embarkation-60th Division		
Miscellaneous	Notes For Entrainment Part I-General	15/06/1916	15/06/1916
Heading	Appendix II to War Diary of 181st Infantry Brigade June 1916		
Miscellaneous	181st Inf Bde Order No. 1	27/06/1916	27/06/1916
Heading	Appendix III to War Diary of 181st Infantry Brigade June 1916		
Operation(al) Order(s)	181st Infantry Brigade Order No. 3	28/06/1916	28/06/1916
Heading	181st Infantry Brigade War Diary 1st-31st July 1916 Vol. 2		
War Diary	Chelers	01/07/1916	12/07/1916
War Diary	Chelers To Etrun	13/07/1916	13/07/1916
War Diary	Etrun	14/07/1916	31/07/1916
Heading	Attached to 181st Infantry Brigade War Diary for July 1916 Operation Order No.4		
Operation(al) Order(s)	181st Infantry Brigade Order No. 4	04/07/1916	04/07/1916
Heading	Attached to 181st Infantry Brigade War Diary for July 1916 Battalion Relief		
Operation(al) Order(s)	181st Infantry Brigade Order No. 5	12/07/1916	12/07/1916
Miscellaneous	181st Infantry Brigade Order No. 5	12/07/1916	12/07/1916
Heading	Attached to 181st Infantry Brigade War Diary for July 1916 Inter-Orders Battalion Relief No. 1		
Operation(al) Order(s)	181st Infantry Brigade Order No. 5	15/07/1916	15/07/1916
Miscellaneous	Table Of Relief 181st Infantry Brigade	15/07/1916	15/07/1916
Heading	Attached to 181st Infantry Brigade War Diary for July 1916 Inter-Battalion Relief No. II		
Operation(al) Order(s)	181st Infantry Brigade Order No. 7	19/07/1916	19/07/1916
Miscellaneous	Table Of Relief 181st Infantry Brigade	19/07/1916	19/07/1916

Heading	Attached to 181st Infantry Brigade War Diary for July 1916. Order for Bombardment 23-7-16		
Operation(al) Order(s)	181st Infantry Brigade Order No. 8	22/07/1916	22/07/1916
Miscellaneous	Daily Intelligence Summary 181st Infantry Brigade	24/07/1916	24/07/1916
Heading	Attached to 181st Infantry Brigade War Diary for July 1916 Inter-Battalion Relief No. 3		
Operation(al) Order(s)	181st Infantry Brigade Order No. 9	27/07/1916	27/07/1916
Miscellaneous	Table Of Relief 181st Infantry Brigade	25/07/1916	25/07/1916
Heading	181st Infantry Brigade War Diary 1st-31st August 1916 Vol No 3		
War Diary	Etrun	01/08/1916	31/08/1916
Heading	181st Infantry Brigade War Diary 1st 31st Aug. / 16 Relief Orders Nos 10, 12, 13 & 15 Vol. I No. 3		
Operation(al) Order(s)	181st Infantry Brigade Order No. 10	03/08/1916	03/08/1916
Miscellaneous	Table Of Relief 181st Infantry Brigade	03/08/1916	03/08/1916
Operation(al) Order(s)	181st Infantry Brigade Order No. 12	11/08/1916	11/08/1916
Miscellaneous	Table Of Relief 181st Infantry Brigade	11/08/1916	11/08/1916
Operation(al) Order(s)	181st Infantry Brigade Order No. 13	19/08/1916	19/08/1916
Operation(al) Order(s)	181st Infantry Brigade Order No, 15	26/08/1916	26/08/1916
Heading	181st Infantry Brigade War Diary 1st-31st Aug/ 16 Raid By 2/23 London Regt. Vol. I No, 3		
Miscellaneous	Description Of The Raid Carried Out By The 2/23 London Regt.		
Operation(al) Order(s)	181st Infantry Brigade Order No. 11	06/08/1916	06/08/1916
Miscellaneous	181st Infantry Brigade	04/08/1916	04/08/1916
Miscellaneous	Details Of The Raid Itself Timetable Of Same	07/08/1916	07/08/1916
Miscellaneous	Information As Regards The Raid Up To Date	08/08/1916	08/08/1916
Miscellaneous	181st Infantry Brigade 2 T.M.Battery (z.60)		
Miscellaneous	181st Infantry Brigade 3" Stokes Guns		
Miscellaneous	Officer Commanding	08/08/1916	08/08/1916
Heading	181st Infantry Brigade War Diary 1st-31st Aug. 16 Raid By 2/24 Lond Regt Vol. I No. 3.		
Miscellaneous	Headquarters 60th (London) Divn.	29/08/1916	29/08/1916
Miscellaneous	Story of the Raid Made by The 2/24th Lond R. on Night of 28/29th August 1916	29/08/1916	29/08/1916
Miscellaneous	Time Table Of Raid By 2/24th Lond R On Night Of 28/29th August 1916	29/08/1916	29/08/1916
Miscellaneous	On No Account Is Any Telephone		
Operation(al) Order(s)	181st Infantry Brigade Order No. 14	25/08/1916	25/08/1916
Miscellaneous	Scheme For Trench Mortar Co-Operation		
Miscellaneous	Copies		
Miscellaneous	Please Make The Following amendment to your copy of orders issued by O.C. 2/24th London Regt. For raid to take place on night 28/29th August 1916		
Miscellaneous	Raid By 2/24th London Regiment	25/08/1916	25/08/1916
Heading	181st Infantry Brigade War Diary 1st-30th September 1916 Vol. I No. 4		
War Diary	Etrun	01/09/1916	30/09/1916
Heading	181st Infantry Brigade War Diary 1st-30th September 1916 Raid By 2/22 London Regt. Vol. I No.4		
Operation(al) Order(s)	181st Infantry Brigade Operation Order No. 17	02/09/1916	02/09/1916
Miscellaneous	Scheme For Trench Mortar Co-Operation		
Miscellaneous	Amendment	03/09/1916	03/09/1916
Heading	181st Infantry Brigade War Diary 1st-30th September 1916 Reliefs Vol I No. 4		
Operation(al) Order(s)	181st Infantry Brigade Order No. 16	02/09/1916	02/09/1916

Type	Description	Date From	Date To
Operation(al) Order(s)	181st Infantry Brigade Order No. 18	08/09/1916	08/09/1916
Operation(al) Order(s)	181st Infantry Brigade Order No. 19	14/09/1916	14/09/1916
Operation(al) Order(s)	181st Infantry Brigade Order No. 20	20/09/1916	20/09/1916
Operation(al) Order(s)	181st Infantry Brigade Order No. 21	26/09/1916	26/09/1916
Heading	181st Infantry Brigade War Diary 1st-30th September 1916 Carrying Parties-Gas Installation Vol. I No. 4		
Miscellaneous	Addenda to The 2/21 Lond R.	03/09/1916	03/09/1916
Miscellaneous	181st Infantry Brigade Gas Installation Instructions To 2/21st Lond R/	04/09/1916	04/09/1916
Miscellaneous	Orders For Guides		
Miscellaneous	Trench Picquets	04/09/1915	04/09/1915
Miscellaneous	Gas Installation Instructions to 2/21th Lond. R.		
Miscellaneous	Addenda (to 2/22 Lond R.)	05/09/1916	05/09/1916
Miscellaneous	181st Infantry Brigade Gas Installation Instructions To 2/22 Lond. R.		
Miscellaneous	Orders For Guides	05/09/1916	05/09/1916
Miscellaneous	Trench Picquets	05/09/1916	05/09/1916
Miscellaneous	181st Infantry Brigade Gas Installation Instructions To 2/23 Lond R.	06/09/1916	06/09/1916
Miscellaneous	Routes For Carrying Parties		
Miscellaneous	Instructions for Guides for 180th Infantry Brigade		
Miscellaneous	Time Table		
Heading	181st Infantry Brigade War Diary 1st-30th September 1916 Raid By 2/21 London Regt. Vol. I No. 4		
Miscellaneous	Raid By 2/21 Lond. Regt. On Night Of 23/24 Sept 1916		
Miscellaneous	Headquarters 60th (London) Divn, "G"	24/09/1916	24/09/1916
Heading	HQ 181 Infy Bde Vol 5		
Miscellaneous	D.A.G. 3rd Echelon Base		
Heading	181st Infantry Brigade War Diary From 1st October 1916 To 31st October 1916 Vol I No. 5		
War Diary	Etrun	01/10/1916	24/10/1916
War Diary	Etrun Ivergny	25/10/1916	25/10/1916
War Diary	Ivergny	26/10/1916	27/10/1916
War Diary	Ivergny Occoches	28/10/1916	28/10/1916
War Diary	Occoches Fienvillers	29/10/1916	29/10/1916
War Diary	Fienvillers	30/10/1916	31/10/1916
Heading	181st Infantry Brigade War Diary 1st-31st October 1916 Inter Battalion Reliefs Vol I No. 5		
Operation(al) Order(s)	181st Infantry Brigade Order No. 22	02/10/1916	02/10/1916
Operation(al) Order(s)	181st Infantry Brigade Order No. 23	08/10/1916	08/10/1916
Operation(al) Order(s)	181st Infantry Brigade Order No. 24	14/10/1916	14/10/1916
Heading	181st Infantry Brigade War Diary 1st-31st October 1916 Raid By 2/22 London Regt. Vol I. No.5		
Operation(al) Order(s)	2/22 London Regiment Operations Order No. 1	07/10/1916	07/10/1916
Miscellaneous	Preliminary Report Of The 2/22 Lond. R. Raid On 8th Oct/16	16/10/1916	16/10/1916
Miscellaneous	Supplementary To Preliminary Report	09/10/1916	09/10/1916
Miscellaneous	Headquarters 60th (London) Divn. "G"	09/10/1916	09/10/1916
Miscellaneous	2/22 London Regiment Appendix "A"		
Heading	181st Infantry Brigade War Diary (Tactical) 1st-31st October 1916 Vol I No. 5		
Miscellaneous	Weekly Intelligence Summary Of 181st Infantry Brigade	10/10/1916	10/10/1916
Miscellaneous	Daily Intelligence Summary Of 181st Infantry Brigade	10/10/1916	10/10/1916
Miscellaneous	Daily Intelligence Summary Of 181st Infantry Brigade	11/10/1916	11/10/1916

Miscellaneous	Daily Intelligence Summary Of 181st Infantry Brigade	12/10/1916	12/10/1916
Miscellaneous	Daily Intelligence Summary Of 181st Infantry Brigade	13/10/1916	13/10/1916
Miscellaneous	Daily Intelligence Summary Of 181st Infantry Brigade	14/10/1916	14/10/1916
Operation(al) Order(s)	181st Infantry Brigade Order No. 24	14/10/1916	14/10/1916
Miscellaneous	Daily Intelligence Summary Of 181st Infantry Brigade	15/10/1916	15/10/1916
Miscellaneous	Daily Intelligence Summary Of 181st Infantry Brigade	16/10/1916	16/10/1916
Miscellaneous	Weekly Intelligence Summary Of 181st Infantry Brigade	17/10/1916	17/10/1916
Miscellaneous	Daily Intelligence Summary Of 181st Infantry Brigade	17/10/1916	17/10/1916
Miscellaneous	Daily Intelligence Summary Of 181st Infantry Brigade	18/10/1916	18/10/1916
Miscellaneous	Daily Intelligence Summary Of 181st Infantry Brigade	19/10/1916	19/10/1916
Miscellaneous	Daily Intelligence Summary Of 181st Infantry Brigade	20/10/1916	20/10/1916
Miscellaneous	Daily Intelligence Summary Of 181st Infantry Brigade	21/10/1916	21/10/1916
Miscellaneous	Daily Intelligence Summary Of 181st Infantry Brigade	22/10/1916	22/10/1916
Miscellaneous	Daily Intelligence Summary Of 181st Infantry Brigade	23/10/1916	23/10/1916
Miscellaneous	Daily Intelligence Summary Of 181st Infantry Brigade	24/10/1916	24/10/1916
Heading	181st Infantry Brigade War Diary 1st-31st October 1916 Raid By 2/23 London Regt Vol. I No. 5		
Operation(al) Order(s)	2/23 London Regiment Order No. 1	14/10/1916	14/10/1916
Miscellaneous	Report Of Raid Made By The 2/23rd Battalion The London Regt	15/10/1916	15/10/1916
Heading	181st Infantry Brigade War Diary 1st-31st October 1916 Divisional Relief Vol. I No. 5		
Operation(al) Order(s)	181st Infantry Brigade Order No. 25	21/10/1916	21/10/1916
Miscellaneous	Relief Of 181st Infantry Brigade By 8th Canadian Infantry Brigade		
Miscellaneous	The Following Amendments Will Be Made To 181st Infantry Brigade Order No. 25	22/10/1916	22/10/1916
Miscellaneous	Move Of 181st Infantry Brigade To New Area		
Miscellaneous	Billeting Arrangements		
Miscellaneous	G.S./392/14	23/10/1916	23/10/1916
Miscellaneous	Brigade Major	23/10/1916	23/10/1916
Miscellaneous	Use Of Lorries	23/10/1916	23/10/1916
Miscellaneous	Brigade Major	23/10/1916	23/10/1916
Miscellaneous	Use Of Lorries	23/10/1916	23/10/1916
Operation(al) Order(s)	181st Infantry Brigade Order No. 26	26/10/1916	26/10/1916
Miscellaneous	March Table-181st Infantry Brigade		
Miscellaneous	Billeting Table-181st Infantry Brigade		
Miscellaneous	To O.C. 3/3 Field Co. R.E.		
Operation(al) Order(s)	181st Infantry Brigade Order No. 27	28/10/1916	28/10/1916
Miscellaneous	March Table-181st Infantry Brigade		
Miscellaneous	Table "B"		
Miscellaneous	A Form Messages And Signals		
Operation(al) Order(s)	181st Infantry Brigade Order No. 28	29/10/1916	29/10/1916
Miscellaneous	Table "B"		
Heading	181st Infantry Brigade War Diary From 1st November 1916 To 30th November 1916 Vol. I No. 5		
War Diary	Fienvillers	01/11/1916	03/11/1916
War Diary	Fienvillers Brucamps	04/11/1916	04/11/1916
War Diary	Brucamps	05/11/1916	22/11/1916
War Diary	Brucamps Longpre	23/11/1916	23/11/1916
War Diary	En Route	24/11/1916	24/11/1916
War Diary	En Route Marseilles	25/11/1916	25/11/1916
War Diary	Marseilles	26/11/1916	30/11/1916

Heading	181st Infantry Brigade Appendix To War Diary For November 1916 Orders For Move To New Area Vol I No. 6		
Operation(al) Order(s)	181st Infantry Brigade Order No. 29	02/11/1916	02/11/1916
Miscellaneous	Billeting Table		
Operation(al) Order(s)	181st Infantry Brigade Order No. 30	02/11/1916	02/11/1916
Miscellaneous	Billeting Table		
Miscellaneous	Addenda A To 181st Infantry Brigade Order No. 30	03/11/1916	03/11/1916
Miscellaneous	Addenda B To 181st Infantry Brigade Order No. 30	03/11/1916	03/11/1916
Heading	181st Infantry Brigade Appendix II To War Diary For November 1916 Orders For Entrainments For Marseilles On 23rd & 24th Nov / 16 Vol I No, 6		
Miscellaneous	G.S.104	21/11/1916	21/11/1916
Miscellaneous	G.S.104/1	12/01/1916	12/01/1916
Miscellaneous	Programme of Entrainment	23/11/1916	23/11/1916
Miscellaneous	Table Of Personnel Animals And Vehicles	23/11/1916	23/11/1916
Miscellaneous	G.S.104/2	22/11/1916	22/11/1916
Miscellaneous	Programme of Entrainment	24/11/1916	24/11/1916
Miscellaneous	Table Of Personnel Animals And Vehicles	24/11/1916	24/11/1916
Heading	181st Infantry Brigade Appendix III To War Diary For November 1916 Programme Of Training Vol I No. 6		
Miscellaneous	Instructions Regarding Training Issued in Connection with 60th Divn. No. S.G./391	22/10/1916	22/10/1916
Miscellaneous	Suggested Daily Time Table		
Miscellaneous	H.Q. 60th Divn "G" In 10.11.16	08/11/1916	08/11/1916
Miscellaneous	Headquarters 60th (London) Divn "G"	04/11/1916	04/11/1916

WO 95/3032/2

60TH DIVISION
181ST INFY BDE

BDE HEADQUARTERS
JUN - NOV 1916

60TH DIVISION
181ST INFY BDE

SECRET.

W A R   D I A R Y

OF

181ST INFANTRY BRIGADE.

June, 1916.

VOL. I,
NO. I.

WAR DIARY

OF 181st INFANTRY BRIGADE
60th (LONDON) DIVISION

INTELLIGENCE SUMMARY

Army Form C. 2118.

Instructions regarding War Diaries and Intelligence Summaries are contained in F.S. Regs., Part II. and the Staff Manual respectively. Title pages will be prepared in manuscript.

(Erase heading not required.)

For details of move see APPENDIX I.

Place	Date	Hour	Summary of Events and Information	Remarks and references to Appendices
SUTTON VENY	14-6-16		Divnl letter S/399 d 14-6-16 re ORDER of EMBARKATION received. Capt. BEVINGTON 2/22	
			Bn 1 R & CRABBE 2/23 Bn LR leave for overseas in connection with disembarkation & entrainment	Jn-42
	15-6-16		1st day of embarkation. Divnl letter Q/540 re notes for entrainment received. Bde instructions issued in accordance	Jn-42
"	16-6-16		2nd day of embarkation.	
"	17-6-16		3rd " " " . Capt BM EDWARDS, Staff Captain, leaves for overseas for billeting duties	Jn-42
"	18-6-16		4th " " " . Divnl letter S.1.Q1 re Railway time table received.	Jn-42
"	19-6-16		5th " " " . Divnl Train letter C/155 re ration loading time table received	Jn-42
"	20-6-16		6th " " " . Draft received from 1/1st Huntingdon Cyclists, 13 men to 2/21 Bn LR, 12 men to 2/22 Bn & 13 Bn LR	Jn-42
"	21-6-16		7th " " " . Authority received for taking officers up to 34 in number overseas	Jn-42
"	22-6-16		8th " " " . On departure of G.O.C. 60th London Divn. Brig Gen C Mc N Parsons C.B. takes over	Jn-42
"			Command of the Divnl details still to go.	
"	23-6-16		9th day of embarkation. Final Preparations	
"	24-6-16		The Brigade Commenced to entrain for overseas. departure of 181 Inf BDE HQ 2/21, 2/22 Bn LONS. R.	Jn-42
			520 Coy Divnl Train. All entraining was excellently carried out & all trains started well before	
			Scheduled time. Bde HQ & 520 Coy Div Tr. Embarked on S.S. ROSSETTI at SOUTHAMPTON at about 6.30 pm	

A very stormy day wind SW.

WAR DIARY of 181st INF BDE.

INTELLIGENCE SUMMARY.

Army Form C. 2118.

Place	Date	Hour	Summary of Events and Information	Remarks and references to Appendices
HAVRE FRANCE	25-6-16		Ship arrives HAVRE 6 a.m. disembarkation commenced 7 a.m. Troops moved up to No 1 Rest Camp and rested that day. BRIG: visited 2/21 2/22 B'ns L R at No 5 Rest Camp. 2/23, 2/24 B'ns LOND. R. leave WARMINSTER. Weather fine & warm	JHZ
HAVRE & train	26-6-16		BRIG: visits 2/23 & 2/24 B'ns LOND R at No 5 Rest Camp. entrain at POINT I. Commencing noon. train left 2.46 P.M. Details on board. HQ 181 INF BDE. 520 COY DIV T'P: 60 DIV CYCLIST Total 20 Offrs 260 O.R. 73 Horses 17 wagons. Train shunted from 6 pm - 7 pm near MAROMME ½ hour Halts at BRUGIS 9.50 pm - 10.26 pm & ABBEVILLE 4.25 am - 4.55 am. Detrained at ST POL at 7.45 am. met by STAFF CAPTAIN. Troops less Cyclists march to billets at CHELERS BRIG & BDE MAJOR proceed to BDE HQ, BUNEVILLE. 2/21 & 2/22 B'ns LOND. R billeted at ECOIVRES & BUNEVILLE respectively. Orders for move to fresh area issued. ST: CAPT proceeds to foot of area to allot billets. B'de H.Q. opens at CHELERS at 5 p.m. 2/23 & 2/24 B'n LOND R detrain at PETIT HOUVIN & ST POL respectively & march into billets at VILLERS BRULIN & CHELERS. 12.50 PM 2.30 P.M. HQ 301 FAB & A BATTY remain at GOUY-EN-TERNOIS. All other units in area by 8.30 P.M. Weather cool & gusty. Wind SW.	APP II JHZ
BUNEVILLE	27-6-16			

WAR DIARY
INTELLIGENCE SUMMARY
181 INF BDE.

Army Form C. 2118.

Place	Date	Hour	Summary of Events and Information	Remarks and references to Appendices
CHELERS	28.6.16		Numerous secret papers received from 51st HIGHLAND DIV our G.S.I. Maps received & issued all Bns resting. Orders received & issued re move of 2/21 & 2/22 Bns LOND R up to forward area to be attached to 154 INF BDE for instruction. Weather wet & squally. Wind SW	APP III Mtz
"	29.6.16		Lecture to officers of 2/23 2/24 Bns LR by Corps Cdr SIR CHARLES FERGUSSON on discipline etc. Explanation of front trenches by B.G.G.S. CHARLES. 2/23 2/24 Bns proceed marching astray met fighting. 181 MG Coy arrive TINQUES & are billeted at HERLIN LE VERT. 1000 gas helmets received for instructional purpose. Secret order No 30 received from 154 INF BDE. 2/21 & 2/22 LOND R move up to forward area for instruction by 154 INF BDE. Weather wet and gusty. Wind SW.	APP IV Mtz
"	30.6.16		2/23 2/24 Bns continue training in back area. Brig Gen PARSONS CB BDE MAJOR & SIGNALLING OFFICER proceed at 4.30 PM to 154 INF BDE HQ. ½ No 4 Sec Sig Coy ordered to move up to 154 INF BDE area for attachment on 1-7-16. Weather fine SW wind. 1 Offr 3 OR each 2/23 2/24 LR attend TM school at LIGNY-ST FLOCHEL till 4-7-16. 1 Offr 2 NCOs per Coy 2/23 2/24 LOND R commence Grenade course 51 Div at HERMAVILLE till 6-7-16	Mtz

MOVE OVERSEAS.

SECRET.

APPENDIX I

to

WAR DIARY

of

181ST INFANTRY BRIGADE.

June, 1916.

BRIGADE NOTES FOR ENTRAINMENT

Ref. Divisional Letter Q/540 dated 15-6-16.

PART 1. GENERAL

1. Each Battalion will detail an Officer to take over the Unit's train. If the Battalion travels by more than one train, one Officer per train will be detailed. This Officer should be Senior, and will be in charge of the train from the moment he takes it over to the time the troops detrain (Vide Divisional letter) In England, after detrainment; he will again go over the train with a Railway Official, and note any damage done en route. The same Officer should be employed overseas. On completion, he will render a report to Brigade Headquarters as to how all details of the journey were carried out, noting hour and times of detrainment, detrainment of personnel, horses, baggage, and notes of anything that he may consider important.

2. All ranks should be carefully informed of all details as regards the entraining and disentraining routine.

3. O.C. Units will render a Marching out State to a Brigade representative on reaching WARMINSTER Station. A Marching in State will be rendered to Brigade Headquarters immediately on arrival at the detraining place overseas. *R.T.O.*

4. Each Unit will arrange for its Military Police, under an Officer, to be detailed to control traffic at the Railway Station, whilst troops are entraining. A carriage must be set apart for the men thus employed. Further details as to this para. will be issued later.

5. O.C. Units to arrange for the necessary labels, as mentioned in the Divisional letter (Colour Blue)

PART II. TRANSPORT

1. Attention is called to para. b, Divisional Letter.
These Officers and men must be detailed immediately the number of trains allotted to the Unit is known.

2. O.C. Units will make arrangements for their Transport Officers to be present during the entrainment of one of the Infantry Units of the 180th. Infantry Brigade.

3. Special attention is drawn to para. (h).

4. Baggage wagons of units will join their respective units on the day prior to entraining, and will move to the Station with the Units' 1st. Line Transport. The horses of these wagons will be picketted out. O.C. Units will make arrangements for accommodation for the drivers.

PART 111. RATIONS

1. A time table re the issuing of the Baggage & Supply Wagons is to be forwarded to this office by the O.C. Divisional Train, and on receipt, Units will be notified.

2. Attention is drawn to the fact that each trainload must be self contained as regards messing arrangements. O.C. Units should warn Officers that suitable arrangements must be made as to their messing up to their arrival at the concentration area overseas.

(Signed) J.M.HOMLICK
Captain,
Brigade Major,
181st. Infantry Brigade.

Sutton Veny,
16-6-16.

SECRET

RAILWAY TIME-TABLE

181st INFANTRY BDE.

Train No.	UNITS	Officers	Other Ranks	Horses	Guns	Veh. 6-wh.	Veh. 2-wh.	Bicycles	From	To	Starting Time. June	Starting Time	Arrival June	Arrival Time
X.1194 X.1196	2/21st Ldn. Regt.	17 17	498 497	32 32	-- --	9 8	2 2	-- --	WARMINSTER	SOUTHAMPTON Dks.	24th "	10.5am 11.30am	24th "	12.10 p.m. 1.30 p.m.
X.1298 X.1300	2/22nd Ldn. Regt.	17 17	498 497	32 32	-- --	9 8	2 2	-- --	" "	" "	" "	12.20pm 1.30pm	" "	2.30 p.m. 3.45 p.m.
X.1202	(H.Q. 181st Infy. Bde (Section Div. Sig.Coy. (Coy. Div. Train	7 1 4	27 26 56	26 6 29	-- -- --	6 1 5	1 1 1	4 -- 4	"	"	} 25th {	3. 0pm	"	5.10 p.m.
X.1612 X.1614	2/23rd Ldn. Regt.	17 17	498 497	32 32	-- --	9 8	2 2	-- --	" "	" "	25th "	11. 5am 12.20pm	25th "	1.15 p.m. 2.30 p.m.
X.1616 X.1618	2/24th Ldn. Regt.	17 17	498 497	32 32	-- --	9 8	2 2	-- --	" "	" "	" "	1.40pm 3. 0pm	" "	3.50 p.m. 5.10 p.m.

NOTE - It is most important that the train loads, and that the units specified as allotted to each train, upon which the Embarkation Staff base their arrangements in allotting troops to ships are very strictly adhered to. Any discrepancy between the authorised train load and the numbers arriving in the train leads to complication, inconvenience and discomfort to the troops, and delay in embarkation.

SUBJECT :- Move Overseas

1. Table for arrival of Units at station.

June 24th.

Unit	Transport	Troops
1st ½ 2/21st.Bn.L.R.	8-35 a.m.	9-20 a.m.
2nd.½ 2/21st.Bn.L.R.	9-50 a.m.	10-35 a.m.
1st ½ 2/22nd.Bn.L.R.	10-50 a.m.	11-35 a.m.
2nd.½ 2/22nd.Bn.L.R.	12- 5 p.m.	12-50 p.m.
H.Q. 181st.Inf.Bde. }		
No.4 Sec.Div.Sig.Coy.}	1-30 p.m.	All Troops of this train arrive with the Transport
520 Coy.Div.Train }		

June 25th.

1st.½ 2/23rd.Bn.L.R.	9-35 a.m.	10-20 a.m.
2nd.½ 2/23rd.Bn.L.R.	10-50 a.m.	11-35 a.m.
1st.½ 2/24th.Bn.L.R.	12-10 p.m.	12-55 p.m.
2nd.½ 2/24th.Bn.L.R.	1-30 p.m.	2-15 p.m.

O.C. Units will arrange to leave their respective Camps so as to arrive at the station at the times laid down above. The O.C. No. 4 Sec. Div. Sig. Coy. will march to Brigade Headquarters, No. 2 Camp, arriving there at 11 a.m., preparatory to moving.

2. Table of Fatigue Parties needed for entraining

(a) Infantry Trainload (½ Battalion)
1. 1 Officer i/c Train & 1 N.C.O.Assistant.
2. 1 Officer & 6 N.C.O's & men for control of traffic in and around station.
3. 1 Officer, 1 Sergt. & sufficient men with the drivers to supply 1 man to each horse, for loading horses, 52 in number
4. 1 Officer, 3 N.C.O's & 30 men to load vehicles.
The Officer i/c Train will arrange for the carriages marked for these fatigue parties to be in the rear of the train.
The compartments for police & prisoners and stretcher bearers & sick should be next to the fatigue men's carriages.
The two compartments next to the engine must be left unoccupied, and the doors kept locked.

3. Documents needed at entrainment station:-
(a) Warrant.
(b) March out state to be handed to R.T.O. at station.

4. For Table of Fatigue Parties needed for detrainment and embarkation, see instructions for entrainment and embarkation, Part 1, page 5.
For Returns needed see page 6.

5. Special attention is drawn to Instructions for the Voyage &c., &c., Part 11, for procedure on board ship & on arrival overseas.

6. In the compiling of nominal rolls of Officers, Units must be most careful to comply strictly with the orders & specimen copies as laid down in W.O.letter 100/G.M/2804 (A53) dated 24-9-15 issued to Units from this Office dated 20-4-16.

- 2 -

7. Complete Table of Returns to be rendered before, during and after the journey.

   (a) **Before Leaving.**

   1. Nominal Roll of all Officers of Unit, showing name & address of next of kin - to War Office.
   2. Nominal Roll of all Officers, Warrant Officers, N.C.Os. and men of Unit - to Officer i/c Records. This should show next of kin.

   (b) **At Entraining Station.**

   3. Warrant for train-load.
   4. Marching-out State to R.T.O.

   (c) **On Detraining.**

   5. Statement showing number of train-load to be handed by Senior Officer of train to Embarkation Officer.
   6. Shortage Return, showing any shortage from the standard allotment of the train-load, expressed in terms of "Officers", "Other Ranks", "Horses" and "Prs. of Wheels", to be handed to Embarkation Officer.

   (d) **On the Ship.**

   7. Landing Return, showing the actual number of all ranks of Unit that will land, casualties of journey to be shown, & details of casualties on the back. Attached to this a Nominal Roll of the Officers of the Unit actually landing with the Unit. This to be handed to the Military Officer commanding the ship.

   (e) **On Disembarkation.**

   8. Nominal Roll of Officers of the Unit to Disembarking Staff Officer for transmission to A.G., G.H.Q.; for this return see W.O.Letter 100/G.M./2804 (A.G.3.) d/24.9.15.

   9. Nominal Roll of Officers, Warrant Officers, N.C.Os. & men with each man's A.F.B.103 attached. (No. 2 return is a copy of this one, less A.F.B.103). These documents are taken by the Orderly Room Sergeant or other N.C.O. who proceeds from the Unit to join the A.G's. Office at the base, if possible, otherwise they are forwarded by post addressed to
   This should show A.A.G. i/c Records,
   next of kin. General Headquarters, 3rd Echelon,
   (A.G's. Office at the Base.)

   (f) **On arrival at Concentration Area.**

   10. Marching-in State to be rendered to Bde.H.Q. immediately on arrival at detraining station.

NOTES. In Nos. 1, 2, 8 & 9 all Officers, N.C.Os. & men proceeding overseas who are not actually seconded to another Unit must be shown. Any ranks only temporarily attached to another Unit must be shown, e.g. an officer or man temporarily attached for the voyage to Bde. H.Q. should be shown by the Unit on these returns and not by Bde.H.Q. Similarly in the case of No. 9 return, the A.F.B.103 of a man temporarily attached to Bde. H.Q. will be handed in by the Unit he belongs to.
In the case of No. 7 however, the Nominal Roll attached to the Landing Return, shows only the actual officers of the Unit crossing on the Boat with the Unit, so that in this return, if an officer is attached for the journey to Bde.H.Q. he will be shown on the Nominal Roll handed in by the Bde.H.Q. and not on that of his actual Unit even if it be the same boat.

Contd.

8. On landing overseas, when moving through the town, the greatest care must be exercised by Drivers whilst moving over "Pavée". This type of road is most slippery and Transport Officers should be warned to caution their men to use extreme care, especially whilst turning corners. Horses must <u>not</u> be swung sharply round them. It is also absolutely forbidden for Transport to move at any rate faster than a walk.

9. The attention of Os.C. Units is drawn to the great necessity of seeing that all ranks promptly and accurately carry out any orders that may be given them during the journey. Orders as to non-smoking as when below decks on the voyage must be rigidly enforced. Exact punctuality must be insisted on. Men both before embarkation and after disembarkation must not be allowed to wander away on their own.

10. As the Censor Stamps for Units will not be received till arrival overseas, it is probable that the men will only be able to send off F.S.Postcards. These can be obtained at any Rest Camp. Men should be cautioned that it is a serious crime to send off letters from a civilian Post Office & that all civilian mails are searched for these sort of letters.

11. Under no circumstances are men allowed to give away their badges or buttons as souvenirs. This is a very common practice, and must not be allowed to commence in the Brigade. Offenders should be very severely dealt with.

INSTRUCTIONS RE ENTRAINING FOR H.Q., 181st INFANTRY BDE.,
No. 4 SECTION, 60th DIV. SIG. COY., and 520th COY.,
DIVISIONAL TRAIN.

1. The Personnel and Transport of the H.Q. 181st Infantry Brigade (less the 3 Chaplains and their Batmen) and No. 4 Sec. Div.Sig.Coy. will parade on the parade ground just north of Bde. H.Q. at 12.10 p.m. when the final roll call will be carried out. The Unit will then move off to the Station. All details as to labelling, marking of horses and kits to be complete on this parade.

2. The O.C. 520th Coy. Div. Train will make his own arrangements as to reaching the Station. He should arrive there at 1.25 p.m. and have his fatigue parties immediately ready for their various work. He will report on arrival to the R.T.O.

(signed) J.N.HORLICK.
Captain.
Brigade Major.
181st Infantry Brigade.

SUTTON VENY,
23.6.16.

OVERSEAS MOVE

LOADING TIME-TABLE AND GROUPING – TUESDAY, June 20th to SATURDAY, June 24th inclusive – FRESH RATIONS

DATE	TIME	S.O. 179th Bde.	TIME	S.O. 180th Bde.	TIME	S.O. 181st Bde.	TIME	S.O. Divl.Troops
TUES. June 20th	7.30 to 8.30	Pioneers ×; 2/13×; 2/14×; B.H.Q.; 2/15; 2/16; 2/4 F.A.; 518 Co. A.S.C.	8.30 to 9.30	D.H.Q.; B.H.Q.; 2/17; 2/18; 2/19; 2/5 F.A.; 2/4 F.Co.R.E.; Cas.C. Stn; 519 Co. A.S.C.	9.30 to 10.30	Signals ×; 3/3 F.Co.R.E.×; C.R.E.; B.H.Q.; 2/21; 2/22; 2/23; 2/24; 2/6 F.A.; 1/6 F.Co.R.E.; Cyclists; 520 Co. A.S.C.	10.30 to 11.30	300 Bde.×; 517 Co. A.S.C.; 301; 302; 303; Yeo.; M.V.S.; D...C.
WEDY. June 21st	7.30 to 8.30	B.H.Q. ×; 2/15; 2/16×; 2/4 F.A.×; 518 Co. A.S.C.×	8.30 to 9.30	D.H.Q.×; 2/5 F.A.×; 2/4 F.Co.R.E.×; Clg.Stn.×; B.H.Q.; 2/17; 2/18; 2/19; 519 Co. A.S.C.	9.30 to 10.30	C.R.E.; B.E.Q.; 2/20; 2/21; 2/22; 2/23; 2/24; 2/6 F.A.; 1/6 F.Co.R.E.; Cyclists; 520 Co. A.S.C.	10.30 to 11.30	C.R.×; 303 Bde.×; 301; 302; Yeomanry M.V.S.; D...C.
THUR. June 22nd	–	Nil	8.0 to 9.0	B.H.Q.×; 2/17×; 2/18×; 519 Co. A.S.C.×	9.0 to 10.0	2/6 F.A.×; 1/6 F.Co.R.E.×; C.R.E.×; B.H.Q.; 2/20; 2/21; 2/22; 2/23; 2/24; Cyclists; 520 Co. A.S.C.	10.0 to 11.0	301 Bde.×; 332 Bde.; Yeomanry; M.V.S.; D...C.
FRID. June 23rd	–	Nil	–	Nil	9.0 to 10.0	B.H.Q.×; 2/20×; 2/21×; 2/22×; Cyclists ×; 520 Co. A.S.C.×; 2/23; 2/24	10.0 to 11.0	302 Bde.×; Yeo.×; M.V.S.×; D...C.
S.TY. June 24th	–	Nil	–	Nil	–	Nil	10.0 to 11.0	D...C.×; 2/23×; 2/24×

(×) Units drawing their last Fresh Ration.

OVERSEAS RATIONS

DAY	TIME	S.O. 179th Bde.	TIME	S.O. 180th Bde.	TIME	S.O. 181st Bde.	TIME	S.O. Div. T's.
TUESDAY June 20th	3.0 to 4.0	Pioneers, 2/13, 2/14	–	Nil	2.0 to 3.0	(Signals, 3/3 F.Co. (R.E.	4.0 to 5.0	500 Bde. Base Details, 517 A.S.C.
WEDNESDAY June 21st	3.0 to 4.0	B.H.Q., 2/15, 2/16, 2/4 F.A., 518 A.S.C.	2.0 to 3.0	D.H.Q., 2/5 F.A., 2/4 F.Co. R.E., Casualty Clg. Station	–	Nil.	4.0 to 5.0	C.R.A., 303 Brigade.
THURSDAY June 22nd	–	Nil.	3.0 to 4.0	B.H.Q., 2/17, 2/18, 2/19, 519 A.S.C.	2.0 to 3.0	C.R.E., 2/6 F.A., 1/6 F. Co. R.E.	4.0 to 5.0	301 Brigade
FRIDAY June 23rd	–	Nil.	–	Nil.	3.0 to 4.0	B.H.Q., 2/20, 2/21 2/22, Cyclists, 520 A.S.C.	4.0 to 5.0	302 Brigade Yeomanry, M.T.S.
SATURDAY June 24th	–	Nil.	–	Nil.	–	Nil.	4.0 to 5.0	D.A.C., 2/23, 2/24

SECRET.

PROGRAMME NO. 32.

ORDER OF EMBARKATION - 60th DIVISION.

Index No.	UNIT	From	To
	JUNE 18th		
I	Divisional Supply Column	Avonmouth	Rouen
	JUNE 21st		
II	Divl. Ammunition Sub-Park	do	do
III	Motor Ambulances	do	do
	1ST DAY - JUNE 21st		
IV	1/12th L.N.Lancs. Reg.(Pioneer Bn)	Southampton	Havre
V	2/13th London Regiment	do	do
VI	2/14th ditto	do	do
VII	2/5th London Bde. R.F.A.	do	do
VIII	H.Q. & 517 Coy. Div. Train	do	do
IX	H.Q. & No. 1 Sec. Div. Sig. Co.	do	do
X	3/3rd London Field Co. R.E.	do	do
	2nd DAY - JUNE 22nd		
XI	Divisional Headquarters	do	do
XII	Hd.Qrs. Divl. R.A.	do	do
XIII	(H.Q.179th Inf. Bde. Sec.Sig.) (Co. & 518th Co. Div. Train.)	do	do
XIV	2/15th London Regiment	do	do
XV	2/16th ditto	do	do
XVI	2/8th London Bde. R.F.A. (How)	do	do
XVII	2/4th Field Coy. R.E.	do	do
XVIII	2/4th London Field Ambce.	do	do
XIX	2/5th London Field Ambce.	do	do
XX	2/2nd London Casualty Clg.Stn.	do	do
	3rd DAY - JUNE 23rd.		
XXI	(H.Q. 180th Inf. Bde. Sec. Sig.) (Co. & 519th Co. Div. Train.)	do	do
XXII	2/17th London Regiment	do	do
XXIII	2/18th ditto	do	do
XXIV	2/19th ditto	do	do
XXV	2/6th London Bde. R.F.A.	do	do
XXVI	H.Q. Divl. R.E.	do	do
XXVII	1/6th London Field Coy. R.E.	do	do
XXVIII	2/6th London Fd. Ambce.	do	do
	4th DAY - JUNE 24th.		
XXIX	2/20th London Regiment	do	do
XXX	(H.Q. 181st Inf. Bde. Sec. Sig.) (Co. & 520th Co. Divl. Train.)	do	do
XXXI	2/21st London Regiment	do	do
XXXII	2/22nd ditto	do	do
XXXIII	2/7th London Bde. R.F.A.	do	do
XXXIV	60th Div. Cyclist Coy.	do	do
XXXV	(H.Q. 1/1st Hants Yeomanry) (Squadron 1/1st Hants Yeo.)	do	do
XXXVI	60th Mobile Veterinary Sec.	do	do
XXXVII	60th Sanitary Section	do	do
XXXVIII	2/23rd London Regiment	do	do
XXXIX	2/24th ditto	do	do
XL	Divl. Ammunition Column	do	do

NOTES FOR ENTRAINMENT.

Q/540.

PART I - GENERAL.

With reference to the move of the Division, memo No. S/399 dated 14th instant, circulated to all concerned, the G.O.C. 60th (London) Division directs that arrangements shall be made for an Officer of the Unit concerned to take over the train as soon as it arrives at the Railway Station at which the Troops are to be entrained. This Officer will mark off carriages and trucks, allotting them to Companies, Sections, etc. He should provide himself with chalk for this purpose.

In this country the Officer in charge of the train will be accompanied by an Official of the Railway Company when taking over the train and will note broken glass or straps. The Official of the Railway Company will sign the list of deficiencies before Troops entrain. The Officer in charge of the train will be accompanied by a N.C.O. to assist him in this work.

Troops for entrainment are not to go on to the siding or platform until 20 minutes before the train starts.

Before Troops move on to the siding or platform to entrain, all carriage doors will be opened.

No Officer or man is allowed on the siding or platform -- except for the purposes of entrainment or for the supervision thereof. Troops will march on the siding or platform in fours if such is possible.

Special carriages should be detailed for the fatigue parties. *for Shelter Bearers and* Carriages for fatigue parties employed in loading horses and wagons will be as far as possible arranged for next to the trucks. One Compartment must be reserved for Police, and one for men who may be taken ill on the journey. *and prisoners*

Each carriage load of men will be in charge of an N.C.O. or an old soldier who will form up his party opposite the door, and on the signal, will march them into the carriage, taking his own seat nearest to the platform. The signal for the men to entrain will be three whistles. Men will be drawn up, awaiting the signal, facing the engine and will move into the carriages, carrying their rifles at the short trail.

Until the train moves off, no shouting, cheering or talking will be allowed. When once the train has started, the men can cheer, *and sing.*

Rifles and, if necessary, accoutrements are to be placed carefully on the racks and packs on the floor underneath the carriage seat. When overseas travelling in trucks, on no account will men be allowed to sit with their legs out of the doors of the compartments, several accidents having taken place in France owing to disobedience, or neglect of this order.

The Officer in charge of each train will ascertain and notify to all concerned when and where and for how long the train will stop, and on the whistle being sounded at such places, those who wish to go out of the train may do so, leaving their arms and equipment in the carriages. The N.C.O. or old soldier in charge of each carriage is responsible for the quick return of the occupants of his carriage.

(-2-)

No animals, other than horses and Mules will be allowed on any account to accompany the Division overseas. The Police have instructions to detain any dogs, pet animals etc.

The allowance of Kit, as laid down in Regulations, must in no case be exceeded.

A quarter of an hour before the arrival of the train at its destination, men will put on their packs and equipment and take their rifles in their hand. On the arrival the sounding of a whistle three times will be a signal for the men to detrain. Each carriage will detrain separately and will form up on the platform, facing the engine under the charge of the N.C.O. or old soldier referred to above.

The whole party with the exception of any fatigue parties detailed to assist in unloading the Regimental Transport etc. will be marched off by signal or by a whistle. No bugling, shouting or loud talking is to be permitted during detraining.

The O.C. Unit will render to a Staff Officer of the Brigade, a Marching-out State, at the time of the entrainment of the Unit and he will forward a Marching-in State to Brigade Headquarters, so as to reach Divisional Headquarters at point of detraining overseas not later than two hours after the arrival of the train.

Officers Commanding Brigades and Divisional Troops entraining will, in direct communication with the R.T.O. and the A.P.M. (and after the departure of the A.P.M. on the 22nd instant with the D.A.Q.M.G.) arrange for the control of vehicular and pedestrian traffic at the Railway Station at which troops are entraining.

The arrangements should be so ordered that no person, other than the troops entraining and the members of the travelling public are admitted to the Railway Station or immediate precincts, at the time of departure of the Troops.

The arrangements must be controlled by an Officer.

With a view to prevent the loss of rifles and equipment during the journey to the concentration area overseas a label will be attached to each man's equipment and rifle in the following form:-

No. ....
Rank ....
Name ....
Company ....
Unit ....
Brigade ....

In the case of the Rifle the label may be pasted to the Butt of the Rifle.

It is suggested that these labels should conform to the authorised colours of the Brigades or Divisional Troops concerned.

After the troops have disembarked an Officer will be detailed by the Officer Commanding the Unit accompanied by an N.C.O. & Ship's Officer, to go round the whole ship and ensure that nothing belonging to the Troops has been left behind.

The labels referred to above, will be kept on the rifles and equipment until the troops arrive in their billets in the Concentration area where they will be carefully collected and destroyed under the supervision of the Officers.

PART II - TRANSPORT.

(a) In the case of Infantry Units, the fatigue party for loading horses and vehicles should arrive with the transport an hour and a half, and the main body should arrive three quarters of an hour before the time of departure of the train; in the case of other units, all transport wagons and other vehicles, all horses and mules and the troops travelling on the same train are to be at the Station an hour and a half before the time of departure.

(b) The fatigue parties should consist of enough men to provide, with the drivers, one man for each horse and thirty for the vehicles for each train, with an Officer in charge of each party. Immediately on arrival at the Station the fatigue parties should take off their equipment, pile or ground arms, and fall in ready for work. Drivers should not attempt to lead horses into trucks with rifles in their hands, or slung.

(c) On arrival at Warminster Station the transport should halt with the head of the column opposite the R.T.O's. Office. The first vehicle is driven straight for the Station building and wheeled square to the right to bring it straight for the loading dock, the horses are unhooked and led to the side of the horse loading platform, one fatigueman with each driver, bits are taken out, headropes down, feed bags off, and traces secured; as soon as the horses are unhooked from the first vehicle the next moves up, the column moving up all the time, the fatigue party man-handles each vehicle on to the trucks as soon as to horses are unhooked, all end-loading at this Station.

A definite system should be similarly adopted at Codford Station by arrangement between O.C. Mounted Units and the R.T.O. Codford.

As the first vehicles have to be hauled the whole length of the trucks it is well to have the lightest in front, i.e. carts and limbered G.S. wagons. The heavy G.S. wagons are conveniently loaded last. The two-wheeled vehicles should be kept together in pairs, as they are loaded two to a truck.

The Railway Officials will lash the vehicles, any assistance they require being provided by the fatigue party.

As the horses are ready for loading they are led up the ramps at each end of the horse-loading-platform and loaded into the trucks, beginning in the middle, loading two or more trucks at a time, an Officer and as many N.C.O's. as are available should superintend the loading of the horses.

Drivers should take the feed bags into the carriages with them.

A similar procedure will be adopted at all entraining stations, the above notes being taken as a guide.

(d) Loaded vehicles must be carefully packed and the sheets well tied down, and no packages left loose on the floors of the trucks containing wagons.

(e) As the poles have to be taken out of G.S. wagons it should be ensured beforehand that all bolts and pins draw easily.

(f) Loaded wagons must not exceed 8 feet in height from the ground.

(g) It is advisable that Transport Officers of later entraining units should come down and watch the entrainment of earlier units.

(h) It is of the utmost importance that units should be at the Station at the times detailed. On an overseas move the trains must be despatched to time, and this cannot be done unless the stated time for loading is allowed. It is well to remember that it is apt to take a long time to get loaded wagons out of camps in the dark.

Officers should bear in mind that the loading must be completed at least twenty minutes before the time of departure to allow the train to be "made-up".

The Officer Commanding each Unit or portion of Unit entraining will bring a warrant for his train-load and exchange it for a ticket at the Booking Office.

AMMUNITION.

The Small Arm Ammunition ordered to be carried by each man will be issued on the day prior to the departure of the Unit concerned.

RATIONS

Entraining and Embarkation.

Baggage and Supply Wagons together with horses and drivers will be issued to Units by the A.S.C. prior to departure, according to the time table at time and place to be arranged in direct communication between the O.C., Divisional Train and O's.C. Divisional Troops and Infantry Brigades concerned. The Supply Wagons on issue to Units will contain one day's Field Ration, and will be covered with the Tarpaulin and properly lashed down. These rations will not be consumed except in case of emergency until arrival at the concentration area.

The Baggage Wagons at the time of issue will be loaded by the A.S.C. with fresh rations up to and including breakfast on the day following the day of departure of the Units concerned. These rations will be unloaded at once on receipt, and the wagons reloaded with the Unit's baggage.

The unexpended portion of these rations will be carried by the men in their haversacks on entrainment.

For consumption during the voyage, in addition to the unexpended portion of these rations for the day of entrainment, each man will be provided with preserved rations by the Embarkation Commandant at the port of embarkation, and will take ashore with him the unexpired portion of the ration for the day of disembarkation, being dependent on this for the remainder of that day's food.

Each trainload must be self-contained as regards messing arrangements.

Officers of Units must make their own necessary arrangements to conform with the above.

Forage for horses on the voyage will be provided by the Embarkation Officer at the port of embarkation.

Disembarkation.

On entraining at the port of disembarkation the following supplies in addition to the unconsumed portion of the current day's ration will be entrained with the troops.

(a) On each soldier one Iron Ration, but men to be warned that this is not to be consumed without a definite order from a responsible Officer.

(b) In Supply Wagons - 1 day's ration.

(c) In coaches or vans, sufficient rations for the journey including rations for the day of detrainment.

With reference to (c) above it is advisable to distribute rations before commencing the journey, as there is little chance of distributing rations en route.

Forage and buckets for watering animals on the trains must be placed so that they are readily available during the journey.

On arrival in the Concentration Area the Supply Wagons in charge of Units will be unloaded as quickly as possible and the O.C., A.S.C. Companies concerned will arrange to collect these wagons, and from this time forward the one man per wagon provided to A.S.C. by Units as loaders will be attached to A.S.C.

Cooking.

There will be no arrangements for cooking on board ship other than the provision of boiling water for the making of tea.

P. MALCOLM.

Lieut-Col.
A.A. & Q.M.G.
60th (London) Division.

SUTTON VENY,
15th June 1916.

BILLETING ORDERS.

SECRET.

APPENDIX II
to
WAR DIARY
of
181ST INFANTRY BRIGADE.

June, 1916.

Ref. LENS Sheet 11 1/100,000. R.F. 181st INF.Bde. ORDER No. 1,
Chateau Buneville,
27-6-18-

1. The 2/21, 2/22, 2/23, 2/24 Bns.L.R. Detachment 3/3 Coy.R.E., 2/6 Fld.Amb. will move into billets today as under.

	Route	
2/21 Lond.R.	"	PETIT HOUVIN STATION-BUNEVILLE-TERNAS-LIGNY-ST.FLOCHEL-TINQUES.
2/22 "	"	TERNAS-LIGNY-ST.FLOCHEL-TINQUES-BETHENCOURT-VILLERS BRULIN.
2/23 "	"	BUNEVILLE-TERNAS-LIGNY-ST.FLOCHEL-TINQUES-BETHENCOURT.
2/24 "	"	ROELLECOURT-TINQUES.
Det.3/3 Coy.R.E.	"	ROELLECOURT-BAILLEUL-AUX-CORNAILLES-CHELERS.
2/6 Fld.Amb.	"	TERNAS-LIGNY-ST.FLOCHEL-TINQUES.

Unit.	Starting Point.	Time.	Distance.	Billet.	Other Units Billets.
2/21 Lond.R.	X rds. ¼ mile south of Q in FRAMECOURT.	1 p.m.	12 miles.	BETHENCOURT) VANDELICOURT)	....
2/22 Lond.R.	BRIQIE. ½ mile East of last E in BUNEVILLE.	1 p.m.	12 "	BETHONSART.	.... 520 Coy.A.S.C CHELERS.
2/23 Lond.R.	Station, PETIT HOUVIN.	When detrained.	11 "	VILLERS BRULIN.	....
2/24 Lond.R.	Station, ST.POL.	do.	8 "	CHELERS.	.... 302 Bde.R.F.A
Det.3/3 Fd.Coy. R.E.	X roads ¼ mile north of first C in OCOCHE.	1 p.m.	10 "	GUESTREVILLE.	.... at TINQUES & TINQUETTES.
2/6 Fld.Amb.	Road junction ½ mile east of T in NEUVILLE-AU-CORNET.	12.45 p.m.	10 "	GUESTREVILLE.	....

2. Billetting Parties will be sent on immediately.
3. A report will be rendered to Bde.H.Q. immediately on arrival in billets.
4. All reports before 5 p.m. to Bde.H.Q. CHATEAU,BUNEVILLE, after 5 p.m. CHATEAU, CHELERS.
5. Acknowledge.

(signed) J.N.HORLICK.
Captain.
Bde.Major.
181st Infantry Brigade.

302nd Bde. R.F.A. notified separately. 181st Inf.Bde.H.Q. & 520TH Coy.A.S.C. marched direct from station to CHELERS.

MOVE - 2/21 & 2/22
TO FORWARD AREA.

SECRET.

APPENDIX III
to
WAR DIARY
of
181ST INFANTRY BRIGADE.

June, 1916.

S E C R E T.   181st INFANTRY BRIGADE. ORDER NO.3.

Ref. LENS sheet 11 100,000
     FRANCE " 51c N.E. 20,000

1. The 2/21st and 2/22nd Battalions, London Regiment, will move up for instruction, and be attached to the 184th Infantry Brigade to-day, as under:-

   2/21st Bn.Lond.R.

   Route. VANDELICOURT - HAUTES - AVESNES - LOUEZ

Starting Point	Time	Distance	Destination
Road Junction 200X West of L in TINCQUES	6-45	10½ miles	LOUEZ

   2/22nd. Bn. L.R.

   Route. SAVY - HAUTES - AVESNES - MAROEUIL

Starting Point	Time	Distance	Destination
X Roads 100X North of first L in VILLERSBRULIN	7-30	9 miles	MAROEUIL

2. O.C. Units will arrange for the necessary billetting parties to go forward as soon as possible on receipt of these orders. The 2/21st. LONDON REGIMENT party to report to Headquarters 184th. INF. BDE. ETRUN. The 2/22nd. LONDON REGIMENT party to report to the TOWN MAJOR, MAROEUIL. The O.C's these parties will arrange to guide their units in on arrival.

3. The transport of 2/21st. LONDON REGIMENT will be withdrawn to ETRUN on arrival of unit at LOUEZ.

4. No troops to pass the point B.30.d.5.3. (Ref. Sheet 51c.N.E.) before 9-30 p.m.

5. These Units, on reaching their destination, are entirely under the orders of the Brigade they are attached to.

6. Acknowledge.

H.Q. 181st. Inf. Bde.
    26-6-16.

(Signed) J.N.HORLICK
          Captain,
          Brigade Major,
          181st. Inf. Bde.

Copies to
1. file
2. 2/21st. Bn. L.R.
3. 2/22nd. Bn. L.R.
4. H.Q. 184th. Inf. Bde.
5. Town Major MAROEUIL
6 & 7 War Diary.

SECRET.

181ST INFANTRY BRIGADE.

———————

WAR DIARY.

———————

1st - 31st JULY, 1916.

———————

VOL. I.   No. 2.

-----------oOo-----------

WAR DIARY

of 181st INFANTRY BRIGADE

INTELLIGENCE SUMMARY.

(Erase heading not required.)

Army Form C. 2118.

Place	Date	Hour	Summary of Events and Information	Remarks and references to Appendices
CHELERS	1-7-16		2/23, 2/24 3rd LOND R Continue training in back area. 181 M.G. Coy moves up to ACQ for instruction under 154 INF BDE also ½ No 4 Sec SIG Coy. BRIG GEN PARSONS CB & BDE MAJOR return to CHELERS 7.30 p.m. STAFF CAPTAIN attached HQ 154 INF BDE. Weather fine SW wind	[sig]
"	2-7-16		2/23 LOND R send working party 80 men to No 8 RE PARK SAVY. 2/23, 2/24 3rd LOND R Continue training in back area. 2/24 LOND R send 4 Platoons to ATUMER'S to be instructed in Consolidating Craters. 2 Offrs 4 NCOs go ST POL for ANTI GAS Course.	[sig]
"	3-7-16		2/23, 2/24 LOND R Continue training in back area. 2/23 LOND R send working party 100 ORs No 8 RE PARK SAVY. 2/23 LOND R bath men during day at SAVY. Nominal roll forwarded Div of 2nd GRENADE Course HERMANVILLE. Staff Captains Conference ordered 9.30 am HERMANVILLE 9.30 am 4-7-16. Details re courses affecting units in forward Area forwarded 154 INF BDE. Weather fine and warm SW wind. Numerous documents forwarded 154 INF BDE 2/21 2/22 LOND R	[sig]

WAR DIARY
of 181st INFANTRY BRIGADE
INTELLIGENCE SUMMARY

Army Form C. 2118.

Place	Date	Hour	Summary of Events and Information	Remarks and references to Appendices
CHELERS	4.7.16		2/23 LOND R find party for consolidation of craters at AGNIERES. 2/24 LOND R trekking at TINQUES. OPERATION ORDER No 4 issued (APPI). 1000 Instructional MILLS grenades received. 200 to 2/23, 300 to 2/24 LOND R. Telegram received from 60 Div postponing move up to forward area of 2/23, 2/24 LOND R to forward area subsequent on receipt of 51 Div order No 60. 154 INF BDE ORDER No 32 received and acknowledged. All attention for move made good. Brig Gen CDG goes up to 154 INF BDE accompanied by Capt LYDIATT Bde Bombing Offical. Weather Sultry violent thunder storm from 2.15 PM – 5 PM. Very slight SW wind between 1-2.	APPI
"	5.7.16		2/24 LOND R find 100 OR to work at Nos RE Park SAVY from 9am – 5pm. 2/21 2/22 TM parties for school 51 Div at LIGNY ST FLOCHEL due at 9 am fail to arrive, despatched during day by motor lorry. 2/21 2/22 LOND R Grenade Class arrive HERMAVILLE instead of on 6th inst. 2/23 LOND R send 2 Coys to bathe during day at TINQUES. 151/60 154 INF BDE OP ORDER 32 and 2/23 2/24 LOND R orders for move up received acknowledged. Weather fine warm, wind mild S.W.	

WAR DIARY
of 181 INFANTRY BRIGADE
INTELLIGENCE SUMMARY

Army Form C. 2118.

Place	Date	Hour	Summary of Events and Information	Remarks and references to Appendices
CHELERS	6-7-16		2/23 LOND R leaves for forward area 7.45am 2/24 LOND R leaves for forward area 5pm. 6th ARGYLL and SUTHERLAND HIGHLANDERS come back in afternoon. All these units moved under direct orders from 51 DIVN. 2 inch Medium TM BATTERY attached Bde. arrive MAROEUIL and is attached 154 INF BDE. Weather sultry, slight rain about 5pm. Wind SW. 2/22 LOND R detailed for consolidation of craters on 10th vice 8th inst. 2/21 LOND R on 8th vice 10th. 7th A & S HIGHLANDERS detailed for working party No 8 RE PARK SAVY)5th inst. 2/23 LOND R consolidate craters.	[signature]
CHELERS	7-7-16		Weather Sultry & Stormy - Wind SW. All Battalions in forward area. BRIGADE MAJOR attached to 154th BDE.	[signature]
CHELERS	8-7-16		Weather fine & warm - Wind S. 2/21 Bn find party for consolidation of Craters at AGNIERES. 2/21 LOND R arrives from forward area 9 P.M. leaving left MAROEUIL at 1.30 PM. 154 INF. BDE ORDER No 33 received and acknowledged.	[signature]

WAR DIARY
of 181st INFANTRY BRIGADE
INTELLIGENCE SUMMARY.

Army Form C. 2118.

Place	Date	Hour	Summary of Events and Information	Remarks and references to Appendices
CHELERS	9-7-16		Weather fine & warm. Wind light S.S.W. 2/21 LOND. R. sent working party of 50 O.R. to No 8 R.E. Park SAVY - Party of 5 officers (with batmen) and 5 N.C.Os. left for III ARMY Infantry School at AUXI LE CHATEAU - One section of 181st T.M. BATTERY leaves LIGNY ST FLOCHEL T.M. SCHOOL at 6 P.M. for MARŒUIL. BRIG. GEN. returns from 154th BDE. & brings with him 51st DIV Operation order No 61.	
"	10-7-16		Weather fine and warm. Wind S.S.W. 2/22 LOND R. send party for consolidation of craters at AGNIERES. GO DIV Secret letter G/572 received re Instructions in the use of telephones in the trenches. Also PROVISIONAL DEFENCE SCHEME AND RELIEF ORDERS. (No I.) 154 INF. BDE ORDER No 34 received re Relief of trenches. Bde MAJOR rejoins Brigade.	
"	11-7-16		Weather dull & warm. Some rain in morning. Wind W. 2/21 LOND find party of 50 men for work at R.E. PARK SAVY. 10th & 1 N.C.O. detailed from 2/21 LOND R. to attend DIVN ANTI GAS SCHOOL (FREVIN-CAPELLE) on 15th inst. DIV Secret letters G/s 82 and G/s 86 received 2/60 TRENCH MORTAR BATTY and No I SECTION 181 TRENCH MORTAR BATTY commence relief of 2/51 T.M. BATTY and No I SECTION 154 T.M. BATTY at 6.30 PM. Relief complete 7.5 PM.	

WAR DIARY

of 181 INFANTRY BRIGADE.

INTELLIGENCE SUMMARY.

(Erase heading not required.)

Army Form C. 2118.

Place	Date	Hour	Summary of Events and Information	Remarks and references to Appendices
CHELERS	12-7-16		Weather dull and cold. Some rain in afternoon. Wind fairly strong S.W. Conference at RED HOUSE, ETRUN at 11 a.m. attended by O.C. Bde M.G. Coy. T.M. Batty, 3/3 F. Coy R.E., Bde Bombing Offr, Bde Sigs Offr. Defence Scheme and all details as to line discussed. BRIGADE PROVISIONAL DEFENCE SCHEME issued. DIVNL G/S/64 re TELEPHONE Precautions issued. DIVNL G/S/67 on use of T.M's received and issued. 181 INF BDE ORDER No 5 issued. No 2 Section 181 T.M. BATTY completed relief of 154 T.M. BATTY at 9.30 pm. 151 M.G. Coy moves to MAROEUIL from A.C.Q. H.Q. of 2/60 and 181 T.M. BATTYS at MAROEUIL. 2/21 LOND R sent party of 200 O.R. and Offrs to consolidate Craters at AGNIERES. 2 NCO's 2/21 LOND R detailed for Musketry Course at MACHINE GUN SCHOOL CAMIERS on 20th inst. 1 Offr. 2 NCO 2/21 LOND R detailed for SNIPING COURSE at A.C.Q. commencing 14th inst. 1 Offr & 2 NCO's each from 2/21 & 2/21 LOND R's detailed for PHYSICAL TRAINING COURSE at DIVNL School, HERMAVILLE. 17th inst.	App II
CHELERS TO ETRUN	13-7-16		Weather dull and cold. Some rain. Wind fairly strong S.W. 181 INF BDE relieves 154 INF BDE in RIGHT SECTOR, 14th Division on right. 179th BDE on left. 2/21 LOND R leave CHELERS 9 am and march to ETRUN. 2/23 LOND R relieve 4th SEAFORTH HIGHLANDERS in RIGHT 1. 2/24 LOND R relieve 7th A & S Highlanders in RIGHT 2. 2/22 LOND R

WAR DIARY

Army Form C. 2118.

or

INTELLIGENCE SUMMARY.

(Erase heading not required.)

of 181 INFANTRY BRIGADE

Place	Date	Hour	Summary of Events and Information	Remarks and references to Appendices
CHATEAU LA ETRUN	18.7.16 Continued		Relieve 2 Coys 2/23rd at BARI MONTON and ARR CENTRALE and 2 Coys 2/24th at ECURIE and SOUTHERN REDT. These four points are commonly called "C" area x form Bde RESERVE. 2 Platoons 1/12th LOYAL NORTH LANCS (PIONEERS) are also quartered in ECURIE. Relief complete 6.35 p.m. Casualties o/w 2/24 Lond R 4 killed (1 wounded). Germans explode a mine opposite M34 to the left of RIGHT 2. at 7.115 p.m. No damage done.	[signature]
ETRUN	14.7.16		A wet morning, fine afternoon wind NW. A very quiet morning at along Bde front. 14th Division on right bombarded enemy's front heavily between 3am and 4.30am. Enemy's artillery more lively in the afternoon. At 5.35pm he put several shells (77mm) in rapid succession over L21 wounding one man. Enemy MG's fired at junction of BONNAL and G (BOYAN) at 2am. Our artillery fired 10 light shells in direction of THELUS at wisp'n all shot, 6 duds. MG Sniping Post fired at LOOPHOLE with armour piercing bullets & put it out of action. The left of the BRIGADE extended from M34 to VICTOIRE AVENUE exclusive. This is taken over by 2/24 LOND R. All Officers & men of 51st DIVN left in line for instructional purposes ordered to be withdrawn, also mining fatigue found by 8 A&S HIGHLANDERS	[signature]

Army Form C. 2118.

WAR DIARY
of 5th INFANTRY BRIGADE
INTELLIGENCE SUMMARY.

(Erase heading not required.)

Place	Date	Hour	Summary of Events and Information	Remarks and references to Appendices
L'TRUX	15-7-16		A Beautiful warm day, light SW wind. The day opened quietly with the exception that ANZAC was shelled intermittently from 8 am onwards with 5.9. H.E. Hostile artillery however became very active on Right I especially between 4.25–4.27 causing considerable damage and some casualties. 2 M Gunners were killed in LSF & the emplacement (concrete) knocked about. Our TMs did some good shooting during the day. Great difficulty was experienced in obtaining Artillery Retaliation some 20 minutes elapsing, when obtained the enemys guns promptly ceased, but not before two of life was occasioned. The 9'23 L.F. Sniping Offr scored a hit opposite L.22. General improvement of trenches is as carried on prior to bombardment. Relief orders issued.	APP II
"	16-7-16		A dull morning and wet afternoon, strong SW wind. An instentation relief was carried out during the day, and for the first time of doing this, things went most smoothly. The Relief started at 1PM and was complete at 8PM. The 151 M G Coy also relieved during the night 16/17. There was very little activity on either side during the day. In the evening 11:45 pm the enemy bombarded our lines heavily with TMs which damaged our trenches and killed 3 men and 18 pm retaliated with effect. At 10pm one of our listening posts wounded a German whom they brought	APP III

WAR DIARY
or
INTELLIGENCE SUMMARY.

Army Form C. 2118.

of 181 INFANTRY BRIGADE

Place	Date	Hour	Summary of Events and Information	Remarks and references to Appendices
ERUN	Cont. 16-7-16		him, he however died without recovering consciousness, he was No 211 Cpl GRENADIER HEINRICH RICHTER 1st GARDE RES. DIV. 64 RES INF BDE. Our MGs dispersed enemy transport on LILLE ROAD & fired effectively on crossroads at 18.a.1.65	
"	17-7-16		A damp misty morning, better afternoon. V. slight E wind in morning veering to NW in afternoon. A very quiet morning indeed. Our guns shewed some activity in the afternoon. G.O.C. Divn had an interview with Brig at G.30 P.M. Physical Training School at HERMAVILLE commences. Also second course of ANTI GAS SCHOOL. FRÉVIN CAPELLE. Considerable M.G. & Artillery activity during the night	
"	18-7-16		A damp cold morning, fine evening. NE wind. A perfectly normal day with the usual intermittent TM and Artillery activity. EcuRIE was shelled by 5.9 HE during the afternoon. M.G. indirect fire was effective on LILLE ROAD during the night 17/18. An officers patrol visited the crater at A.32.b.1.5 (50 x N of Sap 28) but found it unoccupied. An enemy patrol got into Sap 24. A.22.b.7.1. and hurriedly retreated on hearing outpost. CHEMIN CREEK again reconnoitered about by Bn. T.M.O. Quiet night	

WAR DIARY

INTELLIGENCE SUMMARY

of 1st INFANTRY BRIGADE

Army Form C. 2118.

Place	Date	Hour	Summary of Events and Information	Remarks and references to Appendices
ETRUN	19-7-16		A bright warm morning. Slight NE wind veering to NW in afternoon. With the exception of TM activity along most of the Bde front all was fairly quiet till about 10 a.m. A Squadron of about 25 BRITISH AEROPLANES flew over our lines at 7.50 a.m. During the course of the morning a heavy German TM shell scored a direct hit on a MG emplacement and killing 2 men. Lewis BONNEL and GRANT collector made good progress. One officer and 8 men 2/24 LR left for LEWIS GUN Course at ETAPLES.	[signature]
"	20-7-16		A fine warm day. A slight NW wind. Bde held conference at ADVANCED BDE HQ at 10 a.m. attended by ARTY GROUP CDR, MG OC, DO TM. OC 2/23 LR. A certain amount of hostile French Mortar fire during the day. Also shelling. ANZIN shelled in afternoon. Our guns & TMs retaliated effectively. A&M into "B" relief was carried out during the day. One man 2/22 LONR R was killed, 50 men for 2/22 LONR R, 70 men for 2/23 LONR R. The following drafts arrived 50 men for 2/23 LONR R. 70 men 2/24 LONR R. a rather poor looking lot, composed of various LONDON Bn's. The 1/2 joined their Regt. at ETRUN. The remainder were billeted at MAROEUIL. The 36th (JACOBS) HORSE came under MAROEUIL for MINING PARTIES took in Bde area, & are attached for rations to Bde. 6 officers & naturoffrs & 310 O.R. During evening out night The BONNAL in Right I was badly knocked about by TM fire	APP. IV [signature]

Army Form C. 2118.

WAR DIARY
of 87 INF BRIGADE

INTELLIGENCE SUMMARY.
(Erase heading not required.)

Instructions regarding War Diaries and Intelligence Summaries are contained in F. S. Regs., Part II. and the Staff Manual respectively. Title pages will be prepared in manuscript.

Place	Date	Hour	Summary of Events and Information	Remarks and references to Appendices
ETRUN	21.7.16		A very warm bright day. Wind Easterly. A certain amount of Artillery activity on our front. About 30 HE 4.2 shells were put into ECURIE during the morning. The front line was also heavily bombarded by TM's of all calibres. The sector was visited by the G.O.C. Div'n during the day. The enemys "TRAVELLING CIRCUS" was the chief cause of the hostile artillery activity & apparently departed about 3 PM. CAPT MACDONALD 2nd R reported for duty as Ass. STAFF CAPTAIN vice CAPT V BEVINGTON ?/12 LOND R. to 129th INF BDE. Quiet night.	
"	22.7.16		A very warm day, beautiful evening NE wind. The normal amount of artillery and TM activity. Orders issued re the proposed bombardment for 23-7-16 and likewise orders re time of same received from CRA. The BRIG and BDE MAJ visit H'strn BDE HQ at ARRAS re bombardment and other matters. Night very quiet. Several patrols visited the GERMAN wire during the night.	APP V
"	23.7.16		A fine warm day, beautiful evening NW wind. A quiet morning. At 8.15 PM our TM's started a slow bombardment of enemys front. At 8.30 PM 2 BATTYs of 18 PRS, 1 BATTY 4.5 HOWITZERS & the CORPS HEAVY GUNS (6" HOWs & 4.7) commenced bombardment of enemys trenches & TM positions ably assisted by the TMs (medium & light) & trench MG fire. The bombardment continued until	

Army Form C. 2118.

WAR DIARY
of 181 INFANTRY BRIGADE
INTELLIGENCE SUMMARY.
(Erase heading not required.)

Place	Date	Hour	Summary of Events and Information	Remarks and references to Appendices
ECURIE	Contd. 23.7.16	4.10 PM	and was most successful. The Field Guns shooting especially well in all. Some 50 4.5" How Shells, 150 18-Pr Shells, 850 3" TM, 0 120 2" TM shells were put into the German lines. Few duds were observed. During this bombardment the enemy remained quiescent & only made a feeble retaliation at 4:30 PM. It is to be hoped that considerable damage was done to his trenches. At 9.30 PM a very heavy fire was opened by the enemy on the trenches held by the 11th Divn. Continuing until 10.30 PM. The ECURIE Garrison was warned to stand by in its battle positions, & the 2/22 Long R in Divnl Reserve to be ready to move at a moment's notice. Likewise a d detail back at ETRUN. The Stand to for Divnl Reserve & all other troops back was cancelled at 11.15 PM. The Stand to of the ECURIE Garrison cancelled at "Stand to" 24th inst	JHD
"	24.7.16		A dull day NNW wind. A quiet day. The usual TM and artillery intermittent activity on patrol the night before were very active (23/24) a Lewis enerunts round the crater opposite Sap 24 ended in our driving off the enemy's patrols. During the evening 9.30 our M.G's searches the enemy's dumps and lines of communication up to his support trenches with indirect fire. At 3.30 PM the 14th Division bombarded the enemy's trenches on our right heavily until 4.30 PM	

Army Form C. 2118.

WAR DIARY

of 181 INFANTRY BRIGADE

INTELLIGENCE SUMMARY.

(Erase heading not required.)

Instructions regarding War Diaries and Intelligence Summaries are contained in F. S. Regs., Part II. and the Staff Manual respectively. Title pages will be prepared in manuscript.

Place	Date	Hour	Summary of Events and Information	Remarks and references to Appendices
ETRUN	Contd 24-7-16		The BRIGADE BOMBING SCHOOL opened at ETRUN at 9 a.m. It is a weekly course. The Class arriving each Sunday evening & leaving following Sunday midday. One officer one NCO & privates from each Bn. Staff Bde Bo. Capt LIDDIATT 2/Lt SGt SANDS H/ei Two Junior SgGs 2/Lt B/m (These tent to be changed each fortnight). A mixed class of 2 Officers & 4 NCOs went to Divn Ph Training School at HERMAVILLE. A quiet night.	[sig]
ETRUN	25-7-16		A dull muggy day turned to an exceptionally quiet day, with practically no TM or Artillery Activity on either side. The G.O.C. Divn paid a visit to the night subsector and inspected the junction with the 4th Infantry Brigade. About 4 P.M. the enemy shelled the HILL Road by our dump. Secret letter received stating that 146 Division less Artillery was to be relieved by 21st Division less artillery by 30 July. During the night 24/25 there was the usual patrol and indirect M.G. fire the HILL Road being especially carefully searched. Fresh instructions ref S.O.S Signal and retaliation issued to all concerned	[sig]

WAR DIARY
or
INTELLIGENCE SUMMARY.

Army Form C. 2118.

of — 181 INFANTRY BRIGADE

Place	Date	Hour	Summary of Events and Information	Remarks and references to Appendices
ETRUN	26.7.16		A very dull murky morning, brighter in the afternoon. Wind very slight N-NW. An exceptionally quiet day along the whole Brigade front. The enemy mildly shelled the BARRICADE in the LILLE ROAD with whizz-bangs about 9.30 a.m. a ROCLINCOURT quite heavily with 4.2 HE about the same time. Our field guns made several direct hits on the enemy's front line trenches during the day, likewise our TM's. The gunners enacted a considerable amount of work to be got through during the day. During the evening information was received that the Artillery "STRAFE" arranged for 27th had been postponed, that we were exploding a mine to the NORTH of Rcl area and that a BRITISH airship would cruise over during the night. During the night 26/27 our patrols were very active the enemy's line being thoroughly examined from SAP 20 (A 23 a & 25 9) to SAP 26 (A 22 c 40 20) and onwards. An enemy patrol was also seen out between SAPS 20 & 21 about 1 am composed of some 12 men. Night very quiet	Initial
ETRUN	27.7.16		A very dull murky morning, brighter in the evening. Wind N.N.W. The quietest day that there has been on the front since the Brigade has been in the line. Several patrols were out in night. A Sniper's post was knocked out in RIGHT 2 by our Rifle grenades. A great amount of work was done owing to lack of shelling on the part of the enemy. Our field guns in the afternoon	

WAR DIARY or INTELLIGENCE SUMMARY

Army Form C. 2118.

of 181 INFANTRY BRIGADE

Place	Date	Hour	Summary of Events and Information	Remarks and references to Appendices
ETRUN	27-7-16		Shot exceptionally well. 181st Inf Bde Order No 9 was issued to all concerned. The night was very quiet. Extraordinary heavy dews are falling during the early hours of the day	APP VI
"	26.8.16		A foggy misty morning. Beautiful afternoon, strong NNW wind. A very quiet morning, late on there was considerably more hostile activity in T.M. & artillery fire. The Bde major inspected the BONNET and GRAND COURETIOR trenches in company with the OC 3/5 Field Coy RE, a large amount of work has been done in these trenches, and in RIGHT I no further assistance is required from the RE, the trenches having been well deepened throughout this part of the line. In RIGHT 2 there is still a considerable amount of work to be done in both trenches. The GRAND COURETIOR being especially bad towards the left. The BRIGADIER & CRA (GEN SIMPSON-BAIKIE B) inspected the site proposed for the HEAVY TM. LT EVATT Divn. T.M.G. GAS instructor observated the trenches. In the evening about 7:40 PM quiet a flock of 26 aeroplanes was brought down by the enemy, a direct hit being registered. The machine burst into flames & airplanes down landing near ROCLINCOURT. The relief was carried out without incident, in spite of a hostile Observation Balloon going up about 2 PM for 10 minutes, whilst our platoons were moving up the ANZIN road. Apparently they were observed, as immediately afterwards Universal Shells were burst over our Communication Trenches, as the	

Army Form C. 2118.

WAR DIARY
or
INTELLIGENCE SUMMARY.

6/781 INFANTRY BRIGADE

(Erase heading not required.)

Place	Date	Hour	Summary of Events and Information	Remarks and references to Appendices
ETRUN	Contd. 28-7-16		Enemy howrs. shelled our "DOWN" trenches. No harm was done. Very heavy firing & can note from 9.30 PM onwards, believed to be a GERMAN MINE attack.	[initials]
ETRUN	29-7-16		A really beautiful Summers day. Wind very slight now. The morning was normally quiet during the afternoon hostile TM's were very active on the left of RIGHT 2 doing considerable damage to SPOONER AVENUE. One or two Sapos and the BOYAU. Two men were killed and five men were wounded. At 5 PM our field guns A.S. Howitzers & the Corps Heavy Artillery shelled the enemy support trenches & suspected TM positions situated on the right flank of the 179th Bde on our left. Considerable damage appeared to be done. The enemy did not retaliate very much achiefly when he did on our RIGHT 2. With TM's and 4"2 "WOOLLY BEARS". The "P"1 & "D"1 & recent 2 patrols during the night to examine the enemy wire, this was found to be strong & in good condition. Germans do not appear to patrol to any extent. The 6/4th B/Sc (2nd Div) relieved the 1st SrB/Sc on our right during the course of the day. It was ascertained that not only did the pilot of the aeroplane shot down escape with only a few burns, but that to get rid of the burning petrol, he three looped the loop whilst descending.	[initials]

WAR DIARY
INTELLIGENCE SUMMARY

Army Form C. 2118.

of 181 INFANTRY BRIGADE.

(Erase heading not required.)

Place	Date	Hour	Summary of Events and Information	Remarks and references to Appendices
ETRUN	30.7.16		Another beautiful day, very hot. practically no wind (NE) Another day on the whole Bde. front. During the previous night our Vickers guns searched the LILLE road during the night, and enemy Vickers guns were very active searching the LILLE road in their turn. News was received of the Russian having captured 7300 officers & 15000 guns. Night quiet. We sent out 3 Patrols a long various points of our line to examine hostile wire, which was reported strong.	[signature]
ETRUN	31.7.16		Beautiful day, very hot. Very slight NW wind. NE16. Nothing to report along Bde front, except the usual TM & Bgd Bang activity. A considerable amount of work has been got through during the day. TM Course for the 50% of reserve Stokes Gun Batty. personnel detailed for course commencing 1-8-16. Also names forwarded for LG Course at ETAPLES Commencing 8-8-16. Names of Captains & 4 NCOs forwarded for Infantry Course at 3rd Army School 8-8-16. Report received from 64 INF BDE on our right as to suspicious discharge of white smoke from enemy's lines & later about 1 am we were informed of the same fact by 60 Div. Nothing however came of it, and a quiet night was passed along the whole BDE front.	[signature]

[signature]
BRIG-GENL
Comdg 181st Inf Bde

1577 Wt.W10791/1773 500,000 1/15 D.D.& L.   A.D.S.S./Forms/C.2118.

SECRET.　　　　　　　　　　　　　　　　　　　　APPENDIX I.

Attached To

181ST INFANTRY BRIGADE

WAR DIARY.

For JULY, 1916.

OPERATION ORDER No. 4.

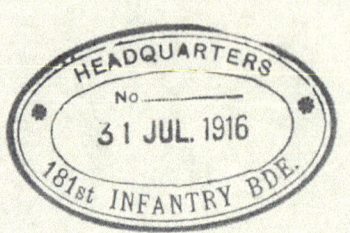

SECRET No. 7

181ST. INFANTRY BRIGADE ORDER NO.4

Ref. LENS Sheet 11.R.F. $\frac{1}{100,000}$ H.Q. 181ST. INF. BDE.

FRANCE " 51.c.N.E. R.F. $\frac{1}{20,000}$ 4-7-16.

1. The 2/23rd. and 2/24th. BATTALIONS LOND. R. will move up on the 5th. inst. for instruction, and will be attached to the 154TH. INF. BDE. as under:-

    2/23rd. LOND. R.
    Route via. HAUTES-AVESNES

Starting Point	Time	Distance	Destination
Road junction ¼ mile S of Church VILLERS-BRULIN	7-0 p.m.	About 10 miles	LOUEZ

    2/24th. LOND. R.
    Route TINQUES -- HAUTES-AVESNES

Starting Point	Time	Distance	Destination
Southernmost House CHELERS.	6-20 p.m.	About 11½ miles	MAROEUIL

2. O.C. Units will arrange for the necessary billeting parties to precede their units. The O.C. 2/23rd. LOND. R. party to report to HQRS. 154TH. INF. BDE., ETRUN at 4 p.m. The O.C. 2/24TH. LOND. R. party to report to the TOWN MAJOR, MAROEUIL, at 4 p.m. The O's C. these parties to arrange to guide their units in on arrival.

3. The Transport of 2/23RD. LOND. R. will be withdrawn to ETRUN on arrival of unit at LOUEZ.

4. No troops to pass the point E.30.d.5.3. (Ref. Sheet 51.c.N.E.) before 9-30 p.m.

5. These Units, on reaching their destination, are entirely under the orders of the Brigade that they are attached to.

6. The usual certificates on leaving billets to be forwarded to this office immediately on departure.

7. Acknowledge.

(Signed) J.N.HORLICK
Captain,
Brigade Major,
181st. Infantry Brigade.

Copies to:-

1. File
2. 2/23rd. LOND. R.
3. 2/24th. LOND. R.
4. H.Q. 154TH. INF. BDE.
5. TOWN MAJOR, MAROEUIL.
6. 60TH. DIVISION.
7 & 8. WAR DIARY.

NOTE:- 4 Platoons 2/23rd. LOND. R. remain behind at VILLERS BRULIN, attend CRATER CONSOLIDATION Course on 6th. inst., and rejoin Bn. at LOUEZ that evening.

SECRET.   APPENDIX II.

Attached To

181ST INFANTRY BRIGADE.

W A R   D I A R Y.

For JULY, 1916.

~~8008~~ - BATTALION RELIEF.
(from instructions)

SECRET.   COPY No......3....

181st INFANTRY BRIGADE
ORDER No. 5.

Ref. FRANCE Sheet   12.7.16.
51^c $\frac{1}{40,000}$.

1. The 2/21 London Regt. will move from the back area to ETRUN on the 13th inst. at 9 a.m. in accordance with 51st Divisional Order No. 61 dated 8.7.16 & 154th Inf. Bde. order No. 34 d/10.7.16, moving via TINQUES-ARRAS road.

2. On reaching Road Junction E.29.b.8.5, troops will proceed by platoons at 100 yards intervals, single wagons at a similar interval.

3. On arrival at ETRUN, supply, baggage and any extra wagons will be unloaded and will be sent back in accordance with instructions which will be issued later.

4. Only 20 horses and 4 chargers will be stabled in ETRUN. The remainder of the horses and two limbers will be sent back immediately after unloading to ACQ, where they will report to the Transport Officer, 2/22 London Regt.

5. On arrival at ETRUN, 3 Coys. of the 2/21 London Regt. will be in Divisional Reserve and on one hour's notice. 1 Company will be in Bde. Reserve and will be on ½ hr. notice.

6. Acknowledge.

                                                    Captain.
                                                Brigade Major.
                                            181st Infantry Brigade.

12.7.16.

Copy No. 1 - Filed.
 "   "   2 - 2/21 L.R.
 "   "   3 & 4 - War Diary.

SECRET. COPY No. 4

181st INFANTRY BRIGADE
ORDER No. 5.

O.S.5

Ref. FRANCE Sheet
$51^c \frac{1}{40,000.}$

12.7.16.

1. The 2/21 London Regt. will move from the back area to ETRUN on the 13th inst. at 9 a.m. in accordance with 51st Divisional Order No. 61 dated 8.7.16 & 154th Inf. Bde. order No. 34 d/10.7.16, moving via TINQUES-ARRAS road.

2. On reaching Road Junction E.29.b.8.5, troops will proceed by platoons at 100 yards intervals, single wagons at a similar interval.

3. On arrival at ETRUN, supply, baggage and any extra wagons will be unloaded and will be sent back in accordance with instructions which will be issued later.

4. Only 20 horses and 4 chargers will be stabled in ETRUN. The remainder of the horses and two limbers will be sent back immediately after unloading to ACQ, where they will report to the Transport Officer, 2/23 London Regt.

5. On arrival at ETRUN, 3 Coys. of the 2/21 London Regt. will be in Divisional Reserve and on one hour's notice. 1 Company will be in Bde. Reserve and will be on ½ hr. notice.

6. Acknowledge.

Captain.
Brigade Major.
181st Infantry Brigade.

12.7.16.

Copy No. 1 - Filed.
"   " 2 - 2/21 L.R.
"   " 3 & 4 - War Diary.

SECRET.   APPENDIX III.

Attached To

181ST INFANTRY BRIGADE

W A R   D I A R Y.

For JULY, 1916.

ORDERS
INTER - BATTALION RELIEF No. I.

SECRET.   Copy No. 14

181st Infantry Brigade Order No. 6.

———oOo———

Reference – Maps 51B & C   Saturday,
            Trench Map.   15th July, 1916.

... ...

1. Battalions in front line will be relieved by Battalions in reserve on evening of 15th inst. according to attached table. ~~Relief to be complete by 7.0 p.m.~~ *The leading Platoon 2/21 LOND R to reach AN21N Communication trench by 1 PM* Details will be arranged by O.Cs. concerned.

2. 2/24th London Regt. will take over Control Posts by 11 a.m. on 16th inst. from 2/21st London R.

   1 Corporal & 3 men   at Church ANZIN
   1 Corporal & 3 men   at Railway Bridge ETRUN.

3. The O.C. 2/23 London R. will take over the command of the ECURIE defences from O.C. 2/22nd London Regt.

4. The Company at ABRI CENTRALE (2/23 London R.) is under the command of O.C. 2/21st London R. The companies at ABRI MOUTON and SUNKEN ROAD (2/23rd London R.) are under the command of O.C. 2/22nd Lond.R.

5. Hourly NOT ½-hourly progress reports will be rendered according to system arranged at Conference.

6. Acknowledge.

                                                  J. Hulick
                                                  Captain.
                                                  Brigade Major.
                                                  181st Infantry Brigade.

Issued at 7.30 p.m. by Orderly.

Copy No. 1   2/21st   No. 9   179th Inf.Bde.
        2   2/22nd   10   60th Div. "G".
        3   2/23rd   11   Staff Captain.
        4   2/24th   12   O.C. Art.Group.
        5   181st M.G.Co.   13   File.
        6   181 T.M.Btty.   14   War Diary.
        7   2/3rd R.E.
        8   41st Inf.Bde.

TABLE OF RELIEF.

181ST INFANTRY BRIGADE.

UNIT.	FROM.	TO.	IN RELIEF OF.	REMARKS.
2/21 London Regt.	ETRUN.	RIGHT I.	2/23 London Regt.	The Order of Relief will be as follows:- The 2/21 L.R. will relieve the 2/23 L.R., who will in turn relieve the 2/22 L.R, who in their turn will relieve the 2/24 L.R., who return to ETRUN.
2/22 London Regt.	Bde. Reserve.	RIGHT II.	2/24 London Regt.	
2/23 London Regt.	RIGHT I.	BDE. RESERVE.	2/22 London Regt.	
2/24 London Regt.	RIGHT II	ETRUN.	2/21 London Regt.	

Os.C. Units will arrange for the necessary guides to meet the incoming Units.
The 2/21 London Regt. will move up from ECRUN to ANZIN by platoons at 100 yds. intervals, especial care being taken to avoid congestion at entrance to ANZIN "UP" Trench.

15.7.16.

SECRET.   APPENDIX IV.
———————   ——————————

                        Attached To

                  181ST INFANTRY BRIGADE

                  W A R   D I A R Y.
                  ————————————————

                     For JULY, 1916.
                  ————————————————

              INTER - BATTALION RELIEF No. II.
                  ————————————————

SECRET.   Copy No......12.....

181ST INFANTRY BRIGADE ORDER No. 7.

Reference - Maps 51B & C.   Wednesday,
           Trench Map.   19th July, 1916.

....

1. Battalions in front line will be relieved by Battalions in reserve on afternoon of 20th inst. according to attached table. The leading Platoon 2/24 London Regt. to reach ANZIN Communication Trench by 3 p.m.

2. The 2/22 London R. will take over Control Posts by 12 noon on 20th inst. from 2/24 London R.

   1 Corporal & 3 men   at CHURCH ANZIN.
   1 Corporal & 3 men   at Railway Bridge ETRUN.

3. The O.C. 2/21 London R. will take over the command of the ECURIE defences from O.C. 2/23 London Regt.

4. The Company at ABRI CENTRALE (2/21 London R.) is under the command of O.C. 2/23 London Regt. The companies at ABRI MOUTON and SUNKEN ROAD (2/21 London R.) are under the command of O.C. 2/24 London R.

5. Hourly progress reports will be rendered according to attached system.

6. Os.C. Units will arrange for necessary guides to meet the incoming Units: 2/22 London R. guides to be at ANZIN CHURCH at 2.50 p.m.

7. Acknowledge.

                                              Captain.
                                           Brigade Major.
                                        181st Infantry Brigade.

Issued at 7.30 p.m. by orderly.

Copy No. 1 2/21st.   7. 41st Inf.Bde.
         2 2/22nd.   8. 179th "   "
         3 2/23rd.   9. O.C. Art.Group.
         4 2/24th.   10. 181 T.M.Battery.
         5 181 M.G.Coy.   11. File.
         6 3/3rd R.E.   12. War Diary.

P.F.4

TABLE OF RELIEF.

181ST INFANTRY BRIGADE.

UNIT.	FROM.	TO.	IN RELIEF OF.	REMARKS.
2/21 LONDON R.	RIGHT I.	BDE. RESERVE.	2/23 LONDON R.	The 2/21st & 2/23rd Relief to be complete by 4 p.m. All Coys. of both Bns. to be in position by that hour.
2/22 LONDON R.	RIGHT II.	DIVL. RESERVE ETRUN.	2/24 LONDON R.	
2/23 LONDON R.	BDE. RESERVE.	RIGHT I.	2/21 LONDON R.	
2/24 LONDON R.	DIVL. RESERVE ETRUN.	RIGHT II.	2/22 LONDON R.	

The Company (2/24 L.R.) proceeding to take over the Right firing line of RIGHT II will move up via ARIE - AVE.MOUTON - AVE.FANTOME.

The remaining three companies (2/24 L.R.) via BETHUNE AVE. - ENIVERSAIRE.

19.7.16.

SECRET.   APPENDIX V.

Attached To

181ST INFANTRY BRIGADE

WAR DIARY.

For JULY, 1916.

ORDERS FOR BOMBARDMENT.
23 — 7 — 16

SECRET   NO ....

181st INFANTRY BRIGADE ORDER No. 8

------oOo------

Ref:- ROCLINCOURT Trench Map   Headquarters
            1/10,000   181st Infantry Bde
                                      22nd July 1916.

1. The enemy's Front and Second Lines opposite the Right Sector, and their T.M.Positions will be bombarded tomorrow at a time to be notified later, by the guns of the Right Artillery Group, Centre Group Howitzer Battery and the Corps Heavy Artillery as under :-

    THE FIELD GUNS (2 Batteries) will bombard the enemy's Front Line trenches.

    The 4.5 HOWITZER BATTERY will engage the emplacements
    at   A.22.b.44.50
                    A.23.b.45.57
                    A.22.b.41.82

    HEAVY ARTILLERY will bombard the Second Line Trenches.

2. The 2" and 3" Trench Mortars will co-operate as under :-
    (a) 15 minutes before the start of the bombardment our Trench Mortars will open on the German Trenches at a slow rate of fire, sufficient to draw retaliation from the hostile T.M's. It is essential that the enemy should be induced to man their T.M's for retaliation by the time the bombardment commences (3 rounds per gun in this period from both the 2" T.M's and 3" Stokes Guns).
                                                    two
    (b) When the bombardment commences the/2" T.M's in RIGHT I will cut the German wire in front of Saps 20 and 21 (A.23.d.2.5. and A.23.c.9.8.) firing 50 rounds per gun.
    The one 2" T.M. in RIGHT II will fire on the hostile T.M. position at A.16.c.95.15, firing 25 rounds.
    (c) The 3" Stokes Mortars after commencement of the bombardment will fire on selected positions of the German front line trenches along the whole front of the Sector, 50 rounds per gun being fired. They will then stand by to counteract retaliation on completion of bombardment.

3. By 5 minutes before the time that the bombardment is due to commence all infantry will have been withdrawn from the Saps and from the fire steps of the BONNAL and will have taken shelter in their dug-outs. They will be ready to man the parapets however, at a moments notice. Infantry will remain in their dug-outs at the discretion of the O.C. Subsector after the cessation of the bombardment, in case of retaliation.
    The above entails the Garrison of the GRAND COLLECTEUR being very much on the alert.
    The bombardment will be carefully watched from this line and its course carefully noted. All men not actually engaged in observation must be under shelter throughout the sector.

4. M.G.Teams will be ready to mount their guns in the shortest possible time, but will remain under cover until that moment.

5. O.C.Subsectors and ECURIE Defences will be responsible that all units in their Subsector are warned as to the bombardment in plenty of time.

6. Any reference to the affair will be referred to as the "CHURCH PARADE FOR SUNDAY AFTERNOON".

7. Acknowledge.

                                        Captain
                                        Brigade Major
                                        181st Infantry Brigade

22-7-16

CONFIDENTIAL.   I.S.11.

DAILY INTELLIGENCE SUMMARY
of
181ST INFANTRY BRIGADE.

From 10 a.m. 23.7.16 To 10 a.m. 24.7.16.
----

1. **OPERATIONS.**

   (a) There was the usual amount of T.M. activity during the day, at 3.15 p.m. as a prelude to the prearranged bombardment, our T.Ms. opened a slow fire on hostile front line and T.M. positions, this successfully drew retaliation by 3.25 p.m. At 3.30 p.m. the bombardment commenced continuing till 4.10 p.m. The field gun shooting was good, many direct hits on enemy's parapets being observed. The 4.5" Howitzers also made good shooting. At 3.40 p.m. one of our 6" Howitzers threw a large quantity of planks etc. into the air, almost 150 yds. west of the LILLE ROAD in the German support line. The bombardment ceased at 4.10 p.m. The enemy made but feeble retaliation. Our T.Ms. materially assisted the guns during the bombardment & our 2" damaged the German front & support line trenches, cutting several gaps in his wire opposite Saps 20 & 21 (A.23.c.9.4 & A.23.c.7.8). Our Stokes guns fired some 300 rounds during the 40 minutes.

   At 3.30 p.m. our M.Gs. firing from LOA, LOB & LOC searched enemy's communication trenches at A.24.b.25.95 to A.18.d.0.65, A.24.c.16.88 to A.17.d.31.22, & A.17.b.3.3 to A.17.b.55.0, firing 750 rounds from each gun.

   The gaps made in enemy wire opposite Saps 20 & 21 (A.23.c.9.4 & A.23.c.7.8) were kept under Lewis gun fire during the early part of the night & the enemy were hindered from repairing them.

   (b) At 11.55 p.m. and again at 3.15 a.m. raids with bombs & rifle grenades were made by enemy bombers on our Sap 30A (A.22.a.8.7). Our bombers at once proceeded to scatter this party & they threw half a dozen Mills bombs & there was some fire from Stokes Gun which quieted the enemy.

   About 4.30 p.m. several heavies (Shrapnel) burst in the vicinity of ABRI MOUTON (A.23.a.5.6), no damage was done.

   Hostile M.Gs. tried to search LILLE ROAD between 11.45 p.m. and 12.30 a.m. but there was nothing to search for.

   (c) One of our patrols exploring the crater at the head of Sap 24 (A.22.d.70.95) encountered a strong party of the enemy patrolling in and around the crater at 3.40 a.m. A brisk exchange of bombs occurred, the enemy eventually retired, no enemy wounded or dead were found.

   Two bombers went out from Sap 32A (A.16.c.6.1.) and bombed a spot where a machine gun was concealed. They claim to have been successful in destroying this target.

   The enemy patrolled more freely and were fired on in several cases.

2. **INTELLIGENCE.**

   The strange curlew call reported in Divnl. Intelligence report, apparently emanated from us as it is the rallying call of the 181st M.G.Coy.

   A great deal of commotion was caused among enemy transport by our searching M.G.fire on the night of the 22/23rd.

   The enemy have apparently more or less located our 2" T.M. position at A.23.c.40.40 as Coy.H.Q., which is near the emplacement had about 50 T.M. & aerial torpedo bombs round it during the course of the afternoon.

   At 8.5 p.m. a carrier pigeon was seen to approach from direction of ECURIE and pass over our lines, thence over enemy lines flying in a northerly direction.

   Red lights were sent up from enemy's lines opposite right of Right Coy's. Sector about 10.30 p.m. but nothing followed.

/Contd.

DAILY INTELLIGENCE SUMMARY
    (Continued)

I.S.11.

-2-

3. GENERAL.
    (a) The Fallen Aeroplane is certainly a well-built sniper's position. There is a plate in centre of the debris which has been fired on & hit without apparent results.
    (b) Our aircraft were busy throughout the day. At 8.15 p.m. one of our biplanes flew over enemy's lines under fire, it was seen to burst into flame but was able to get back & descended in rear of our lines.

4. WORK DONE.
    (a) Repairing & rebuilding fire & support trenches where damaged by hostile bombardment. A number of saps were also repaired.
    Nine boxes of ammunition were recovered by SEC.LIEUT. NORBURY of the Bde.M.G.Coy. from the W emplacement (A.22.d.7.5), this officer who was in full view of the enemy while doing so ran great risk of being crushed by the rest of the emplacement collapsing.

24.7.16.

                      Brig.-General.
                      Cmdng. 181st Infantry Brigade.

SECRET.   APPENDIX VI.

Attached To

181ST INFANTRY BRIGADE

W A R   D I A R Y

For JULY, 1916.

INTER - BATTALION RELIEF No. 3.

SECRET.   Copy No. 12

181ST INFANTRY BRIGADE ORDER No. 9.

Reference - Maps 51 B & C.   Thursday,
            Trench Map.   27th July, 1916.

... ...

1. Battalions in front line will be relieved by Battalions in reserve on afternoon of 28th inst. according to attached table, under arrangements to be made by C.Os. concerned. The leading platoon 2/22 London Regt. to reach ANZIN Communication Trench by 1 p.m.

2. The 2/23 London R. will take over Control Posts by 12 noon on 28th inst. from 2/22 London R.

       1 Corporal & 3 men   at   CHURCH ANZIN.
       1 Corporal & 3 men   at   RAILWAY BRIDGE, ETRUN.

3. The O.C. 2/24 London R. will take over the command of the ECURIE Defences from O.C. 2/21 London R.

4. The Company at ABRI CENTRALE (2/24 London R.) is under the command of O.C. 2/21 London R. The Companies at ABRI HOUTON and SUNKEN ROAD (2/24 London R.) are under the command of O.C. 2/22 London R.

5. No Companies of the 2/21 London R. will move from present positions until actually relieved by Companies of the 2/24 London R.

6. Hourly progress reports will not be rendered but on completion of the relief will be reported in accordance with code issued with Relief Order No. 7.

7. Os.C. Units will arrange for necessary guides to meet the incoming Units: 2/24 London R. guides to be at ANZIN CHURCH at 12.50 p.m.

8. Acknowledge.

                                                Captain.
                                          Brigade Major.
                                   181st Infantry Brigade.

Issued at 7.30 p.m. by orderly.

Copy No: 1 2/21st.   7. 41st Inf.Bde.
         2 2/22nd.   8. 179th "   "
         3 2/23rd.   9. O.C.Art.Group.
         4 2/24th.   10. 181 T.M.Battery.
         5 181 M.G.Coy.   11. File.
         6 3/2rd R.E.   12. War Diary.

P.F.4.

TABLE OF RELIEF.

181ST INFANTRY BRIGADE.

UNIT.	FROM.	TO.	IN RELIEF OF.	REMARKS.
2/21 LONDON R.	BDE. RESERVE.	R I.	2/23 LONDON R.	Order of relief as follows:- 2/23 to relieve 2/24. 2/24 to relieve 2/21. 2/21 to relieve 2/22.
2/22 LONDON R.	DIVNL. RESERVE. HEBUT.	R II.	2/24 LONDON R.	
2/23 LONDON R.	R I.	DIVNL. RESERVE. HEBUT.	2/22 LONDON R.	
2/24 LONDON R.	R II.	BDE. RESERVE.	2/21 LONDON R.	

The Company (2/22 L.R.) proceeding to take over the Right Firing Line of R II will move up via
AKHIN – AVELUCHTON – AVE.PORTER.
The remaining three companies (2/22 L.R.) via HEBERN AVE. – ABEYVILLERIE.
The 2/23 L.R. will move from HEBUT to points of 6 minute intervals.

25.7.16.

SECRET.

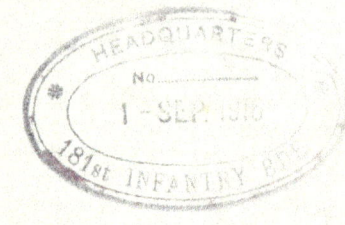

181ST INFANTRY BRIGADE

WAR DIARY.

1st - 31st AUGUST, 1916.

Vol. I. No. 3.

---------------oOo---------------

Army Form C. 2118.

WAR DIARY
—of— 181st INFANTRY BRIGADE
INTELLIGENCE SUMMARY.
(Erase heading not required.)

Instructions regarding War Diaries and Intelligence Summaries are contained in F.S. Regs., Part II. and the Staff Manual respectively. Title pages will be prepared in manuscript.

Place	Date	Hour	Summary of Events and Information	Remarks and references to Appendices
ETRUN	1-8-16		A Beautiful day, wind East. A normal day along all the Bde front, perhaps slightly more TM activity on the Right of Right I than usual. During the night B1/1 The enemy attempted to bomb Sap 26 B but were driven off, 3 of the enemy being hit. The enemy have made their front line trenches with large notice boards probably as a guide to their guns. The personnel of the 50% reserve for the 181 TM Battery left for LIGNY-ST ROCHER all except the 2/22 POND R. party arrived late for two motor lorries provided at ECOIVRES. A quiet night, except for our MG activity	Sgd
ETRUN	2-8-16		A Beautiful Day. Wind West. A quiet morning, afternoon rather uneasy, enemy fires a number of HE & "B" shells in the vicinity of ABRI MOUTON about 6 pm. Stokke Aeroplanes very active, passing over ETRUN. MARŒUIL & ACQ were bombed during the day. A British Aeroplane brought down near Adv Bde STO. The enemy shelled it heavily with Shrapnel & then heavies, eventually scoring a direct hit & destroying it. Stokes TMs active during evening on Row I and occasionally during the night, otherwise the situation was normal.	Sgd

WAR DIARY
INTELLIGENCE SUMMARY

Army Form C. 2118.

of 18th INFANTRY BRIGADE.

Place	Date	Hour	Summary of Events and Information	Remarks and references to Appendices
ETRUN	3-8-16		A beautiful day, slight SW wind. Nothing unusual occurred on the Brigade front during the day. The new Coy of the 2/4 Bn LOND R and the 6 down Ams also the 2 Pioneer Platoons garrisoning ECURIE practiced "BATTLE QUARTERS" during the day, it took 30 minutes before everyone was in position. Considerable hostile aeroplane activity during the day, bombs being dropped in various places. The Brigadier had interviews with both the CRA and DIVNL GENERAL. Intimation was received during the evening that the 6/4th Bn 8th Bde 2nd Divn on our right intended filling up the trench connecting their trench to our post in SAP 20 with wire, the OC 2/21 LOND R was duly notified. G. Summerigh.	J.M.D.
ETRUN	4-8-16		A dull morning, beautiful afternoon, slight N. Wind. During night 3/4 our Heavy Howitzers fired on THELUS in answer to hostile bombardment of ACQ Naval TM activity on both sides. It was reported during the morning that one of our STOKES MORTARS had been knocked out by a direct hit from a shell & 50 rounds of ammunition blown up. Patrols busy as usual. RE proceeding on new dug out scheme. LEWIS GUN COURSE at ÉTAPLES opened 1 B/SC BOR from 2/21, 7/22 LOND R. at 11.15pm our 18/Pro Neer Cutting wire of posts Sap 23. Apparently with success. Considerable damage was done	J.M.D.

WAR DIARY
of 181 INFANTRY BRIGADE
INTELLIGENCE SUMMARY.
(Erase heading not required.)

Army Form C. 2118.

Instructions regarding War Diaries and Intelligence Summaries are contained in F. S. Regs., Part II. and the Staff Manual respectively. Title pages will be prepared in manuscript.

Place	Date	Hour	Summary of Events and Information	Remarks and references to Appendices
ETRUN	5.8.16		Beautiful day, not so warm, fresh N'otherly wind. During night 4/5 our M.Gs were active, firing on enemy dumps, tramways, etc. During the morning the G.O.C. 64 B'de G.S.O.I 63div & G.S.O.I 21 Div and B'de Major made a thorough inspection of junction of the Brigade and arranged for a division at Duisans relations. About 11.15 a.m. the enemy apparently struck one of our Observation Balloons with a shell as the observer jumped out with parachute, & the Balloon slowly crumpled & was hurriedly pulled down. There was a certain amount of shelling during the day. At 8.30 p.m. we received the orders from 60 Div ack to Stand by GAS ALERT, until being informed this was cancelled about 4.15 p.m. At midnight the enemy opened a bombardment on our immediate right, continuing until 12.35 A.M. he had apparently seen a grass cutting patrol. 3 N.C.Os from B'de at Sniping School H.C.Q. About midnight our howitzers fired several rounds at distant targets. Beyond bombardment night was normal. During the afternoon Div inter Battalion relief was carried out. Were without casualties.	A.D.S.R. / J.M.S. / APP I
ETRUN	6.8.16		Beautiful day. Wind ANE, fady strong. The day was normal, very little artillery activity. TMS active as usual. At 10.30 PM a raid on the German trenches was carried out by the 179th B'de on our left. Men go forward to Divisions for Lewis Gun Course at ETAPLES commencing Aug 12th 2/23 Bn MDR Operation orders received for the operation to-morrow.	J.M.S.

1577 Wt.W10791/1773 500,000 1/15 D. D. & L.   A.D.S.S./Forms/C. 2118.

WAR DIARY

INTELLIGENCE SUMMARY

Army Form C. 2118.

of 1/81 INFANTRY BRIGADE.

Place	Date	Hour	Summary of Events and Information	Remarks and references to Appendices
ETRUN	7.6.16		A Beautiful Day. Wind N.E, fairly fresh. The day was unusually quiet during the morning. There being just the normal T.M. activity on both sides. All final arrangements for the Raid were made during the morning and everything cut and dried as far as possible. All the necessary people being warned as to the time of ZERO. A final addition was made in the evening of the firing of a white rocket after the Recall signal as a guide to the raiding party. By 6.30 PM. Inf Brig. and 151st MAJOR arrived at BATTLE H.Q.R.S. Both sides were exceedingly quiet before the operation. Commenced. the distant gunfire of the Somme fighting could be distinctly heard. For details of the operations see App II. There was a false GAS alarm about 10 PM which caused considerable trouble, otherwise after the "CEASE FIRE" signal matters were quite quiet. During the raid our M. Guns were very active firing on the Crossup. See PM. TRAINING COURSE at HERMANVILLE. Commenced 10/T 2M.Co[?] each from M[?]/[?]/[?]/2/2.0 NR	APP II.
ETRUN	8.6.16		A Beautiful Day, wind N.E. The Brigadier returned to REAR H.Q.R.S. about 10am. The G.O.C. DIVN visited the trenches & H.Q. of 2/23 LOND R. in Connection with the raid. LT. FAINT was evacuated during the day to the 42nd C.C. Station. he was badly wounded by Shrapnel in arms, legs or feet. The day was unusually quiet, there being no active artillery activity on the part of the enemy at all	

WAR DIARY
or INTELLIGENCE SUMMARY.

Army Form C. 2118.

of 151 INFANTRY BRIGADE

Place	Date	Hour	Summary of Events and Information	Remarks and references to Appendices
ETRUN	Contd. 8.8.16		not even his TM's firing. very enemy flags and boards are continually being put up at different places along the enemy's front. work was again recommenced in the Sector. The RE (213 Fd Coy) starting on several dug-outs in the Sector. During the night, search was made for the missing men, but with no success at all. 3 NCO's from the D/21 Lord R commenced a Sniping Course at NCCC. 4 officers & 4 NCO's 10 each from each Bde commenced an Infantry Training Course at AUXI LE CHATEAU. The night was quiet on the whole front.	[signature]
ETRUN	9.8.16		Beautiful day, N E wind. It was noticed during the course of the 8th inst that the enemy trenches had been badly knocked about by our Shellfire during the bombardment on the evening of the 7th inst. A normal day in the line. The Position for the Lag TM was finally selected & the RE party told off to work on it. The BRIGADIER wrote [illegible] NOW ST KIOI, 182 Bde Hqs where he was received by H.M. THE KING at 3.45 PM. About 7 pm the enemy put 5 Heavy Shells into ANZIN. Our MG's fired several thousand rounds during the night on the enemy's tramways, dumps etc. Several patrols went out, and search was again made for the missing men without avail, 3 rifles & bayonets and a bag of bombs were however brought in. night quiet	[signature]

WAR DIARY

of 181 INFANTRY BRIGADE

INTELLIGENCE SUMMARY

Army Form C. 2118.

Place	Date	Hour	Summary of Events and Information	Remarks and references to Appendices
ETRUN	10-8-16		A damp muggy morning. Wind NW. it cleared up towards evening. The B.G. Major went over the work to be done at the junction with the 13th on the right with Capt. Montgomery OC Pioneer Coy (1/1/2 Ln L.N.V.C.S.). 1 Offr. 1/4 OR Commenced ArtillerY & T.M.S course at REVIN CAPELLE (3 days). During the day our Stokes guns blew a complete gap in the enemy's front line trench. The g's as usual fired about 3000 rounds during the night 9/10th. Hostile T.M's during the night did a great deal of damage to Saps 24 & 26 killing 3 and wounding 5 men. A Lewis Gun was also knocked out. The connecting trench between our right & the B.De on our right (64th) was commenced & traverses made. The Big T.M emplacement was also started.	M.E.
ETRUN	11-8-16		A beautiful day. Wind NW. The B.G. regarded attended a Divisional Conference at ECOUVRES at 11 a.m. with reference to the method of holding the line. Our light guns and T.M's were both active during the day, otherwise a normal day. During the evening an aeroplane dropped a German Pamphlet apparently an answer to the book "J'accuse". The Patrols went out during the night. There was a certain amount of aeroplane activity on our front during the day. The CoRPS CoMr visited the line. 3 h COs 1/23 to Snipers Course (3 days) at ACQ. Night normal.	F.E.

Army Form C. 2118.

WAR DIARY of 181 INFANTRY BRIGADE.

INTELLIGENCE SUMMARY.

(Erase heading not required.)

Place	Date	Hour	Summary of Events and Information	Remarks and references to Appendices
ETRUN	12-6-16		A beautiful day, exceedingly hot. Wind N.E. The B'de Major accompanied The O.C. 2/23 Lond.R. in an inspection of the Saps 23, 24, 26a, 26B with reference to withdrawing the advanced posts in the observation line. Capt Col DICOTT 2/21 Lond R who was voluntarily up in front wiring, although his Bn was in rest, in the morning must have been worn & pushed forward & brooded The German front line. The day was normal in activity, our guns smashed up the lips of some craters just to the North of the LIHE road, & our heavies put several shells into THELUS. Our snipers claim 3 Huns hit during the day. In the evening the Allied T.M's fired at their usual target of the junction of THE BONVAL and CHENINCREUX doing a certain amount of material damage. At 2am (13) a combined strafe of Craters XIX & XIXa was carried out by a field gun battery, 1 2" T.M. & 2 Stokes with good effect & judge by the hostile retaliation. The usual M.g activity. 7 patrols sent out on our front. At 5.45 pm a hostile T.M. shot put our emplacement (in g) M.S.D. killing two men & wounding two. Aeroplanes active during the day. 1 Offr & 5 men to LEWIS Gun course. Golf Course LE TOUQUET. B'de Sig Offr & NCO's Sig Scot. 2 NCO's each Bn to 13 Sq R.F.C. for instruction in communication between infantry & R.F.C. Operation Orders issued for Inter-Bn relief.	C.O.P.T

WAR DIARY

INTELLIGENCE SUMMARY

Army Form C. 2118.

of 2/1st INFANTRY BRIGADE.

(Erase heading not required.)

Instructions regarding War Diaries and Intelligence Summaries are contained in F. S. Regs., Part II. and the Staff Manual respectively. Title pages will be prepared in manuscript.

Place	Date	Hour	Summary of Events and Information	Remarks and references to Appendices
ETRUN	13-8-16		Very heavy rain in the early morning. A hot oppressive day. Wind puffy westerly. The Staff Capt: visited the water supply in company with R.E. A quiet morning. The Relief was carried out without any hitch, the all complete coming in at 7 p.m. Between 6.30 & 7 a.m. our light gun bombarded the enemy's front line opposite Saps 21 & 23 with excellent effect. Hostile TM again bombarded the Bewmn at L1.2 & L2.3 doing considerable damage. Our Snipers claim one hit & our post in SAP 21 also hit a man. The gas were active as usual. 1 Officer 4 O.R. 2/24 Lond R to ANTI GAS School at FREVIN CAPELLE. A normal night.	Fritz
ETRUN	14-8-16		A dull day, heavy showers in the afternoon. Q.S.W. wind gusty, quite strong at times. Enemy fired HE methodically most of the morning at our Field gun batteries. Information received that our BATTLE HQ are to be handed over to XIth Corps as they are in that Corps area and a new one to be selected. One was selected in HIGH STREET, ECURIE (intrepid). Our TM's were very active during the day damaging the enemy's front line trenches considerably. One of our Snipers claim a hit. An Corps action during the night 3 O.R. 2/21 Lond R to Sniping School at ACQ. The Crater Consolidation Course at MONIGRES Commenced 2 Offrs 8 O.R. 2/24 Lond R also Physical Training Course at HERMAVILLE 1 Offr 4 O.R.	WD

Army Form C. 2118.

WAR DIARY
or
INTELLIGENCE SUMMARY

of 181 INFANTRY BRIGADE

(Erase heading not required.)

Instructions regarding War Diaries and Intelligence Summaries are contained in F. S. Regs., Part II. and the Staff Manual respectively. Title Pages will be prepared in manuscript.

Place	Date	Hour	Summary of Events and Information	Remarks and references to Appendices
ETRUN	15.8.16		An oppressive morning. Violent storms of rain during the day. Wind strong & gusty S.W. G.v.g. quiet morning up to 8 a.m. The Corps Heavy Artillery bombarded the enemy T.M. positions from 5 – 5.15 p.m. Our T.M's did considerable damage to the enemy's front line. Our artillery dug The trenches were bombarded 5.0" for 1½ hours, a dug out was blown in and a machine gun and emplacement was knocked out. Our Snipers claimed 4 hits. M. Gs active as usual from 10 pm to midnight	JN
ETRUN	16.8.16		A warm dull day. Slight showers of rain in the evening. Wind S.W. A quieter day. Arty. as from our four field gun batteries & Stokes guns and one 2" mortar bombarded the enemy's wire from a support trench vicinity for 2 minutes. The enemy expecting an infantry attack immediately fired the S.O.S. Signal red rockets breaking into two, after a three minute rest our 4 Stokes suddenly reopened with 30 bursts in the fast trench. The 4 Stokes fired about 300 shells. The results were most satisfactory. Artillery reply was feeble. Light A.S. Forbes Adjt of the 181 M.G. Coy is as most unfortunately shot through the head and killed whilst firing from the open emplacement in the PANTONG. He was an excellent officer & is a very great loss to the Bde.	JN
ETRUN	17.8.16		An oppressively close day. With Reminders storms of rain in the afternoon, including a severe thunder about 8 p.m. Wind very variable N - N.W. An exceptionally quiet morning and afternoon. The enemy firing much below his usual number of T.M's and Fizz Bangs. Our Snipers snipers a German. The night to see quiet except for the normal M.G. fire 3 men 2/4 to 2/8 R commenced a Sniping course at A.T.Q. 2 N.Cos 181 M.G. Coy commenced Artists Course at MAGNY CAMEL	JN

Army Form C. 2118.

WAR DIARY
of 181 INFANTRY BRIGADE
INTELLIGENCE SUMMARY
(Erase heading not required.)

Instructions regarding War Diaries and Intelligence Summaries are contained in F. S. Regs., Part II. and the Staff Manual respectively. Title Pages will be prepared in manuscript.

Place	Date	Hour	Summary of Events and Information	Remarks and references to Appendices
ETRUN	18.8.16		A beautiful morning, though very misty, heavy rain in the afternoon. Wind N.W. very mild. Another quiet morning, artillery from troops up just behind ROCLINCOURT fired a considerable amount during the morning, exploding the enemy's trenches. Our T.M⁵ were active throughout the day, making very good shooting. T.G⁵ active as usual during the night. Several patrols also went out during the night, but no very definite results were obtained. A new class for the crater consolidation course at AGNIÈRES was commenced. 2 OFFICERS 8 O.R. The weather has rather impeded the work on the improvement of the line. The new method of water supply in the sector (by means of pressure through the 4" main) working most satisfactorily.	JHL
ETRUN	19.8.16		A very wet morning although it cleared up a bit in the evening. Chilly all day. Wind N.W. a quite strong. During the morning ECURIE and MADAGASCAR were shelled by the enemy, no damage being done. As our T.M and Artillery activity increases that of the enemy is steadily decreasing. A Divisional Staff Officer inspected the saps on our RIGHT front during the morning. Our Mortars were again very active during the day, and a few gun knocked about our O.P pretty badly near the LINE Road, exposing an iron structure itself Aerial Torpedoes caused two casualties near Sap 20 or our right about 2.15 p.m. Our general repair and keep work proceeded satisfactorily during the day. The enemy were very quiet during the night till 1 a.m which appear as if a relief were taking place as suspected, our guns throughout the night bombarded their main communication trenches. The night was otherwise quiet except for the usual T.M.G activity.	JHL

Army Form C. 2118.

WAR DIARY
of 181 INFANTRY BRIGADE
INTELLIGENCE SUMMARY

(Erase heading not required.)

Place	Date	Hour	Summary of Events and Information	Remarks and references to Appendices
ETRUN	20.8.16		A dull cold day, with a strong N.W. wind. Our T.M's were not quite so active during the day. Gas Retalgung bombarded the enemy's support line with good effect about 7.30 p.m. our advanced Lewis gun caused much annoyance and damage to the enemy's trenches during the day. Enemy were quiet. Trench mortar. Two patrols out a usual M.G activity on enemy's dumps, a considerable amount of smoke was observed from the enemy's trench during the early morning. 3 O.R's Rank to Shipong Camp at M.O.Q. 1 Officer 4 O.R. to RUTIGA'S School at PREVIN CAPELLE. Quiet night.	JM2
ETRUN	21.8.16		A nice day, rather cold, wind N.W. ⊕ Very quiet in early morning. Usual T.M. activity on 18 pr twice silenced hostile TM's during the afternoon. Our Snipers claim one hit on our Right. Our M.G's fired at enemy tramway and dumps during the night and also silenced hostile M.G. which was firing on LILLE Road Barricade & Dump. A good amount of aerial activity during the day. 1 Offr & 1 NCO from 1/2 Lond R. to METEMNVILLE for a Physical Training Course. A normal night. The Relief of B.N's in front line was carried out during the day without any trouble. 1 man of the 2/sd Lond R. killed. 1 man 1/23 Lond R. wounded	JM2 APPI
ETRUN	22.8.16		A Beautiful day, much warmer. Wind very slight westerly. Usual T.M and artillery activity in the morning especially directed on our new portion of trench connecting with the 61st Int B'de on our right. Our 60 pr TM's & Stokes were very busy in the Right Sub sector and did a good amount of damage to the enemy's trenches. Enemy fired Aerial Torpedoes without testing out the fuses, it thus appear that there are inexperienced troops opposite us. Two patrols went out without discovering anything of importance. Our aerial activity was normal. The 1/4 Lond R. sent 2 Officers & 8 O.R to AGNIERES for the Gates Caustic show Course. Work proceeding most satisfactorily in the Scots	JM2

Army Form C. 2118.

WAR DIARY
or
INTELLIGENCE SUMMARY

of 161 INFANTRY BRIGADE.

(Erase heading not required.)

Instructions regarding War Diaries and Intelligence Summaries are contained in F. S. Regs., Part II. and the Staff Manual respectively. Title Pages will be prepared in manuscript.

Place	Date	Hour	Summary of Events and Information	Remarks and references to Appendices
ETRUN	23-8-16		A wee morning, rain in evening, practically no wind, what there was S.E. A quiet day apart from our artillery shelling the German support & reserve line trenches periodically during the day. Our TM's also fairly active. Enemy very quiet. The usual patrols were out during the evening & our MG's were active during the night. 3 men from 2/10 LONDR to HQ 2/5 MIDDX came. A good deal of work got through.	JMH
ETRUN	24-8-16		A beautiful day, wind very slight & East in morning veering round to NW through the course of the day. We shelled the enemy intermittently throughout the day, & at 9 pm carried out a burst of rapid fire. We again heavily bombarded the enemy trenches with Artillery & TM fire. The enemy fired a few shells on ETRUN at about 4 pm & our kitns a civilian & wounded 2 children. The during the evening sent a fathway through his wire just south of the BILLETOAD. About from M.G.'s a quiet night. (other H.Q. from 2/10 LOND to PREVINCAPELLE for an anti gas course.)	JMH
ETRUN	25-8-16		A very close muggy day, rain in afternoon, very little wind. S.E. Our TM's were extremely active during the day and our Stokes guns violently bombarded the enemy's trenches at 3.45 pm. 5.30 pm & 7 + 8 pm. The enemy's trenches and wire was severely damaged. The enemy retaliated chiefly on our left damaging a Stokes Gun & knocking in 30 yards of trench in the BURMAH. 4 men wounded. Our M.G's were very active and three patrols including one INDIAN (2/5 CIH) patrol were out, nothing special to report. Hostile aeroplanes were more active than usual during the day, no less than 5 coming over our lines. All trains with reference to the Raid to be carried out by the 2/24 LOND R. completed, with the exception of final instructions.	JMH

Army Form C. 2118.

WAR DIARY
—OR— 181 INFANTRY BRIGADE.
INTELLIGENCE SUMMARY
(Erase heading not required.)

Instructions regarding War Diaries and Intelligence Summaries are contained in F. S. Regs., Part II. and the Staff Manual respectively. Title Pages will be prepared in manuscript.

Place	Date	Hour	Summary of Events and Information	Remarks and references to Appendices
ETRUN	26-8-16		A muggy day inspite of strong SW wind. Severe storms of rain in the morning. Our TMs fired intermittently during the day and our Artillery was active, especially between 3pm & 7.30pm. An 18ptr which had been put into position in front of ECURIE did good work firing some 60 rounds. It was however located about 5pm & heavily shelled by 5.9 & 4.2 howitzers. The Battery CO CAPT CRAIG. 3 o.R. B BATTY being killed & 4 of the crew wounded. The gun itself however was untouched & was withdrawn during the night without loss. Several patrols were out during the night, but had nothing important to report. The 3/5 & 2/4 Field Coys R.E. engaged in special work in the front line (BONNAL) assisted by 2 officers 40 o.R. of Q Coy ARMY TROOPS RE made satisfactory progress. Q Coy details were billeted in dugouts in ARIANE west of BETHUNE Road. Other work very impeded by the bad weather. 2 officers & 8 o.R of the 1/22 LOND R to AGNIERES for instruction in CRATER Consolidation.	*[init]*
ETRUN	27-8-16		A warm day. very heavy rain during the morning early and again at intervals throughout the day. Wind SW and quite strong varying from 10 to 14 M.P.H. The morning was quiet our TMs & those of the enemy were intermittently active. Our TMs were again exceedingly active on our right. The enemy's front line being most severely knocked about very little retaliation followed about 10.30pm. The enemy fired 3 Shells to which gave off sulphurous clouds of smoke. Our M G's were active as usual during the night & the enemy shewed increased activity in this line against our left. Suspected content during the night. The 2/23 LOND R sent 1 officer 2 o.R & the 2/24 2 o.R to the Lewis Gun School at FREVIN CAPELLE. CAPT R.C.A. MORGAN WESTMINSTER DRAGOONS attached to B'de for instruction in Staff Duties.	*[init]*

WAR DIARY
6/1st INFANTRY BRIGADE
INTELLIGENCE SUMMARY

Army Form C. 2118.

Place	Date	Hour	Summary of Events and Information	Remarks and references to Appendices
ETRUN	26-9-16		Overcast muggy day with showers of rain. Wind S.E. About 3am a party of GERMANS attempted to bomb S.A.P. 31. they were driven off by rifle fire. Not quite so much T.M. activity on our front as usual & a consequent increase in hostile T.M. fire. 5.9" H.E. shells were fired at the Bn north about 5pm. 2 more Sulphur Shells were fired about 10pm. News was received during the day that ROUMANIA had declared war on AUSTRIA. A large notice board with this in GERMAN was posted at the head of one of our SAPS. Hostile M.G. activity. Special work in the trenches proceeding satisfactorily. All the final preparations for the 2/24th LONDON R. RAID completed. 2/23 LONDON R. sent 1 officer & 1 N.C.O. to CAMIERS & 1 officer to CAMIERS for Musketry Course also 1 officer & 4 men to HERMAVILLE for Physical Training. Br. Major visited DIV. as to Special Work being done.	Jmt APP III. Jmt APP I.
ETRUN	29-9-16		A horrible Day, with Terrifically Heavy Rain & Thunder Storm in the afternoon and again at night. Wind EAST. At 2.10 PM the 3/2th LONDON R. carried out a Raid of two CRATERS (xxxxixa) opposite to GERMAN's. They all returned safely. All quiet for the rest of the day except for intermittent T.M. activity along the front. 20 H.E. Shells were fired into ECURIE about 11 am I think. No result - water train and Trolley line damaged. The later Bn. Relief was carried out without incident during the day. 1 officer & 8 men to LEWIS Gun School at ETAPLES. 2/19 LONDON R. carried out a very successful raid on the enemy capturing 8 and ? swallowing ? no Casualties.	Jmt
ETRUN	30-9-16		A really Terrible Day, clearing a gale from veering in morning from almost South to North in afternoon. heavy rain also at intervals. The Trenches quite flooded out and weeks of work destroyed. Conference of CO.s ref Special operations at ECURIE 3pm. The G.O.C. DIV. visited the BDE HQ during the morning. Not so much activity as usual, as all hands were on clearing trenches & pumping. Special Work proceeding well in spite of the weather. 2 officers & S.O.R. 2/23 LONDON R. to CRATER Consolidation Course at AGNIERES	Jmt

…

Army Form C. 2118.

WAR DIARY
or
INTELLIGENCE SUMMARY
of 181 INFANTRY BRIGADE
(Erase heading not required.)

Place	Date	Hour	Summary of Events and Information	Remarks and references to Appendices
ETRUN	31-8-16		A nice warm day. Strong wind SW. The usual I'm activity video. Hostile Artillery more active than usual. 5.9"s shelling intermittently our firing line & Support trenches, a large proportion of shells were blind. Usual M.G. activity at night	Initials

J M Hulile.
Captain
Brigade Major
for Brigadier-General
Comdg 181st Infantry Bde

SECRET.   APPENDIX I.

                        181ST INFANTRY BRIGADE.
                        ─────────────────

                          W A R   D I A R Y.

                          1st - 31st AUG./16.
                        ─────────────────

                   RELIEF ORDERS Nos. 10, 12, 13 & 15.
                        ─────────────────

                             Vol. I. No. 3.

                        ─────────o0o─────────

SECRET.   Copy No...13....

181ST INFANTRY BRIGADE ORDER No. 10.

Reference - Maps 51 B & C   Thursday,
            Trench Map.   3rd August, 1916.

1. Battalions in front line will be relieved by Bns. in reserve on afternoon of 5th inst. according to attached table, under arrangements to be made by C.Os. concerned. The leading platoon 2/23 L.R. to reach ANZIN Communication Trench by 3.0 p.m.

2. The 2/21 L.R. will take over Control Posts by 12 noon on 5th inst. from 2/23 L.R.

       1 Corporal & 3 men   at   CHURCH ANZIN.
       1 Corporal & 3 men   at   RAILWAY BRIDGE, ETRUN.

3. The O.C. 2/22 L.R. will take over command of the ECURIE Defences from O.C. 2/24 L.R.

4. The Company at ABRI CENTRALE (2/22 L.R.) is under the command of the O.C. 2/23 L.R.
   The Companies at ABRI MOUTON and SUNKEN ROAD (2/22 L.R.) are under the command of O.C. 2/24 L.R.

5. Os.C. 2/22 and 2/24 L.R. will so arrange their relief that ECURIE is not left ungarrisoned at any time during the relief, and that the Company at ABRI CENTRALE is relieved by 3.30 p.m., at that hour all trenches east of LILLE RD. must be clear of troops of 2/22 & 2/24 L.R.

6. Completion of relief will be reported to Brigade H.Q. as per attached code.

7. Os.C. Units will arrange for necessary guides to meet the incoming Units: 2/21 L.R. guides to be at ANZIN CHURCH at 2.50 p.m.

8. Acknowledge.

                                                      Captain.
                                                    Brigade Major.
Issued at 7.30 p.m. by orderly.   181st Infantry Brigade.

Copy No. 1   2/21st   8.   179th Inf.Bde.
         2   2/22nd   9.   O.C. Art.Group.
         3   2/23rd   10.   181 T.M.Battery.
         4   2/24th   11.   Pioneer Coy. ECURIE.
         5   181 M.G.Coy.   12.   File.
         6   3/3rd R.E.   13.   War Diary.
         7   41st Inf.Bde.

P.F.4.

TABLE OF RELIEF.

181ST INFANTRY BRIGADE.

UNIT.	FROM.	TO.	IN RELIEF OF.	REMARKS.
2/21 Lond.R.	R I.	DIVNL. RESERVE, ETKUN.	2/23 Lond.R.	
2/22 Lond.R.	R II.	BRIGADE RESERVE.	2/24 Lond.R.	
2/23 Lond.R.	DIVNL. RESERVE, ETKUN.	R I.	2/21 Lond.R.	
2/24 Lond.R.	BRIGADE RESERVE.	R II.	2/22 Lond.R.	
The 2/23 L.R. will move from ETKUN to ANZIN by Platoons at 5 minute intervals.				

3.8.16.

SECRET.   Copy No......13......

181st INFANTRY BRIGADE ORDER No. 12.

Reference – Maps 51 B & C.   Friday,
          Trench Map.   11th August, 1916.

...   .

1. Battalions in front line will be relieved by Bns. in Reserve on afternoon of the 13th inst., according to attached Table, under arrangements to be made by Os.C. concerned. The leading platoon 2/21 L.R. to reach ANZIN Communication Trench by 1 p.m.

2. The 2/24 L.R. will take over control posts by 12 noon on the 13th inst. from 2/21 L.R..

3. The O.C. 2/23 L.R. will take over command of the LOURIE Defences from O.C. 2/22 L.R.

4. No companies of the 2/22 L.R. will move from present positions until actually relieved by companies of the 2/23 L.R.

5. Completion of relief will be reported to Brigade H.Q. as per attached code.

6. Os.C. Units will arrange for necessary guides to meet the incoming Units: 2/23 L.R. guides to be at ANZIN CHURCH at 12.50 p.m.

7. Acknowledge.

                                        (sgd) T.N. MORLICH
                                                    G.
                                                  Captain.
                                              Brigade Major.
                                           181st Infantry Brigade.

Issued at 7.30 a.m. by orderly.

Copy No. 1. 2/21.   8. 179th Inf.Bde.
         2. 2/22.   9. O.C.Art.Group.
         3. 2/23.   10. 181 T.M.Battery.
         4. 2/24.   11. Pioneer Coy. LOURIE.
         5. 181 M.G.Coy.   12. File.
         6. 3/3rd Fld.Co.   13. War Diary.
         7. 64th Inf.Bde.

P.F.4.

TABLE OF RELIEF.

181ST INFANTRY BRIGADE.

UNIT.	FROM.	TO.	IN RELIEF OF.	REMARKS.
2/21 LOND. R.	DIVNL. RESERVE. ESRUN.	R I.	2/23 L.R.	
2/22 LOND. R.	BRIGADE RESERVE.	R II.	2/24 L.R.	
2/23 LOND. R.	R I.	BRIGADE RESERVE.	2/22 L.R.	
2/24 LOND. R.	R II.	DIVNL. RESERVE. ESRUN.	2/21 L.R.	

The 2/21 L.R. will move up from ESRUN to ASELN by platoons at 5 minute intervals.

11.8.16.

SECRET.   Copy No..........

181ST INFANTRY BRIGADE ORDER No. 13.

Reference - Maps 51 B & C   Saturday,
            Trench Map.   19th August, 1916.

  ...   .

1. Battalions in the front line will be relieved by Bns. in reserve on the afternoon of the 21st inst. according to Table below, under arrangements to be made by Os.C. concerned. The leading platoon 2/24 L.R. to reach ANZIN Communication Trench by 3 p.m.

2. The 2/22 L.R. will take over Control Posts by 12 noon on 21st inst. from the 2/24 L.R.

3. The O.C. 2/21st L.R. will take over command of the ECURIE Defences from the O.C. 2/23 L.R.

4. Os.C. 2/21st and 2/23rd L.R. will arrange their relief so that it is completed by 3.45 p.m.

5. Completion of the relief will be reported to Brigade H.Q. as per attached Code.

6. Acknowledge.

UNIT.	FROM.	TO.	IN RELIEF OF.
2/21 Lond.R.	R I.	Brigade Reserve.	2/23 Lond.R.
2/22 " "	R II.	Divnl. Reserve.	2/24 " "
2/23 " "	Brigade Reserve.	R I.	2/21 " "
2/24 " "	Divnl. Reserve.	R II.	2/22 " "

The 2/24 L.R. will move up from ETRUN to ANZIN by platoons at 5 minute intervals.

                                                Captain.
                                                Brigade Major.
                                                181st Infantry Brigade

Issued at 7.30 a.m. by orderly.

Copy No. 1. 2/21.   8. 179th Inf.Bde.
         2. 2/22.   9. O.C.Art.Group.
         3. 2/23.   10. 181 T.M.Battery.
         4. 2/24.   11. Pioneer Coy.ECURIE.
         5. 181 M.G.Coy.   12. File.
         6. 3/Ord Fld.Co.   13. War Diary.
         7. 64th Inf.Bde.

SECRET.   Copy No. 13

181ST INFANTRY BRIGADE ORDER No. 15.

Reference - Maps 51 B & C.   Saturday,
            Trench Map.   26th August, 1916.

...   .

1. Battalions in the front line will be relieved by Bns. in reserve on the afternoon of the 29th inst. according to Table below, under arrangements to be made by Os.C. concerned. The leading platoon 2/22 L.R. to reach ANZIN Communication Trench by 1 p.m.

2. The 2/23 L.R. will take over Control Posts by 12 noon on 29th inst. from the 2/22 L.R.

3. The O.C. 2/24 L.R. will take over command of the ECURIE defences from the O.C. 2/21 L.R.

4. Completion of the relief will be reported to Brigade H.Q. as per attached Code.

5. Acknowledge.

UNIT.	FROM.	TO	IN RELIEF OF.
2/21 Lond.R.	Brigade Reserve.	R I.	2/23 Lond.R.
2/22 Lond.R.	Divnl. Reserve.	R II.	2/24 Lond.R.
2/23 Lond.R.	R I.	Divnl. Reserve.	2/22 Lond.R.
2/24 Lond.R.	R II.	Brigade Reserve.	2/21 Lond.R.

6. The 2/22 Lond.R. will move up from ETRUN to ANZIN by platoons at 5 minute intervals.

                                                  Captain.
                                              Brigade Major,
                                           181st Infantry Brigade.

Issued at 7.30 a.m. by orderly.

Copy No. 1.   2/21.   8.   179th Inf.Bde.
         2.   2/22.   9.   O.C.Art.Group.
         3.   2/23.   10.   181 T.M.Battery.
         4.   2/24.   11.   Pioneer Coy. ECURIE.
         5.   181 M.G.Coy.   12.   File.
         6.   3/3rd Field Co. 13. War Diary.
         7.   64th Inf.Bde.

SECRET.   APPENDIX II.

181ST INFANTRY BRIGADE.

WAR   DIARY

1st - 31st AUG/16.

RAID BY 2/23 LONDON REGT.

Vol. I.   No. 3.

----------------oOo----------------

SECRET.

DESCRIPTION OF THE RAID CARRIED OUT BY THE 2/23 LONDON REGT.

GS/61B

2" T.Ms. During the dates 4th, 5th & 6th August, the 2" T.Ms. registered on the enemy's wire at the two points actually to be cut on the night of the raid, (A.23.c.99.77 & A.23.d.10.67) and also on other points along the Brigade front. The moment exact registration had been obtained, no more shots were fired on the two points above-mentioned.

The actual registration was carried out by one Mortar firing from all four emplacements in turn, whilst the other Mortars were especially active on other points of the Brigade front. During the 7th, the German wire and support trenches opposite points of attack were casually shelled at intervals.

3" Stokes Guns. On the above-mentioned dates, the 3" Stokes Mortars also registered on the targets selected for them, the general scheme being, one gun to take on a supposed M.G. emplacement behind the German front line at A.23.d.1.6, one gun to spray front line trench to be raided, two guns to shell support and junctions of communication trenches, all fire to be stopped on Infantry moving forward to the assault. The remaining two guns (2 have been disabled during the last fortnight) to be ready to take on any hostile M.Gs. which might open between points A.23.a.36.40 and A.23.a.10.35 and enfilade the raiding party on its return. All points were satisfactorily registered by the evening of the 6th inst.

During the afternoon of the 7th inst. the 4.5 howitzers fired 30 rounds at a strong point behind German support line in rear of trench to be attacked and 30 rounds at an alternative target just S. of the LILLE RD.

ON NO ACCOUNT IS ANY TELEPHONIC MESSAGE TO BE SENT
WITH REFERENCE TO THESE ORDERS PRIOR TO ZERO ....

SECRET   Copy No. 14

181st INFANTRY BRIGADE
ORDER No. 11
------oO------

Reference - 51 B. N.W.1   Headquarters,
            Edition 2 B   181st Infantry Bde.
            1/10,000   6th August 1916
   Trench Maps.

1. The enemy's front line trench between points A.23.c.99.77. and A.23.d.10.67 will be raided by a party of the 2/23rd Lond. R. on the evening of August 7th, with the object of securing a prisoner.

2. The Raiding Party will consist of 2 Officers, 4 N.C.O's and 36 privates of the 2/23rd Lond. R.

3. The O.C.2/23rd Lond. R. will arrange all details and issue all orders as to the Infantry operations in so far as they concern the raiding party, and all other troops in his subsector.
   In addition to the Company, 2/22nd Lond. R. situated at ABRI CENTRALE, he will have at his disposal, 2 Squadrons CENTRAL INDIA HORSE situated at CHEMIN CREUX and ABRI CENTRALE and approximately 100 Officers and men 185th TUNNELLING Company CHEMIN CREUX.

4. The O.C.181st Machine Gun Company will arrange to sweep with fire the main GERMAN communication trenches, tramways and any portions of the GERMAN second line that he can enfilade.

5. The Artillery Preparation and Co-operation is being arranged by the C.R.A. 60th DIVISION, and will include a Bombardment to the North in the vicinity of ARGYLE CRATER.

6. The Trench Mortar Co-operation Scheme has been issued Separately (Appendix A).

7. The Operations commence, at a time to be notified later, called ZERO.
   At ╬ 20 minutes a shower of RED Rockets will recall the Raiding Party.
   On the return of the party the "CEASE FIRE" signal will be notified by a shower of GREEN Rockets.

8. At ZERO all men of "A", "B" and "C" Battalions who are not engaged in special work will be as far as possible under cover, and standing by ready for emergencies, with a sentry on each dug-out. Each S.O.S. Rocket stand will have a special man told off, whose duty it will be to fire the rockets in case of necessity. Officers Commanding R.1 and R.2 will use their own discretion as to when they consider it advisable to return to normal conditions, and will inform Brigade Headquarters on so doing by sending the code message -   "MESSENGER JUST LEFT"
   The O.C. ECURIE GARRISON will be informed of the cessation of "stand to" by Brigade Headquarters.

9. The O.C. 2/24th LOND. R. holding R.II will arrange to assist the RAID with his LEWIS GUN fire and RIFLE GRENADES.

10. The O.C.2/22nd LOND. R., commanding ECURIE defences, will arrange for the VICKERS and LEWIS Guns at his disposal to be ready for immediate mounting
                                                    contd.

11. The O.C.Coys. 2/22nd LOND. R. situated at ABRI CENTRALE, ABRI MOUTON and SUNKEN ROAD will each send an officer to report to the H.Q. of their respective Sub-Sectors by 9 p.m. 7-8-16

12. The Company and 2 Lewis Guns of 2/21st LOND. R. detailed as Brigade Reserve will be on 20 minutes notice from ZERO until notified to the contrary.

Communicated to O C 3/3 F⁰ Coy RE under separate cover.

13. The O.C. 3/3rd Field Company R.E. will arrange that all men under his command are clear of the trenches by 9 p.m. 7-8-16.

14. The O.C.185th Tunnelling Company R.E. will arrange that all men of his Company are in their dug-outs by 8.30 p.m. The portion of his Company at CHEMIN CREUX coming under the orders of O.C. 2/23rd LOND. R. for tactical purposes. The portion at ARIANE coming directly under the orders of G.O.C. 181st INFANTRY BRIGADE. If conditions are normal tunnelling work may be recommenced at 3 a.m. The O.C.185th Tunnelling Company will be informed by Brigade Headquarters when conditions are normal.

Communicated to O C C I H under Separate cover.

15. The O.C. 2 Squadrons CENTRAL INDIA HORSE situated at CHEMIN CREUX and ABRI CENTRALE will arrange for his men to be in their dug-outs by 8.30 p.m.

Communicated to O C 230ᵗʰ A T RG Coy under separate cover.

16. Personnel of the 230th ARMY TROOPS R.E.Coy. will come under the command of O.C. ECURIE Defences for tactical purposes.

ditto

17. The O.C. 2/6th Field Ambulance will arrange for an officer to be in attendance at the COLLECTING POST on WEST of ROUTE de LILLE (A.28.c.1.1.) by 8 p.m. 7-8-16.

18. If prisoners are taken, Battle Brigade Headquarters will be immediately informed as to numbers, they will be taken to Advanced Dressing Station, ANZIN G.7.b.8.9. under Battalion arrangements via "GENIE" "Down" trench, where they will be handed over to LIEUT. REYNOLDS, 2/21st LOND. R., who will immediately bring them to Rear Brigade Headquarters in an ambulance *[×Car]* which will be provided for the purpose, and report to the Staff Captain who will immediately inform Divisional Headquarters by telephone. All details will be given to LIEUT REYNOLDS by the Staff Captain, to whom he will report at 6 p.m. 7-8-16.

19. The greatest attention must be paid to the correct usage of the "UP" and "DOWN" Trenches during the operations. There will be no movement except of Troops actually on duty from 15 minutes before ZERO until normal conditions are resumed. Up going troops if meeting down coming troops will invariably take precedence.

20. Arrangements for synchronizing watches will be as follows:-
O.C.Right Arty. Group, Representative 2/24th Lond. R. O.C.181st M.G.Coy., O.C.181st T.M.Battery and O.C.Z/60 T.M.Battery will meet O.C.2/23rd Lond. R. at Hdqtrs. 2/23rd LOND. R. ABRI DES SABLIERES at 4.30 p.m. 7-8-16, when watches will be synchronized. All the above C.O's are responsible for the correct synchronizing of their subordinates' watches.

21. Separate orders as to rations for the night of 7/8th will be issued by the Staff Captain.

22. Reports from 8.30 p.m. to BATTLE BRIGADE HDQTRS.

23. Acknowledge.

Captain
Brigade Major
181st INFANTRY BRIGADE.

Secret

Appendix "A" to O.O.R 11

181st INFANTRY to BRIGADE .11

------oOo------

No 12

HEREWITH INSTRUCTIONS AS TO THE VARIOUS DUTIES TO BE
CARRIED OUT BY Z.60 and 181 T.M. BATTERIES, in CONNECTION
WITH OPERATIONS DATED FOR 7-8-16

... ...

(A) .. During the 4th, 5th, 6th and 7th insts

1. 2" mortars will destroy the enemy's wire at selected points along the Brigade Front, shooting from their normal emplacements and working in conjunction with the 3" Stokes Gun.

2. The two points selected for the wire to be cut (in front of A.23.c.99.77 and A.23.d.10.67) will, if not already done, be carefully registered from all four selected positions on the 5th inst, only one gun being employed for this purpose. Fewer rounds should be fired at these two points than at any other point during the 5th and 6th insts and none at all on the 4th inst.
During the afternoon of the 7th inst, by which time the required two points should have been accurately registered, shells should now and again be put into the wire at these points, in such a manner as to make it appear almost by accident, meanwhile at other points along the line the remaining mortars will be rather more active than usual.

(These two points when registered will not be shot at again until 7th inst)

3. O.C. Z/60 T.M. Battery will arrange that all four mortars are in their selected positions by 8 p.m. 7-8-16.

4. 3" STOKES GUNS will during the above dates register on the points laid down in the attached table, ceasing in the case of the targets of Nos. 1,2,3 and 4 guns immediately a satisfactory result has been obtained. Special attention during these dates should be paid to certain points to be selected by O.C.181 T.M.Battery, in the RIGHT II Subsector. These guns should keep up their activity on other portions of the front, working in with the 2" Mortars till the afternoon of the 7th inst.

(B) 1. The 2" MORTARS and the 3" STOKES GUNS will co-operate with the Artillery on Monday 7th August from ZERO onwards as per attached table.

2. The 2" MORTAR crews after ceasing fire will retire to their dug-outs and stand by ready for emergencies. If the S.O.S. signal is sent up, the guns will be at once mounted and such fire will be opened as the position requires.

3. After bombardment has quietened down Nos. 3 and 4 guns will be transferred to RIGHT 2 area.

4. The 3" STOKES GUNS crews of Nos. 1,2,3 & 4 after ceasing fire will withdraw their guns to the dugouts reserved for them and stand by ready for emergency. If the S.O.S. signal is sent up, the guns will be at once mounted and such fire will be opened as the position may require.
(The

-2-   (+20)

(B) contd.

5. The 3" STOKES Guns Nos. 5, 6 and 7 immediately on the Recall Signal going up (~~+ 25~~ minutes) will open with gun fire on points laid down in Table for 1 minute, then dropping to 5 rounds a minute until the Cease Fire Signal goes up, when they will cease fire and take shelter in the dug-outs selected for them, ready for emergency. If the occasion demands the O.C. these guns will vary his rate of fire or target, bearing in mind that the role of these guns is to prevent hostile M.G's sweeping the ground over which the raiding party has to withdraw.

6. After bombardment has quietened down Nos. 5, 6, and 7 guns will be transferred to RIGHT 2 area.

7. O.C. 181 T.M. Battery will make all arrangements for the siting of both the 2" MORTARS and 3" STOKES GUNS. He will select the most suitable places for storing the necessary ammunition and will arrange direct with the O.C. 2/23rd Lond. R. all details for a carrying party to be detailed to bring up fresh ammunition from the ROCLINCOURT Store in case of necessity, arranging all details as to routes to be followed and places for dumping the ammunition thus brought up. He will also select in conjunction with O.C. 2/23rd Lond. R. the various dug outs that the gun crews will occupy and see that all ranks know their exact positions.
He will be responsible that the necessary amount of ammunition (including that for emergencies) is forthcoming.

8. In the case of any unforeseen emergency arising, the O.C. 181 T.M. Battery must impress on all ranks that it is the duty of the leader on the spot to decide what action he is going to take and to act at once.

9. The Signal for "RECALL FROM ENEMY'S TRENCHES" is:-
A shower of red rockets sent up ~~+ 25~~ at + 20 minutes.

The Signal for "CEASE FIRE" is:-
A shower of green rockets.

10. ~~All watches will be carefully synchronized under orders that will be issued by O.C. 2/23rd Lond.~~ R.

11. Actual time of ZERO will be notified later

12. Acknowledge.

Bde. H.Q.
4-8-16

Captain
Brigade Major
181st Infantry Bde.

DETAILS OF THE RAID ITSELF & TIMETABLE OF SAME.

7th August, 1916.

7.0 p.m. The raiding party arrived at 2/23 Lond.R. H.Q. ABRI DES SABLIERS.

9.0 p.m. 181 M.G.Co. opened its normal indirect fire in short bursts on enemy's tramways and rear communication trenches.
Trench posts placed at all important junctions of main "Up" and "Down" communication trenches.

9.15 p.m. All traffic in Right I stopped.
Raiding party assembled at their starting points:-
No. 1 Group - Sec.Lieut. J.L.HUNT, bombing block of 1 N.C.O. and 4 men and clearing party 1 N.C.O. & 14 men at head of Sap 20 (A.23.c.95.45).
No. 2 Group - Lieut.J.FLINT, bombing block of 1 N.C.O. & 4 men & clearing party of 1 N.C.O. & 14 men at the head of Sap 21 (A.23.c.72.77).

9.30 p.m. The Artillery and T.Ms. opened fire on first objectives.
9.31 p.m. Raiding parties left their respective saps and were heavily fired upon at once by hostile guns and T.Ms. pointing to fore-knowledge of the raid.
No. 1 Group had the first 6 men out wounded at once, this disposed of all their bombing group. This caused a certain delay in this party getting to its starting-off point.
No. 2 Group although shelled, had better fortune and got out without casualties.

9.34 p.m. Artillery barrage lifted to the second objective.
2" T.Ms. ceased fire and crews retired to reserved dugouts and stood by.
Nos. 1, 2, 3, and 4 3" Stokes Mortars ceased fire and crews retired to reserved dugouts and stood by ready for emergencies. By this time the German artillery were replying with vigour shelling "No man's Land", BOHNAL & COLLECTEUR and placing heavy H.Es. around Bn. H.Q.
Numerous flares were also discharged by the enemy including a few red and green ones.

9.53 p.m. Red "Recall" rockets sent up, three minutes later, owing to extreme difficulty of getting rockets to fire.

9.53 p.m. - White rockets fired from ROCADE to guide returning
10.21p.m. raiders, again great difficulty experienced in lighting.

10.21 p.m. All in from Sap 20; 8 men from Sap 21, green "Cease fire" rockets fired.
From this moment artillery fire died away, but up till 10.40 p.m. hostile M.Gs. were very active on the Sapheads 20 and 21.

10.50 p.m. All the party were back except Lieut. FLINT and 3 other ranks, including 1 man killed.
From 10.50 p.m. onwards white guiding rockets were sent up at intervals, in all 90 were fired during the night.
Search party went out under Sec.Lieut.HUNT looking for Lieut.FLINT and the other missing men. About 12.40 a.m. one of the missing men came in and stated that he had left Lieut.FLINT wounded with another man in an old trench. Search parties again went out with this man as guide but as he had lost all idea of the direction by which he had come the parties met with no success.

7.30 a.m. Cries were heard and an Officer's patrol went out and brought in Lieut.FLINT and L/Cpl. Bradley who was with him.

INFORMATION AS REGARDS THE RAID UP TO DATE.

In spite of the great difficulty of getting coherent statement as to what happened from those concerned; in the case of No.2 Group, chiefly owing to the fact that Lieut. FLINT was wounded
the following main points seem to be fairly accurate:-

1. That the enemy was ready for the raid as artillery and T.Ms. were firing into the sapheads 20 and 21 within one minute of zero, and that there were parties of Germans in the front line trench with bombs laid out ready for throwing, also to the fact that these men were ready to fight.

2. That owing to para. 1 No. 1 Group was demoralised by having its first 6 men knocked out immediately on leaving the Sap, and in consequence had barely reached the enemy's wire by the time the "cease fire" signal was sent up.

3. Again owing to para. 1, No. 2 Group, although suffering no casualties with the exception of Lieut. FLINT being wounded through the arm, became split up, the first 3 men Sergt. PLIMM and Ptes. SLAUGHTER and MORRIS reaching the German trench alone in the good time of about 2 minutes, and Lieut. FLINT, Pte. WILSTED and about 7 others, forming apparently the centre portion of the group striking the trench further south. Sergt. KILLICK and the tale end of the group eventually joined Sergt. PLIMM who by that time had sent back the 2 men with him to gain liason. Sergt. PLIMM and his ladder man then made a block, whilst Sergt. KILLICK and party (numbers unknown) worked down south and found no-one. This party all returned when the "Recall" went up.

Lieut. FLINT'S party entered the trench and turned south. Immediately on entering, Pte. WILSTED saw a German standing at the entrance of a dugout with a levelled rifle, WILSTED immediately threw a bomb in his face and the German fell backwards into the dugout, the bomb exploding as he did so. Three more bombs, including one incendiary bomb, were thrown down with apparently most satisfactory results.ˣ Lieut. FLINT and L/Cpl. BRADLEY then dashed down the trench by themselves and met several Germans who showed fight, they killed at least two and the rest fled down three separate dugouts which were then promptly bombed with both Mill's and incendiary bombs. After the latter had burst, screams and groans were heard coming from the dugouts and volumes of smoke and sparks.

ˣPte. WILSTED & 2 others formed a bombing block.

Lieut. FLINT and L/Cpl. BRADLEY then pushed on down the trench until they were eventually met by a party of Germans who threw a bomb at them, wounding Lieut. FLINT in the arms, legs & thigh. The two then retired, picking up a third man on their way, got out of the trench, the two men assisting Lieut. FLINT across the open, until he fainted when L/Cpl. BRADLEY stayed with him whilst the other man went on to get assistance.

4. From the reports of this group, it appears that:-
   (a) The German trench is a very well constructed one built on the lines of the COLLECTEUR, deep, well fire-stepped and traversed, the firesteps being well over 3' from the trench floor. The trench itself was, however, very broad and was very badly knocked about by our fire. This is very satisfactory, as, during the bombardment, only one Stokes Gun had been ranged on it.

/ Contd.

(b) The trench contained a small garrison, a certain number of dugouts, apparently not many, and a very much damaged sniping post. A M.G. heard firing very close by was bombed, it ceased fire and did not open again.

(c) The wire opposite No. 2 Group was very thoroughly cut, some of the party walking through it quite easily, and the remainder crossing it by means wired blankets. This points to a really broad gap having been cut. It is reported that the wire opposite No. 1 Group was in similar condition, but as none of the raiding party crossed it, it is impossible to state with any degree of certainty.

(d) The white tap was of no value as it was almost immediately destroyed by shell fire.

(e) A separate report is being put in as to the efficiency of the rockets fired.

(f) The telephones installed in each of the sapheads were of enormous value, and it is interesting to note that in spite of the fact that both saps were quite heavily shelled, the wires were not in the least injured in either case, and the communications were not interrupted for a moment. The same holds good of all communications back to Advanced Bde.H.Q. only one line being cut by shell fire (that between Right I Bn.H.Q. and Bde.H.Q.). The break was found and repaired inside 5 minutes by linesmen.

(g) The one fatal casualty occurred close to Sap 20 on the return journey.

The total list of casualties sustained is as under:-

Lieut. J.FLINT - seriously wounded.

1 man killed.

11 men wounded.

1 man missing.

5. A further report will be rendered with regard to any Officers or men who are deserving of mention with regard to this operation.

---------oOo---------

Brig.-General.
Cmdng. 181st Infantry Bde.

8.8.16.

181st INFANTRY BRIGADE

2" T.M.BATTERY (Z.60)

GUN	POSITION	Time of opening fire.	Time of ceasing fire.	N⁰.of round to be fired.	TARGET	Approx. Range.	REMARKS
No.1	A.23.c.55.26	Zero	+ 4 mins.	as many as possible.	a path to be cut through enemy's wire opposite POINT A.23.d.10.67.	265 – 270 yards	
No.2	A.23.c.45.40	Zero	+ 4 mins.	ditto	ditto	ditto	
No.3	A.23.c.41.60	Zero	+ 4 mins	ditto	a path to be cut through enemy's wire opposite POINT A.23.c.99.77	ditto	
No.4	A.23.c.37.55	Zero	+ 4 mins	ditto	ditto	ditto	

Total approx. 15

181st INFANTRY BRIGADE

3" STOKES GUNS (181 T.M. Battery)

Gun	Approx. Position	Time of Opening Fire.	Time of ceasing fire	No. of rounds to be fired.	TARGET	Approx Range	REMARKS
No.1	Between Points A.23.c.30.85 and A.23.d.90.80 in or near BONNAL Trench	ZERO -- On Recall Signal (4 being fired) (RED ROCKETS) 20 minutes	+ 4 min -- On "Cease Fire" Signal being fired (GREEN ROCKETS)	80	Supposed M.G. emplacement situated at A.23.d.10.60	270 yards	As heavy a fire as possible to be put in round this point.
No.2				50	Firing line trench from A.23.c.99.77 to A.23.d.10.67	280 yards	This gun to traverse up and down the trench named during the four minutes, firing at an easy rate
No.3				80	Trench junction at A.23. d.03.84 inclusive, also support trench to trench junction A.23.d.10.78 exclusive.	340 yards	Special attention to be paid to trench junction itself and each side of it.
No.4				80	Trench Junction at A.23.d. 10.78 inclusive to point along support line 50 yds. S.E. of above trench jtn.	340 yards	Special attention to be paid to trench jtn itself & both sides of it.
No.5	Between Points A.23.c.45.65 in or near BONNAL Trench and			20 rounds per Gun in first minute, 5 rounds per Gun each succeeding minute	Trench junction at A.23.a. 36.40 and searching fire on adjoining trenches.	270 yards	The O.C. of these guns will act on his own initiative as regards either opening fire before "Zero" or to his rate of fire, after 21 min if hostile M.G's become active in the portion of 400 yards 3rd.
No.6					Trench junction at A.23.a. 10.35 along communication trench to its junction with support line at A.23.a.10.40	250 - 270 yards	
No.7				290 rounds Reserve 110	Trenches and craters around Point A.22.b.90.50	250 - 270 yards	

AMMUNITION REQUIRED - For Guns No.1,2,3, & 4
                " "   " 5, 6, & 7

290 rounds and 110 emergency reserve
60 rounds for 1st minute, allow 20 mins.
until "Cease Fire" at 5 rounds per
minute per gun and 40 rds emergency reserve = 400 rounds
TOTAL AMMUNITION REQUIRED .... 800 rounds.

SECRET.

Officer Commanding,
    2/22
    2/23
    2/24
    181 M.G.
    181 T.M.

Reference 181 Infantry Brigade
Order No. 14   Para 2

Please note that the joint bombardment of German trenches will take place as under:- 7th

From ZERO - 5 minutes ...15.c.7.32 - A.14.c.8.7

5 minutes - Cease Fire   A.15.c.9.85 - A.15.c.1.7

instead of in vicinity of ARGYLE CRESH. This brings it on to the Northern half of RIGHT II subsector from opposite KICK AVENUE to the junction with 179th Infantry Brigade.

The O.C. 2/24th London Regt. will accordingly cause the following bays to be vacated

Bays 31A, 31C, 32A, 32B, 32 C, 33A and 33B during the bombardment, and using his own discretion will reoccupy them as soon as possible after the "Cease Fire" signal has gone up.

JR White
Captain
Brigade Major
181st Infantry Brigade

B.M.
6-8-16

SECRET. APPENDIX III.

181ST INFANTRY BRIGADE.

WAR DIARY.

1st - 31st AUG./16.

RAID BY 2/24 LOND. REGT.

Vol. 1. No. 3.

----------------oOo----------------

G.S.86c.

Headquarters,
    60th (London) Divn.

        All details as to the arrangements and organisation of the raid worked quite smoothly, no hitch of any sort occurring.

        The Raiding Party reach their objective without any difficulty whatever, and throughout the raid, the enemy showed no activity at all, neither attempting to interfere with the raiding party itself, or answering to any extent our Trench Mortar and Artillery fire.

        It appears quite plain that no serious work of any kind has been carried out for some time in the craters raided, no does the front line trench behind them appear to be anything but very weakly held.

        The Artillery and Trench Mortar Support was excellent, and effectively kept the hostile Trench Mortar fire down to a negligible quantity, during the entire operation.

        The O.C. 2/24 Lond.R.'s. report is attached.

        No information has yet been received as to the state of the enemy's wire and trenches. As soon as I have had a personal interview with Sec.Lieut.EARLE, this will be forwarded.

                          (signed) J.N.HORLICK.
                                    Captain.
                                Brigade Major.
                    for Brig.-General,
                         Commanding 181st Infantry Bde.

29.8.16.

STORY OF THE RAID MADE BY
the 2/24th LOND R.
on night of 28/29th August
1916

Reference RAID carried out by Battalion under my command last night 28/29th August on Craters XIX and XIX^a. This RAID was planned with a view to obtaining an identification, Very lights had been seen several nights previously fired from inside the Craters and on early morning 27th a man was seen to be moving round the rear edge, these facts made it appear possible that the Crater was held and certainly patrolled.

The raiding party succeeded in surrounding the Crater as arranged, without being discovered. An enemy machine gun near the LILLE ROAD opened fire in the direction of the party, but no casualties occurred.

The party entered the Craters at ZERO as arranged, but found no enemy or enemy work of any sort.

The old mine shaft is still visible in North Wall of XIX Crater, it could not be discovered in the time how far this shaft ran, possibly well behind enemy front line, Crater XIX is not connected to the enemy front line by any Sap, nor is there any sign of the Crater being held on the North lip by a sentry group. An old trench runs out from the enemy line towards Crater XIX as shown in aeroplane photographs, but ends 20 yards from the Crater and is strongly wired; this trench is not held by the enemy. Bombs were thrown by the party into this trench and wire in front of enemy front line, no reply was received. From observation from these Craters the enemy front line appears to be weakly held, few lights were sent up from this line. The party returned at ∕ 10 minutes as arranged. The Artillery support appeared good and enemy T.M. were in most cases silenced, the enemy appeared to answer only with T.M's and field guns.

No casualties were incurred.

(sgd) J.CROSBIE
Lieut-Colonel
Cmdg. 2/24th London R.

29-8-16

TIME TABLE
of
RAID BY 2/24th LOND. R. ON NIGHT OF 28/29th August 1916

.. ..

1.45 a.m.	Raiding party leave position of assembly.
2. 9 a.m.	Raiding party in position.
	A Group on Western inside lip of Crater XIX
	B Group on Southern lip inside Crater XIXa
	C Group on Northern lip inside Crater XIX
	D Group on Western lip of Crater XIXa
2.10 a.m.-- 2.20 a.m.	D Group sweeps through Crater XIXa and XIX, but find no trace of the enemy. Eastern lips examined and hostile front line bombed.
2.13 a.m.	Artillery and T.M. fire opens.
2.18 a.m.	Stokes T.M's cease fire.
2.20 a.m.	Recall Signal fired. Stokes T.M's open on second objective.
2.21 a.m.	First white guiding rocket fired.
2.24 a.m.	Stokes T.M's Cease fire.
2.30 a.m.	2" T.M's cease fire
2.32 a.m.	2/Lt. BARIE and 11 O.R. reported in
2.35 a.m.	2/Lt. BILTON and 8 O.R. reported in, 6 still missing.
2.44 a.m.	Cease fire signals, all guns cease except Howitzer Battery and 1 18 pr. Battery. Firing of Recall rockets ceased.
2.55 a.m.	Howitzer and 18pr Batteries cease fire.
3.11 a.m.	All in except 5 men, one man slightly wounded by comrades bayonet.
3.50 a.m.	All in except one man.
5.50 a.m.-- 6. 0 a.m.	Search parties out, missing man returns at 6 a.m.

xxxxxxxxxxxxxxxxxxxxxxxxxxxxxxxxx

ON NO ACCOUNT IS ANY TELEPHONE
MESSAGE TO BE SENT WITH REFERENCE
TO THESE ORDERS PRIOR TO ZERO.

From - 15 to close of operations
all lines will be kept clear,
except for messages of a
tactical nature.

Issued by orderly
  Copy No.1   Division "G"
      No.2   C.R.A.
      No.3   2/24th L.R.
      No.4   "
      No.5   "
      No.6   2/21st L.R.
      No.7   2/22nd L.R.
      No.8   2/23rd L.R.
      No.9   181 M.G.Coy
      No.10   181 T.M.Battery
      No.11   Z.60 T.M.Battery
      No.12   Rt. Group Artillery
      No.13   179th Infy Bde.
      No.14   A.D.M.S.
      No.15   3/3rd R.E.
      No.16   185th Tunnel. Coy.
      No.17   38th C.I.H.
      No.18   Staff Captain
      No.19   Filed
      No.20   War Diary

---oOo---

SECRET

181st INFANTRY BRIGADE

ORDER No.14

Reference - 51B N.W.1   Headquarters
       Edition 2C   181st Infantry Bde
       1/10000   25-8-16
       Trench Maps.

1. The 2/24th Bn. London Regt. will carry out a Raid on CRATERS XIX and XIX^a (A.22.b.2.5) on the night of 28/29th August, with the object of securing a prisoner and causing damage to the enemy.

2. The Raiding party will consist of
          2 Officers
          4 N.C.O's
         23 Privates

3. The O.C. 2/24th Lond. R. will arrange all details as to the Infantry Operations in so far as they concern the Raiding Party and all other troops in his sub-sector, who will be entirely under his tactical command during the operations.

4. The O.C. 181st Machine Gun Company will arrange to sweep with fire the main GERMAN communication trenches, tramways and any portions of the GERMAN second line that he can enfilade.

5. The O.C. Right Artillery Group will issue all orders as to Artillery co-operation. Sap 26 will be cleared by - 15 min.

6. For Trench Mortar co-operation scheme, see Appendix "A" attached. O.C.Subsector to arrange with O.C.Trench Mortars as to which Saps it may be necessary to clear. All Saps will be cleared by -15 minutes.

7. The operations will commence at a time to be notified later called ZERO, at + 10 minutes a shower of GREEN rockets will recall the Raiding Party. On the return of the party the "CEASE FIRE" Signal will be notified by the firing of six rockets in the following order RED, WHITE, RED, WHITE, RED WHITE, when the Artillery will cease fire with the exception of the Battery and Howitzers detailed to fire at hostile Trench Mortars. The O.C. 2/24th Lond. R. will notify the O.C. Right Artillery Group as to when he wishes these guns to cease fire.
Captain LIDDIATT Brigade Bombing Officer will arrange to fire white Rockets at 1 minute intervals from the ROCADE trench, commencing 1 minute after the "RECALL" signal and continuing until the "CEASE FIRE" Signal. He will then stand by in case further signals are needed

8. At ZERO all men of "A"(2/23) "B"(2/24) and "C"(2/21) Battalions who are not engaged in special work will be as far as possible under cover, and standing by ready for emergencies, with a sentry on each dug-out. Each S.O.S. rocket stand will have a special man told off, whose duty it will be to fire the rockets in case of necessity. Officers Commanding R.1 (O.C.2/23rd Lond. R.) and R.2 (O.C.2/24th Lond. R.) will use their own discretion as to when they consider it advisable to return to normal conditions, and will inform Brigade Headquarters on so doing, by sending the code message - "MESSENGER JUST LEFT"
The O.C. ECURIE GARRISON (O.C.2/21st Lond R.) will be informed of the cessation of "stand to" by Brigade Hdqrs.

(9. The

9. The O.C. 2/23rd Lond. R. holding R.1 will arrange to assist the RAID with 3 LEWIS GUN fire and RIFLE GRENADES.

10. The O.C. 2/21st LOND R. commanding ECURIE Defences, will arrange for the VICKERS and LEWIS Guns at his disposal to be ready for immediate mounting.

11. The O.C.Coys 2/21st LOND. R. situated at ABRI CENTRALE, ABRI MOUTON and SUNKEN ROAD, will each send an officer to report to the H.Q. of their respective Sub-Sectors by 1.50 a.m. 29-8-16

12. The Company and 2 Lewis Guns of 2/22nd Lond. R. detailed as Brigade Reserve will be on 20 minutes notice from ZERO until notified to the contrary.

13. The O.C. 3/3rd Field Coy. R.E. will arrange that all men under his command are clear of the trenches by midnight 28/29th August. He will warn the O.C's of any Army or Corps R.E. who may be working in the Sector to this effect. (Communicated to O.C.3/3rd Field Coy. R.E. under separate cover.)

14. The O.C. 185th Tunnelling Company R.E. will arrange that all men of his Company are in their dug-outs by 1 am The portion of his Company at CHEMIN CREUX coming under the orders of O.C. 2/23rd Lond. R. for tactical purposes. The portion at ARIANE coming directly under the orders of the G.O.C. 181st Infantry Brigade. If conditions are normal tunnelling work may be recommenced at 6 a.m. The O.C. 185th Tunnelling Company will be informed by Brigade Headquarters when conditions are normal.

15. The O.C. 2 Squadrons CENTRAL INDIA HORSE situated at CHEMIN CREUX and ABRI CENTRALE will arrange for his men to be in their dug-outs by 1 a.m. (Communicated to O.C. C.I.H. under separate cover)

16. Personnel of the 230th ARMY TROOPS R.E.Coy. will come under the command of O.C. ECURIE DEFENCES (2/21st Lond R) for tactical purposes.

17. If prisoners are taken Battle Brigade Headquarters will be immediately informed as to numbers and regiment, they will be taken to Advanced Dressing Station ANZIN G.7.b.8.9 under Battalion arrangements via GENIE down trench, where they will be handed over to an officer to be detailed by the O.C. 2/22nd Lond. R., who will immediately bring them to Rear Brigade Headquarters in a car that will be provided for the purpose, and report to the Staff Captain who will immediately inform Divisional Headquarters by telephone. The officer detailed for this duty will report to the Staff Captain for instructions at 6 p.m. on the 28th inst.

18. The greatest attention must be paid to the correct usage of the "UP" and "DOWN" Trenches during the operations. There will be no movement, except of troops actually on duty from 15 minutes before ZERO until normal conditions are resumed. Up going troops if meeting down coming troops will invariably take precedence.

19. The arrangements for synchronising watches will be as under:- O.C. 2/24th Lond. R. will arrange with O.C.Rt Group Arty., 181 M.G.Coy., 181 T.M.Battery Z.60 T.M.Battery and representative 2/23rd Lond R. as to time and place.

20. Every effort will be made to ensure constant reports as to progress being forwarded to Brigade H.Q., a detailed report as to the operations to reach Bde. H.Q. by 1 p.m. 29-8-16

21. Reports from 8.30p.m. to Brigade Battle Headquarters.
22. Acknowledge

(sgd) J.N.HORLICK Captain
Brigade Major
181st Infantry Brigade.

APPENDIX "A"

SCHEME FOR TRENCH MORTAR CO-OPERATION

PHASE 1

STOKES GUN

GUN	Time of opening fire	Time of ceasing fire	No. of rounds to be fired	TARGET	REMARKS
No.1 & 2	f 3	f 5	50 per gun	Support trench A.23.c.08.42 to A.23.c.01.40	Traversing fire along the sector of trench.
No.3 & 4	f 3	f 5	50 per gun	A.23.c.01.40 to A.22.b.36.92	Traversing fire along the sector of trench.
No.5 & 6	f 3	f 5	50 per gun	Support trench A.15.c.90.25 to A.16.c.75.50	Traversing fire along the sector of trench.
No.7 & 8	f 3	f 5	50 per gun	Support trench A.16.c.75.50 to A.16.c.75.55	Traversing fire along the sector of trench

PHASE 2

GUN	Time of opening fire	Time of ceasing fire	No. of rounds to be fired	TARGET	REMARKS
No.1,2,3, and 4	f 10	f 14	50 per gun	Front line trench A.23.a.12.40 to A.22.b.32.95	No.1 & 3 guns firing in burr bursts.
No.5,6,7, and 8	f 10	f 14	50 per gun	Front line trench A.16.c.80.25 to A.16.c.65.60	N. 5 & 7 guns firing in burr bursts.

TOTAL NUMBER OF ROUNDS 800 / 25 per gun EMERGENCY RESERVE = 1000 rounds
On completion of bombardment O.C. Batteries will be ready to assist in any emergency that may arise.

2" TRENCH MORTARS

No. 1	f 3	f 20		Trench Junction A.23.a.68.42	These Mortars will fire continuously until "CEASE FIRE" signal is sent up
No. 2	f 3	f 20		Trench Junction A.22.b.90.30	
No. 3	f 3	f 20		T.M.Position A.16.d.15.20	
No. 4	f 3	f 20		T.M.Position A.16.c.95.35	

COPIES -

No. 1.   60th Divn.
    2.   181st Brigade.
    3.   "   "
    4.   Right Group Art.
    5.   181st T.M.B.
    6.   2/21.
    7.   2/22.
    8.   2/23.
    9-15.   2/24.
    16.   181st M.G.Coy.
    17.   185th Tun. Coy.
    18.   1/12 L.N.L. Regt.
    19.   Detachment C.I.H.
    20.   Sec.Lieut.EARLE.
    21.   "   "   BILTON.

S E C R E T   Copy No.......

PLEASE MAKE THE FOLLOWING AMENDMENT TO YOUR COPY
OF ORDERS ISSUED BY O.C. 2/24th LONDON REGT. FOR
RAID TO TAKE PLACE ON NIGHT 28/29th AUGUST 1916

Page 1 POINT OF RETURN   for A.22.b.9.29 read
                               A.22.b.19.29

SECRET　　　　　　　　　　　　　　　　　　　　Copy No. 3

G.O.C 181st Inf Brigade

RAID BY
2/24th LONDON REGIMENT
---oOo---

Reference Maps :- NEUVILLE ST VAAST 1/5000
and TRENCH MAPS

To take place on AUGUST 29th 1916

Under 2/Lieut H.L.EARLE and 2/Lieut H.C.BILTON (2nd in command)

OBJECT - To obtain identifications & cause damage to enemy.

JUMPING OFF POINT	A.22.b.22.39 (Crater XII)
OBJECTIVE	A.22.b.18.55 (Crater XIXa and XIX)
POINT OF RETURN	A.22.b.19.29 (Crater XIV)

The party will consist of FOUR GROUPS as under :-

"A" Group   Rear blocking party, under 2/Lieut H.C.BILTON of 1 N.C.O. and 6 men. Duty of this Group will be to prevent any of the enemy discovered in the Crater from retiring on their own front line.

"B" Group   Left blocking party 1 N.C.O. & 3 men. Duty of this Group will be to cover main raiding party.

"C" Group   Right blocking party, 1 N.C.O. & 3 men. Duty of this Group will be to cover main raiding party.

"D" Group   Under 2/LIEUT H.L.EARLE, 1.N.C.O. and 11 men; two of these men to look after ladder and tape, which will be taken into Crater from Sapheads. Duty of this Group, to drive through Crater XIXa then XIX Crater, capture any enemy in either and destroy any works found.

---oOo---oOo---

1. **METHOD OF CARRYING OUT RAID**

    The Crater will be rushed at a time which will be known as ZERO.
    At - 25 minutes the party will leave Crater XIV and proceed to jumping off point (Crater XII), from which point the groups will crawl out to their respective positions in following order :-
    A Group   B Group   C Group   D Group
    All Groups will be in position by ZERO, and the raiding party will be lined out on the near lip, ready to advance. "A" Group will crawl into the crater under cover from the German lines and seize any enemy retreating before "D" Group's advance.

2. PRIMARY OBJECT OF RAID is to secure a prisoner, in any case the party will hold the Craters for 10 minutes and gain as much information of the enemy's positions as possible. They will also endeavour to destroy with bombs any works they may find, and bring back any articles of clothing etc. which would be useful as means to identification.

(Signal

3. SIGNAL FOR WITHDRAWAL at + 10 minutes will be showers of GREEN rockets from Right Companies advanced and Main Headquarters. 2/LIEUT H.L.EARLE will superintend the withdrawal of all parties and remain on the near lip of Crater XIX^a with the 8 Battalion bombers ("B" and "C" parties) to cover retirement.
2/LIEUT H.C.BILTON will lead the retirement, but on reaching Crater XII (the jumping off point), will stay until all the parties have passed him, he will be responsible for counting them.
The retirement will be assisted by two tape men, the first remaining on the near lip of Crater XIX^a with rope ladder, the second remaining laying by the tape between Craters XIX^a and XII, this man will also check numbers. On arrival at point of return (Crater XIV) the party will be again checked by an officer.
A shower of RED, WHITE, RED, WHITE, RED, WHITE rockets will be fired from right companies Headquarters when the party has returned complete. *[This will be the signal for cease fire.]*
The whole raiding party will remain in Crater XIV until they receive instructions to do otherwise from Battalion Headquarters.

4. The men of the raiding party will wear, steel helmets and service dress with puttees, but will NOT wear equipment. All means of identification will be removed, including private letters etc, marking on inside of clothing etc. will be obliterated. Faces will be blacked, and both shoulder straps will be bound with white tape.

5. ARMS CARRIED BY RAIDING PARTY

   "A" Group
       3 bayonet men
       3 bombers
       N.C.O. armed with revolver.

   "B" Group
       N.C.O. armed with revolver, and bombs.
       2 bayonet men
       1 bomber.

   "C" Group
       as for "B" Group

   "D" Group
       N.C.O. armed with revolver
       4 bombers
       5 bayonet men
       1 ladder & 1 tape man

   Each man will carry one MILL'S BOMB in left pocket of tunic.
   Every bomber will carry a LIFE-PRESERVER.
   Every bayonet man will carry 9 rounds in magazine, and 1 in chamber of rifle, with an additional 10 rounds in right hand pocket of tunic.
   BOMBERS - each man will carry 10 bombs, selected men will carry "P" bombs.

6. All ranks will be warned that in the event of their being captured by the enemy, they will on no account give the name of their Regiment, Brigade or Division, but should state their number, name and initials.
Special identity discs will be issued.
No identification marks, such as cockades, number plates etc. must be taken from any prisoner as souvenirs.

(Accommodation

7. **ACCOMMODATION OF RAIDING PARTY**, the party will be garrisoned in Crater XV prior to the Raid.

8. A final reconnaissance will be carried out on the evening of the 28th inst.

9. There will be no movement in the BONNAL from -30 minutes, until "Cease Fire" and down traffic will make way for all up traffic in communication trenches

10. **MEDICAL AID POSTS** a special post will be established in Crater XIV, and casualties will be evacuated direct from there to Aid Post near LILLE BARRICADE, the route to which will be picqueted.

11. **STORES TO BE CARRIED BY MEN**

4	Revolvers.
2	Wire traverser matresses,
110	Bombs.
4	Wire Cutters
	Tape
60	Yards of Strong Cord (each man carrying 6 yards)
17	Life Preservers.
6	Pairs of Hedging gloves.
	Rope ladder -
4	Electric torches.
	Special identity discs.

12. The wire round Crater XIX^a will be cut on afternoon of 28th by T.M's. At + 3 minutes the artillery will bombard the enemy's trench mortar positions and support line, until "Cease Fire" signal is sent up.
    Feint bombardments will be carried out by T.M's

13. An advanced telephone station will be established in Crater XIV.

14. The watches of all concerned in the operation will be sent to Battalion Headquarters to be syncronised at 5 p.m. on the 28th August

15. There will be no password or code used in these operations.

16. Company Commanders will ensure that all Sentry Posts are warned of the operations on hand by -40 minutes.

17. A hot meal will be served to the raiding party on return.

18. ZERO time will be notified later.

19. Acknowledge.

John Crosbie
Lieut-Colonel
Cmdg. 2/24th London R.

25-8-16

SECRET.

181st INFANTRY BRIGADE

WAR DIARY.

1st - 30th September, 1916.

Vol. I.   No. 4.

Army Form C. 2118.

WAR DIARY
or
INTELLIGENCE SUMMARY

of 161 INFANTRY BRIGADE.

(Erase heading not required.)

Instructions regarding War Diaries and Intelligence Summaries are contained in F. S. Regs., Part II. and the Staff Manual respectively. Title Pages will be prepared in manuscript.

Place	Date	Hour	Summary of Events and Information	Remarks and references to Appendices
ETRUN	1-9-16		A dull muggy day. Locality wind very slight. Enemy shelled BARRICADE and PIGEONNIER with 5.9". Quite 50% were duds. At 1.15pm the enemy put 12 high velocity shells into ETRUN & a gun at 1.35pm 10 more. Severely wounding Lt CHISHOLM 1/23 Lond R killing 2 men & wounding 4. Our TMs were active during the afternoon and the XVII Corps shelled heavily WITTERNESSE in retaliation for the shelling of ETRUN. The enemy were very active all day both with TMs & guns. 1/4 Co R I was shelled during the afternoon. 3 men of the 1/24 LOND R (at TCQ on a Sniping Course) CAPT MORGAN WESTMINSTER DRAGOON's bomber attached for instruction were sick and were removed to hospital at AUBIGNY. Special work finished in BONNAR.	
ETRUN	2-9-16		A damp muggy morning. Slight NE wind. Bright Evening. Enemy unusually active in the early morning probably owing to our energetic strafing of them. Our guns fired sharp bursts at intervals during the afternoon at the enemy's trenches. A considerable amount of wire was cut by our TMs. Enemy shelled a certain amount with 5.9's. The Rotor Dump at BARRICADE C was fired at by a M.G. at 10pm. A patrol encountered 4 Germans on the ravine side of a crater opposite SAP 30 A. Nothing of importance happened during the day.	
ETRUN	3-9-16		A fine bright day. Some rain in afternoon. Wind west. Our artillery were active throughout the day. Field guns and TMs fired on wire with success at various points. A Bogan Read was carried out at 2.30 am. without arousing any enthusiasm on the part of the enemy. Supporting line shelled twice during the morning by 4.2" & 5.9". A patrol going out in the daytime to some old cable were not fired on. General work on BONNAR being carried on steadily. Final arrangements made as regards raid to be carried out by 1/22 Lond R. early next morning. 1 officer & 4 NCOs to FREVIN CAPELLE for Aniga Course. 2 officer 8 O.R. to AGNIERES for consolidation of craters. Work commenced on arrangements for Secret Gas installation. See E.O. Div letter G/S 249 r. dated 1-9-16. 40 men 1/23 L R working in LOWER PINZIN	

2449 Wt. W14957/M90 750,000 1/16 J.B.C. & A. Forms/C.2118/12.

Army Form C. 2118.

WAR DIARY
or
INTELLIGENCE SUMMARY

CT/181 INFANTRY BRIGADE

(Erase heading not required.)

Instructions regarding War Diaries and Intelligence Summaries are contained in F. S. Regs., Part II. and the Staff Manual respectively. Title Pages will be prepared in manuscript.

Place	Date	Hour	Summary of Events and Information	Remarks and references to Appendices
ETRUN	4.9.16		A Rough Day with showers of rain in morning and heavy rain during the night. Wind strong SW. The 2/22nd LOND R. had miscarried owing to the party missing their way & striking thick wire the recall signal going before they could get through. The usual Artillery & TM activity during the day. The relief was carried out without incident. The BDE MAJOR visited DIVISION with reference to the GAS INSTALLATION. Our snipers claim two hits. 3 O.R. B/23 L.R to SNIPING SCHOOL AC.Q 10/1 3 O.R. M.G. Coy to M.G. SCHOOL CAMIERS. 1 Officer 3 O.R. from YORK HUSSARS attend Bde Bombing School Q. Coy HKTR Special Bde RE established in line at ATRE CENTRALE, CHEMIN CREUX & PRIANE.	APP I. APP II. MK
ETRUN	5.9.16		A variable day. rain most of the day. Wind light SW. Our artillery was active during the day. Also our TMs especially about 2pm. Enemy's TMs active on our left during afternoon damaging the ROWVAL and cutting some wire opposite L.29 in two places. 3 patrols went out during the night and inspected the enemys wire at various points finding it in good condition. A working party was dispersed by LEWIS gun fire about 4.30pm. Hostile TMs fired a large quantity of duds during the Day. Ringdoves interviewed OCs in line as to the Special operation during morning	MK
ETRUN	6.9.16		A fine day. fresh NE wind. Sir CHARLES FERGUSON CDG XVIIth CORPS visited Bde HQ during the morning. MAJOR FRENCH RMLI attached to the Bde for work with Bde SIGNAL SECTION. Normal Artillery and TM activity in the morning. Enemys TMs and Fizz-Bangs very active in afternoon. 5 patrols went out during the night, mostly in special reconnaissances connected with the forthcoming operations. Several little flares set during the day took preceeding satisfactorily. 20 men in each Subsector working in BDIT & WICK AVEs respectively under RE between BURNAL & COLLECTEUR. 40 men 2/21 LR working in DICKEBEARING Camp Lower ANZIN. LEWIS Gun & TAPLES 10 Officers 80 R 2/22. Orders issued to Bns for carrying parties for installing gas	APP III.

Army Form C. 2118.

WAR DIARY
INTELLIGENCE SUMMARY of 1st INFANTRY BRIGADE

(Erase heading not required.)

Place	Date	Hour	Summary of Events and Information	Remarks and references to Appendices
ETRUN	7-9-16		A Beautiful Warm Day. Wind Strong NE morning, mild in afternoon. Our artillery did a good amount of wire cutting during the afternoon and exchanged a hostile bombing post. The enemy two batteries very much more active of late and this have caused considerable annoyance throughout the day. We had over patrols out during the night a large enemy patrol was also seen. Hostile planes were over our lines and also over ETRUN during the day. Our aircraft also were active. Work progressing very well owing to the good weather. Crater Consolidation party from 2/21 L.R. as before. 3 men 2/21 L.A.C.Q. for A.S. Wipers course. Apparently 2 units 20 km a small raiding party of Germans left our trenches opposite our right flank. We disposed them with rifle fire.	Jntz
ETRUN	8-9-16		A Beautiful warm day. Wind Strong NE in morning mild in afternoon. The Boches started on our right subsector at Stand to 5.30 & fairly annoying all day. Our guns & T.M.s continued wire cutting during the day & in the evening the field guns fired 6 rounds gunfire on the T.M. positions. The enemy still maintain his newly found activity. A certain amount of aerial activity during the day.	Jntz
ETRUN	9-9-16		A really Beautiful day. Wind slight N.E. The Brigadier visited The 179 Int Bde HQ (advanced) S.O.C. G.O. Div visited BDE HQ & interviewed MAJOR S. WRIGHT 9/21 Lond R. & Lt Col BECKETT 2/05 1/12 LNL. He also inspected Bde Transport appx Q. A normal day in the line. The enemy perhaps a bit more active although he was fairly active against Right it. during the afternoon, firing some oil cans a large number often burst being amongst them. Our aircraft were very active during the day. The lower ROSIN is now deckboarded throughout its length. Also THE LABYRINTH. Patrols went out during the night. Trial shots x the GAS installation tested.	Jntz

2449 Wt. W14957/M90 750,000 1/16 J.B.C. & A. Forms/C.2118/12.

WAR DIARY
or 91st INFANTRY BRIGADE
INTELLIGENCE SUMMARY.

Army Form C. 2118.

(Erase heading not required.)

Hour, Date, Place	Summary of Events and Information	Remarks and references to Appendices
ETRUN 10.9.16	A dull muggy day. Wind medium N.E. The GAS Installation was cancelled. Wire cutting proceeded during the day. Enemy motors quite active. Attempts at an ambush were made during the day even the CONDUCTOR with very poor effect. The late B.M. Relief was carried out without incident. At 3am (11th inst) our Artillery demonstrated on the "ROSE" in respect of raid by 179th & 180 RDES. This produced fairly heavy retaliation onto our Right Subsector. 3 men being killed. Both raids were successful. Prisoners being obtained. Enemy patrol active during twilight. Lt. ROBINSON 9/91 L.R. attacked 181 TM Coy very badly wounded during the morning by a Shell. Visit by G.O.C. Dvn in afternoon. Information received that the Divn is now in 1st & not 2nd LR III.rd ARMY. 1 O.R. 9/21 L.R. to OFFICERS for Hawkeley Course. 3 O.R.s RFCC for Sniping Course. 10 O.H. 4 O.R. 2/24 to ANTI GAS School FREVIN CAPELLE.	APP.I.
ETRUN 11-9-16.	A warm morning. Turns mild N.E. rain in afternoon wind veering to N.W. A forward gun near RGht Pres but failed to clear little been & therefore was unable to cut enemy's wire. Our guns a TMS were rather quiet during the day, they however "Staked" the enemy's wire about 11pm to which the enemy replied vigorously, killing two men. The enemy appears to be putting in a lot of work on a unit of the line. A good amount of work got through on our side during the day. Apparently Prisoners are not opposite no 72nd Reg 8th Div. These have moved up from S. of the SCARPE.	

Army Form C. 2118.

WAR DIARY
of 181 INFANTRY BRIGADE
INTELLIGENCE SUMMARY.
(Erase heading not required.)

Instructions regarding War Diaries and Intelligence Summaries are contained in F. S. Regs., Part II. and the Staff Manual respectively. Title pages will be prepared in manuscript.

Hour, Date, Place	Summary of Events and Information	Remarks and references to Appendices
ETRUN 12-9-16	A muggy day, with a few storms, very mild SW wind, nice evening. 2/LTS KINROSS & THEW 2/22 LOND R were both killed about 8am whilst investigating number 19 CRATER. LT KINROSS went out first with PTE THOMAS 2/22 LR & two hit by a bomb. 2/LT THEW Saw this & went out to fetch him with 30/4 men & was himself shot. Enemy again active on our Right especially with trench mortars. Two patrols went out during the evening. One of our aeroplanes dropped right down and fires its M.G. into the enemy's trenches about 7.15pm. Minor repair to trenches carried out. RE proceeding with new dugouts Dugout at ÉCURIE to be the Signallers finished. 3 OTRs & 80 R. BTONIÈRES GSO I. on the Somme fighting & lessons learnt. Lecture by Col. HUMPHREYS GSO I. on the Somme fighting & lessons learnt.	Sgt
ETRUN 13-9-16	A warm dull day, rain about 9pm fresh SW wind. A normal day with the usual intermittent TM activity. Our guns a 2"TM² cut wire steadily during the day, a forward gun brought up to the ROCADÉ trench carrying on explosion in the enemy's lines. Instructions received during the day as to the projected "Gas" attack by the 35th DIV on our Right. Our MGs fired on the enemy's CTs during the night. 3 OR 2/24 LONDON to NCC for a Sniping Course and HOFFHERR & 200 OR, 18 MGNITRES for Special look on the entrenching ground Three. LT SWANSON 2/22LR & NCOs to base for instruction to drafts.	Sig.
ETRUN 14-9-16	A chilly raw day, strong gusty N to NNW wind. We were much more active with our TM³ ow 2" making excellent shooting on the enemy's wire. Our field guns also did some good shooting during the day. The enemy was much quieter and practically no artillery at all. During the evening 30/D Dunstor Batty 4·5 feet came into the Group and took up position in the new Canadier emplacements near MAZIN trench.	Sgt

Army Form C. 2118.

WAR DIARY
or
INTELLIGENCE SUMMARY.

of 181 INFANTRY BRIGADE

(Erase heading not required.)

Instructions regarding War Diaries and Intelligence Summaries are contained in F.S. Regs., Part II. and the Staff Manual respectively. Title pages will be prepared in manuscript.

Hour, Date, Place	Summary of Events and Information	Remarks and references to Appendices
ETRUN 15-9-16	A really beautiful day but quite cold. Strong NW wind. Our TM's and guns were very active on the enemy's support line and wire throughout the day, our Lewis guns keeping the gaps open at night. Throughout the night our M.G's out fired on the enemy's trench junctions, dumps and trolley lines. The enemy replied at intervals to our TM doing a certain amount of damage with T.M's. Very little hostile gunfire. Our aircraft were very busy during the day, & our big guns strafed the Bosches steadily to our north. Great news from THE SOMME. Usual patrols out during the night. Took in dugouts and renovation & preservation of trench proceeding, although hampered by large working parties required by CORPS. 10th x 10 C.R. P 2 S.L.R. to ETAPLES for future Sea Course.	[signature]
ETRUN 16-9-16	A very nice day, cold, Strong NW wind. Not very much activity in the TM line on our part owing to the INTER BN. Relief, but the Artillery continued their wire cutting consistently. The enemy were active throughout the day, one large one blowing a crater 14 feet wide right in our trench. Several patrols but nothing unusual to report. Considerable aeroplane activity. Dug outs & other work progressing. 2/8th & 2/8 R & 2/2 LONGNIERES for Crater Consolidation. 3 O.R. 2/4 L.R. furnished to C.O. for Shipping Course.	[signature] APPENDIX II
	1 late Bn. relief. Camp's outwithout incident	

Army Form C. 2118.

WAR DIARY
or
INTELLIGENCE SUMMARY.

Of 181 INFANTRY BRIGADE.

(Erase heading not required.)

Instructions regarding War Diaries and Intelligence Summaries are contained in F.S. Regs., Part II. and the Staff Manual respectively. Title pages will be prepared in manuscript.

Hour, Date, Place	Summary of Events and Information	Remarks and references to Appendices
ETRUN 17-9-16.	A beautiful warm morning turning cloudy towards evening. Wind SSW. Our TMs and Artillery were active throughout the day. Our 2" and Field guns being engaged in cutting wire which they did successfully in several places. Our d. Guns kept the wire open during the night. The enemy were active also with TMs and Aerial Torpedoes doing a considerable amount of damage to BONNAL. Their artillery was also more active than usual. Patrols out but nothing of importance to report. Our MGs fired on the enemy's dumps during the night. 1 Offr + OR 2/az Lond R to FREVIN CAPELLE for Anti Gas Course. 1 Officer 1 OR of each Bn to 3rd ARMY INFANTRY TRAINING SCHOOL at AUXILE CHATEAU.	fritz.
ETRUN 18-9-16.	A terrible day. Blew and Rained hard all the morning. Clearing up for about 6 p.m. Wind 4 WEST. Our artillery were active throughout the day shelling front & support lines. TITELUS & NINE ELMS. Our 18/pr Battery also did good work cutting wire. Our TMs also cut wire successfully & damaged enemy trenches. Enemy again very active against our Right Subsector & doing several direct hits onto BONNAL. 3 Patrols out opposite the Left Subsector & a great deal of talking was head in the trenches & seemed crowded which points to a relief taking place. Owing to the heavy rain the trenches slipped in in all directions and much good work will have to be done all over again. Both BNs worked extraordinarily well during the night & managed to remove many of the landslides.	

WAR DIARY
INTELLIGENCE SUMMARY.

of 181st INFANTRY BRIGADE. Army Form C. 2118.

(Erase heading not required.)

Hour, Date, Place	Summary of Events and Information	Remarks and references to Appendices
ETRUN 19-9-16	A dull rainy morning and very cold, bright at midday, rain again in the evening. Wind very mild NW. Our artillery & TMs fired throughout the day with good effect on the enemy's trenches & supportline. The greatest of wire cutting was also carried out. The forward gun near the RECODE trench doing a lot of good work. Our MGs fired during the night on the enemy second line. The enemy was very active yesterday both very early in the morning and during the evening somewhat damaging the BONKAL. Patrols inspected the enemy's wire during the night & found it badly damaged. A great deal of work was done during the day & night in repairing the trenches wrought by the rain. 30 R to ACo for a Bombing Course. (Capt L R)	[signature]
ETRUN 20-9-16	A nasty day, cold and showers of rain. Strongish wind NW. The usual artillery & TM activity on enemy's lines and ours. 50 rounds were fired by our 4.5 How: looking for enemy Big TM We also had numerous rifle grenades during the day with good effect. The usual patrols were out opposite Right I. The SAPs being carefully watched as owing to the rain it was impossible to go down them. The o/25 L R tried to raid the enemy's trenches at two points but failed to enter. One of our 2" TMs had a premature burst slightly wounding 3 of the crew & damaging the emplacement. Trenches in a very bad state indeed especially The BONKAL. 20(?) SOR 12a LR to ENGINEERS for Crate Consolidation Course.	[signature]

Army Form C. 2118.

WAR DIARY
or
INTELLIGENCE SUMMARY.

6/181 INFANTRY BRIGADE

(Erase heading not required.)

Hour, Date, Place	Summary of Events and Information	Remarks and references to Appendices
ETRUN 21-9-16	A cold day, but with a good drying NNE wind. The usual Artillery and TM activity on our side at the usual targets. Our Lewis Guns dispersed several enemy working parties during the night. The enemy were much quieter than usual with their TMs than a few days being during the day. The Hong Kong Ragram fired toward the enemy's trenches, but found them ready and had to retire. 2/Lt BILTON was severely wounded and one other man. Two Rounds awfully falling so badly. Our aircraft were active during the day. The enemy also had secret observation Balloons up. My office & 10R from 1/31.1/31.1/23.1LR & 20R from 1/24 LR 16 LIGHT ST KILOMET for a TM Course.	[signature]
ETRUN 22-9-16	A Beautiful Autumn day, rather mild NE. A quieter day than usual owing to the Inter Battalion relief. TMs were however bombarded in the afternoon. Our Lewis Guns kept the gaps in the enemy's wire under fire during the night. There were the usual desultory activity on the enemy's part during the day. One patrol was out. Great air activity on our part during the day, all planes were heavily shelled. The relief was carried out without incident. 3 drums from 2:30 p.m. - 9:30 p.m. 1 officer 6 men 1/24 R & 1/24 R 4 men each from 2/D. 3/22.1/23 LR to LE TOUQUET for Lewis Gun Course.	APPENDIX II. [signature]

WAR DIARY
— or —
INTELLIGENCE SUMMARY.
(Erase heading not required.)

of 181 INFANTRY BRIGADE.

Army Form C. 2118.

Hour, Date, Place	Summary of Events and Information	Remarks and references to Appendices
ETRUN 23-9-16	A Beautiful day. Wind light SE. None at all at 8pm. Our T M's bombarded bottoms of the enemy's during the day and also his wire. Field guns shelled trenches in the vicinity of MINE ELMS. The enemy were very quiet during the whole day, only firing a few rifle grenades. Our snipers claimed a hit. Considerable aerial activity on our part during the day. About 11.30pm. the 2/21st London REGT attempted to raid the enemy trenches but were unsuccessful. 10th Hour 2/23rd L R b CAMIERS for a fortnightly Course.	[signature]
ETRUN 24-9-16.	A Beautiful warm day. Low visibility. Wind light SE. A quiet morning. From 1.30pm to 6.15pm 4.5" Hows. 6" Hows. 2" Mortars a Stokes guns bombarded GERMAN Trenches behind the ANGLE CRATERS apparently with great success. The enemy were also very quiet all day, except about 11am when some dugouts belonging to the 185th TUNNELLING Co'Y. caught fire in CHEMIN CREUX and were manually shelled by 5.9". During the night enemy MG fired on LILLE ROAD dump, all stray shots went high. Enemy wiring party near 500 CRATER was dispersed by Lewis Gun fire. Work progressing on BONNAL & dugouts 2.9th G O R 2/23 LR to GRÉNIÈRES for Crater Consolidation 19th to R 2/23 LR to FREVIN CAPELLE. Antigua School.	APPENDIX IV [signature]

Army Form C. 2118.

WAR DIARY
— or —
INTELLIGENCE SUMMARY.
(Erase heading not required.)

of 181 INFANTRY BRIGADE.

Instructions regarding War Diaries and Intelligence Summaries are contained in F.S. Regs., Part II. and the Staff Manual respectively. Title pages will be prepared in manuscript.

Hour, Date, Place	Summary of Events and Information	Remarks and references to Appendices
ETRUN 25-9-16	Beautiful Day, very mild SE wind. Thorough Artillery & TM activity on enemy front during the day. The 2" TM's completely destroyed a suspected O.P. Our Lewis guns swept the enemy wire in front throughout the night. Enemy wire again very feeble in their response & it is quite evident that the 72nd PRUSSIANS have departed. Our present opponents being neither men such as good Soldiers. Our patrols inspected the GERMAN wire in several places & found it very strong. Considerable aeroplane activity, one of our planes was brought down during the day behind the 179th Bde lines. The occupants were slightly injured. The plane itself was destroyed by shell fire. Work on dug-outs & Big TM emplacement at Bernal proceeding. One man from 181 M.G. Coy to CAMIERS for a M.G. Course.	[signature]
ETRUN 26-9-16	Beautiful Day, very mild S.E. wind. At 10.30 am The XVII Corps Cdr Sir W FERGUSSON presented D.C.M. to W/Cpl BRADLEY 7/53 LR at ECOIVRES afterward there was a demonstration of the GERMAN FLAMMENWERFER and the method of advancing behind & through a smoke barrage, & also barrages with a smoke barrage on artillery flank. Things were quiet up the line, with the usual intermittent TM activity, enemy again exceptionally quiet. Several patrols went out, he bagged two of the enemy in the afternoon. Aeroplanes active. Work progressing well. Several dug outs nearing completion. Good news as to the SOMME Battle came in all day long.	[signature]

Army Form C. 2118.

WAR DIARY
of 15th INFANTRY BRIGADE
INTELLIGENCE SUMMARY.
(Erase heading not required.)

Instructions regarding War Diaries and Intelligence Summaries are contained in F.S. Regs., Part II. and the Staff Manual respectively. Title pages will be prepared in manuscript.

Hour, Date, Place	Summary of Events and Information	Remarks and references to Appendices
ETRUN 27-9-16	A dull day with a little rain in the morning. Strong South wind in morning. The Corps Commander inspected the 2/23 B.n LORD REGT at 11:30 am on the football ground at ETRUN. About 12.30 pm the enemy fired about 20 shells between ANZIN, LOUEZ & MAROEUIL at either our new 9.2" Hows which fired for the first time or at an aeroplane which they brought down near MAROEUIL. Both our light & medium TMs were active throughout the day causing a considerable amount of damage to he wire & parapets. Field guns still inactive owing to tactical ammunition shortage. Enemy again very quiet. Patrols out, nothing to report. Our aeroplanes were active. Work progressing well.	
ETRUN 28-9-16	A cloudy day, very close. Slight showers of rain, very mild SE wind. Our TMs bombarded the enemy front and support lines intermittently throughout the day. Our 2" TMs caused 3 loud explosions in the enemy line. Our heavies bombarded THELUS late in the afternoon. Our MGs fired during the night on hostile trench & trolley junctions. Enemy still quiet, although his MGs were active during the night. A number of patrols went out during the night, nothing important to report. Our aircraft were active. Artillery relief was carried out without incident during the afternoon. 2 offrs & men 2/21 LR to MENIERES for Crater Consolidation	APPENDIX II

WAR DIARY or INTELLIGENCE SUMMARY

of 181st INFANTRY BRIGADE   Army Form C. 2118.

(Erase heading not required.)

Instructions regarding War Diaries and Intelligence Summaries are contained in F.S. Regs., Part II. and the Staff Manual respectively. Title pages will be prepared in manuscript.

Hour, Date, Place	Summary of Events and Information	Remarks and references to Appendices
ETRUN 29-9-16	A misty close day with drizzling rain, wind NE. The G.O.C. Divn visited Right I during the morning. Guns considerably more active on our part during the day, our T.M's being quite active. Gt-mons our trench mortars shelled THELUS and about 4pm a Battery near VIMY. Enemy again quiet except for MG fire during the night. 5 patrols went out during the night, but found out nothing of interest. Work on dugouts & trenches continuing.	[signature]
ETRUN 30-9-16	A very nice bright day. Strongish NE wind.	

Archambault
Brig. Genl.
Comdg 181st Infantry Brigade

SECRET.   APPENDIX I.

181st INFANTRY BRIGADE

WAR DIARY.

1st - 30th September, 1916.

RAID BY 2/22 LONDON REGT.

Vol. I.   No. 4.

------------oOo------------

SECRET   Copy No. 20

ON NO ACCOUNT IS ANY TELEPHONE MESSAGE TO BE SENT WITH
REFERENCE TO THESE ORDERS PRIOR TO ZERO.

181ST INFANTRY BRIGADE

Operation Order No. 17
-----oOo--oOo-----

Reference:-
   51B N.W.1 Edition   Headquarters,
   2C   1/10,000   181st INFANTRY BRIGADE
   TRENCH MAPS   2nd September 1916

1. The 2/22nd Bn. London Regt. will carry out a Raid on the enemy's trenches at A.22.a.93.92 in the early morning of 4th September 1916, with the object of securing a prisoner and causing damage to the enemy.

2. The Raiding Party will consist of
              2 Officers
       3 N.C.O's   24 Privates

3. The O.C. 2/22nd Lond. R. will arrange all details as to the Infantry Operations in so far as they concern the Raiding Party and all other troops in his sub-sector, who will be entirely under his tactical command during the operations.

4. THE O.C. 181st MACHINE GUN COMPANY will arrange to sweep with fire the main German communication trenches, tramways, and any portions of the German second line that he can enfilade, He will fire his usual call from Recall signal/until "Cease Fire" signal.

5. The O.C. RIGHT GROUP ARTILLERY will issue all orders as to Artillery co-operation, saps to be cleared as O.C. 2/22nd Lond. R. may direct.

6. For TRENCH MORTAR CO-OPERATION SCHEME see Appendix "A" attached. O.C. Subsectors to arrange with O.C. Trench Mortars as to which Saps it may be necessary to clear. All Saps will be cleared by - 15 minutes. O.C. 2/21st and 2/22nd Lond. R. to arrange for dug outs for Trench Mortar teams to stand by in.

7. The Operations will commence at a time to be notified later called "ZERO", at / 20 minutes a shower of RED rockets will be fired to recall the Raiding Party. Upon the return of the party the "Cease Fire" signal will be notified by the firing of 6 rockets in the following order:- GREEN WHITE GREEN WHITE GREEN WHITE when the Artillery will cease fire.
Captain LIDDIATT the Brigade Bombing Officer will arrange to fire WHITE Very lights at 1 minute intervals from a point to be selected by him in the SAUSAGE REDOUBT, ECURIE commencing 1 minute after the "Recall" signal and continuing until the "Cease Fire" signal, he will then stand by. T.M.O.

8. At ZERO all men of "A"(2/21) "B"(2/22) and "C"(2/24) Battalions who are not engaged in special work will be as far as possible under cover, and standing by ready for emergencies, with a sentry on each dug-out. Each S.O.S. rocket stand will have a special man told off, whose duty it will be to fire the rockets in case of necessity. O.C's R.I(2/21) and R.II(2/22) will use their own discretion as to when they consider it advisable to return to normal conditions, and will inform Brigade Headquarters on so doing, by sending the code message "Your BM.100 acknowledged" The O.C. ECURIE GARRISON (O.C.2/24) will be informed of the cessation of "Stand to" by Brigade Headquarters by the same signal.
                                                           contd

9. The O.C. 2/21st Lond. R. holding R.I will arrange to assist the Raid with Lewis Guns fire and rifle grenades.

10. The O.C. 3/3rd Field Company R.E. will arrange that all men under his command are clear of the trenches by 1 a.m. 4th September 1916. He will warn the O.C's of any Army or Corps R.E. who may be working in the Sector to this effect.

11. If prisoners are taken Battle Brigade Headquarters will be immediately informed as to numbers and regiment, they will be taken to Advanced Dressing Station ANZIN G.7.b.8.9. under Battalion arrangements via GENIE d down trench, where they will be handed over to an officer of the 2/23rd Lond R. (to be detailed by the O.C. 2/23), who will immediately bring them to Rear Brigade Headquarters in a car that will be provided for the purpose, and report to the Staff Captain who will immediately inform Divisional Headquarters by telephone. The Officer detailed for this duty will report to the Staff Captain for instructions at 6 p.m. on the 3rd inst.

12. O.C. 2/22 Lond. R. will make all necessary arrangements for the synchronization of watches.

13. Every effort will be made to ensure constant reports as to progress being forwarded to Brigade H.Q., a detailed report as to the operations to reach Brigade H.Q. by 1 p.m. 4th September 1916.

14. All reports will be sent to REAR BRIGADE H.Q.ETRUN during the operations. Written dispatches via Battle Brigade H.Q.

15. Acknowledge.

16. The O.C. 185th Tunnelling Coy. R.E. will arrange that all men of his Coy. are in their dug-outs by 1am. The portion of his Coy at CHEMIN CREUX coming under the orders of O.C.2/2kst Lond R. for tactical purposes. The portion at BLUE coming directly under the orders of G.O.C. 181st Infy. Bde. If conditions are normal work may be recommenced at 6 p.m. The O.C.185th Tunnel Coy. will be informed by Brigade Hdqtrs. when conditions are normal.

                                              Captain
                                           Brigade Major
                                       181st Infantry Brigade

Issued by Orderly
  Copy No.1 Division "G"
         2 C.R.A.
         3 A.D.M.S.
         4 179th Infy. Bde
         5)
         6) 2/22 Lond. R.   From - 15 to close of
         7)   operations all lines
         8 2/21st Lond. R.   will be kept clear,
         9 2/23rd Lond. R.   except for messages of
        10 2/24th Lond. R.   a tactical nature.
        11 181 M.G.Coy.
        12 181 T.M.Battery
        13 Z.60 T.M.Battery
        14 Rt. Group Artillery
        15 3/3rd R.E.
        16 185th Tunnel. Coy
        17 38th C.I.H.
        18 Staff Captain
        19 Filed
        20 War Diary.

Appendix "A"

SCHEME FOR TRENCH MORTAR CO-OPERATIONS

PHASE 1

STOKES GUN

GUN	Time of Opening fire	Time of Ceasing fire	No. of rounds to be fired	TARGET	REMARKS
Nos. 1,2, 3 & 4	/5	/8	45	Support Trench A.23.a.08.42 to A.22.b.36.92	The first 5 rounds from each gun will be air bursts. Traversing fire along the sector of trench.
Nos. 5 & 6	/5	/8	45	Support Trench A.22.b.35.50 to A.22.b.20.65	
Nos. 7 & 8	/5	/8	45	Support Trench A.16.c.85.25 to A.16.c.75.55	

PHASE 2

GUN	Time of Opening fire	Time of Ceasing fire	No. of rounds to be fired	TARGET	REMARKS
Nos. 1,2, 3 & 4	/19	/21	30	Front line trench A.23.a.12.40 to A.22.b.32.95	1 and 3 guns firing air bursts
Nos. 5 & 6	/19	/21	30	Support Trench A.22.b.35.50 to A.22.b.20.85	No.5 gun will fire air bursts
Nos. 7 & 8	/19	/21	30	Support Trench A.16.c.85.25 to A.16.c.75.55	No.7 gun will fire air bursts

TOTAL NUMBER OF ROUNDS 360 / 20 ROUNDS per gun EMERGENCY RESERVE = 520 ROUNDS

On completion of bombardment O.C. Batteries will be ready to assist in any emergency that may arise.

1" TRENCH MORTARS

	Phase 1		
	From	To	
No. 1	/5	/20	
No. 2	/5	/20	
No. 3	/5	/20	
No. 4	/5	/20	

2" TRENCH MORTARS

Trench Junction	A.25.c.68.42	Phase 1	
" "	A.22.b.90.30		
" "	A.22.b.30.55		
" "	A.16.c.80.40		

Nos. 1,2,3,& 4 Cease Fire until 5 minutes. All mortars on same trenches Phase 2
(time unknown) afterwards in Phase 1

Copy No. 70.

AMENDMENT

Please amend Phase 1 of Appendix A of Brigade Operation Order 17x issued to-day, to read
Guns and T.M's will open fire at ∓ 10 minutes instead of ∓ 5 minutes.

3-9-16

Captain
Brigade Major
181st Infantry Bde

SECRET.   APPENDIX II.

181st INFANTRY BRIGADE

WAR DIARY.

1st - 30th September, 1916.

RELIEFS.

Vol. I.   No.4.

------------oOo------------

SECRET.
Copy No. 13

181ST INFANTRY BRIGADE ORDER No. 16.

Reference - Maps 51 B & C.
Trench Map.

Saturday,
2nd September, 1916.

1. Battalions in the front line will be relieved by Bns. in reserve on the afternoon of the 4th inst. according to Table below, under arrangements to be made by Os.C. concerned. The leading platoon 2/23 L.R. to reach ANZIN Communication Trench by 3 p.m.

2. The 2/21 L.R. will take over Control Posts by 12 noon on 4th inst. from the 2/23 L.R.

3. The O.C. 2/22 L.R. will take over command of the ECURIE Defences from the O.C. 2/24 L.R.

4. Completion of the relief will be reported to Brigade H.Q. as per attached Code.

5. Acknowledge.

UNIT.	FROM.	TO.	IN RELIEF OF.
2/21 Lond.R.	R I	Divnl. Reserve.	2/23 Lond.R.
2/22 " "	R II.	Brigade Reserve.	2/24 Lond.R.
2/23 " "	Divnl. Reserve.	R I.	2/21 Lond.R.
2/24 " "	Brigade Reserve.	R II.	2/22 Lond.R.

The 2/23 L.R. will move up from ECRUN to ANZIN by platoons at 5 minute intervals.

Captain.
Brigade Major.
181st Infantry Brigade.

Issued at 7.30 p.m. by orderly.

Copy No. 1.	2/21.	8.	179th Inf.Bde.
2.	2/22.	9.	O.C. Art.Group.
3.	2/23.	10.	181 T.M.Battery.
4.	2/24.	11.	Pioneer Coy. ECURIE.
5.	181 M.G.Coy.	12.	File.
6.	3/3rd Field Coy.	13.	War Diary.
7.	64th Inf.Bde.		

SECRET. Copy No. 13

181ST INFANTRY BRIGADE ORDER No. 18.

Reference – Maps 51 B & C.
Trench Map.

Friday,
8th September, 1916.

1. Battalions in the front line will be relieved by Bns. in reserve on the afternoon of the 10th inst. according to Table below, under arrangements to be made by Os.C. concerned. The leading platoon of 2/21 L.R. to reach ANZIN Communication Trench by 1 p.m.

2. The 2/24 L.R. will take over Control Posts by 12 noon on 10th inst. from the 2/21 L.R.

3. The O.C. 2/23 L.R. will take over command of the ECURIE Defences from the O.C. 2/22 Lond.R.

4. No companies of the 2/22 L.R. will move from present positions until actually relieved by companies of the 2/23 L.R.

5. Completion of relief will be reported to Brigade H.Q. as per attached code.

6. Acknowledge.

UNIT.	FROM.	TO.	IN RELIEF OF.
2/21 Lond.R.	Divnl. Reserve.	R I.	2/23 Lond.R.
2/22 " "	Brigade Reserve.	R II.	2/24 " "
2/23 " "	R I.	Brigade Reserve.	2/22 " "
2/24 " "	R II.	Divnl. Reserve.	2/21 " "

The 2/21 L.R. will move up from ETRUN to ANZIN by platoons at 5 minute intervals.

J.R. Macdonald
Captain.
Brigade Major.
181st Infantry Brigade.

Issued at 7.30 p.m.

Copy No. 1. 2/21.   8. 179th Inf.Bde.
        2. 2/22.   9. O.C.Art.Group.
        3. 2/23.   10. 181 T.M.Battery.
        4. 2/24.   11. Pioneer Coy. ECURIE.
        5. 181 M.G.Coy.   12. File.
        6. 3/3rd Fld.Coy.R.E. 13. War Diary.
        7. 64th Inf.Bde.
           106th

SECRET.   Copy No. 13

181st INFANTRY BRIGADE ORDER No. 19.

Reference – Maps 51 B & C   Thursday,
            Trench Map.   14th September, 1916.

00519

1. Battalions in the front line will be relieved by Bns. in reserve on the afternoon of the of the 16th inst. according to Table below, under arrangements to be made by Os.C. concerned. The leading platoon 2/24 L.R. to reach ANZIN Communication Trench by 3 p.m.

2. The 2/22 L.R. will take over Control Posts by 12 noon on 16th inst. from the 2/24 L.R.

3. The O.C. 2/21 L.R. will take over command of the ECURIE Defences from the O.C. 2/23 L.R.

4. Os.C. 2/21 and 2/23 L.R. will arrange their relief so that it is completed by 3.45 p.m.

5. Completion of the relief will be reported to Brigade H.Q. as per attached Code.

6. Acknowledge.

UNIT.	FROM.	TO.	IN RELIEF OF.
2/21 Lond.R.	R I.	Brigade Reserve.	2/23 Lond.R.
2/22 " "	R II.	Divnl. Reserve.	2/24 " "
2/23 " "	Brigade Reserve.	R I.	2/21 " "
2/24 " "	Divnl. Reserve.	R II.	2/22 " "

The 2/24 L.R. will move up from ETRUN to ANZIN by platoons at 5 minute intervals.

                                                        Captain.
                                                        Brigade Major.
                                                        181st Infantry Brigade.

Issued at 7.30 p.m.

Copy No. 1. 2/21.   8. 179th Inf.Bde.
         2. 2/22.   9. O.C. Art.Group.
         3. 2/23.   10. 181 T.M.Battery.
         4. 2/24.   11. Pioneer Coy.ECURIE.
         5. 181 M.G.Coy.   12. File.
         6. 3/3rd Fld.Co. 13. War Diary.
         7. 106th Inf.Bde.

SECRET. Copy No. 13

181st INFANTRY BRIGADE ORDER No. 20.

Reference - Maps 51 B & C. Trench Map.

Wednesday, 20th September, 1916.

[Stamp: HEADQUARTERS 20 SEP 1916 181st INFANTRY BDE.]

1. Battalions in the front line will be relieved by Bns. in reserve on the afternoon of the 22nd inst. according to Table below, under arrangements to be made by Os.C. concerned. The leading platoon 2/22 L.R. to reach ANZIN Communication Trench by 1 p.m.

2. The 2/23 L.R. will take over Control Posts by 12 noon on 22nd inst. from the 2/22 L.R.

3. The O.C. 2/24 L.R. will take over command of the ECURIE defences from the O.C. 2/21 L.R.

4. Completion of the relief will be reported to Brigade H.Q. as per attached Code.

5. Acknowledge.

UNIT.	FROM.	TO	IN RELIEF OF.
2/21 Lond.R.	Brigade Reserve.	R I.	2/23 Lond.R.
2/22 " "	Divnl. Reserve.	R II.	2/24 Lond.R.
2/23 " "	R I.	Divnl. Reserve.	2/22 " "
2/24 " "	R II.	Brigade Reserve.	2/21 " "

The 2/22 Lond.R. will move up from ETRUN to ANZIN by platoons at 5 minute intervals.

[Signature]
Captain,
Brigade Major,
181st Infantry Brigade.

Issued at 7.30 p.m.
Copy
No. 1. 2/21.   8. 179th Inf.Bde.
     2. 2/22.   9. O.C.Art.Group.
     3. 2/23.   10. 181 T.M.Battery.
     4. 2/24.   11. Pioneer Coy. ECURIE.
     5. 181 M.G.Coy. 12. File.
     6. 3/3rd Field Co. 13. War Diary.
     7. 106th Inf.Bde.

SECRET.   Copy No...........

181st INFANTRY BRIGADE ORDER No. 21.

Reference-Maps 51 B & C.
Trench Map.

Tuesday,
26th September, 1916.

1. Battalions in the front line will be relieved by Bns. in reserve on the afternoon of the 28th inst. according to Table below, under arrangements to be made by Os.C. concerned. The leading platoon 2/23 L.R. to reach ANZIN Communication Trench by 3 p.m.

2. The 2/21 L.R. will take over Control Posts by 12 noon on 28th inst. from the 2/23 L.R.

3. The O.C. 2/22 L.R. will take over command of the ECURIE Defences from the O.C. 2/24 L.R.

4. Completion of the relief will be reported to Brigade H.Q. as per attached Code.

5. Acknowledge.

Unit.	FROM.	TO.	IN RELIEF OF.
2/21 Lond.R.	R I.	Divnl. Reserve.	2/23 Lond.R.
2/22 " "	R II.	Brigade Reserve.	2/24 " "
2/23 " "	Divnl. Reserve.	R I.	2/21 " "
2/24 " "	Brigade Reserve.	R II.	2/22 " "

The 2/23 L.R. will move up from ETRUN to ANZIN by platoons at 5 minute intervals.

Captain.
Brigade Major.
181st Infantry Brigade.

Issued at 7.30 p.m. by orderly.

Copy No. 1. 2/21.   8. 179th Inf.Bde.
         2. 2/22.   9. O.C. Art.Group.
         3. 2/23.   10. 181 T.M.Battery.
         4. 2/24.   11. Pioneer Coy. ECURIE.
         5. 181 M.G.Coy. 12. File.
         6. 3/3rd Field Coy. 13. War Diary.
         7. 106th Inf.Bde.

SECRET.   APPENDIX III.

181st INFANTRY BRIGADE

WAR   DIARY.

1st - 30th September, 1916.

CARRYING PARTIES - GAS INSTALLATION.

Vol. I.   No. 4.

----------oOo----------

SECRET.

ADDENDA to the 2/21 Lond.R.
Orders for Gas Installation.

1. The O.C. 2/21 Lond.R. will furnish one man per emplacement to assist the men of the Special Brigade, R.E. in putting back sandbags and closing the boxes. These men to be in position by 9 p.m. daily.

2. There will be one man at each of the following emplacements:-

   (a) Night of 11/12th.

   25
   26
   27
   28
   29
   30
   31.

   (b) Night of 12/13th.

   31
   32
   33
   34
   35
   36
   46
   47
   48
   49
   50

   (c) Night of 13/14th.

   37
   38
   39
   40
   41
   42
   43
   44
   45

3. APPENDIX A - Details as to Guides.
   APPENDIX B - Details as to French Piquets.
   APPENDIX C - Map.
   APPENDIX D - Divisional Letter G/S. 849r.

                                    Captain.
                                    Brigade Major.
                                    181st Infantry Brigade.

5.9.16.

ABSOLUTE SILENCE MUST BE MAINTAINED THROUGHOUT.

SECRET War Diary

181st INFANTRY BRIGADE

GAS INSTALLATION

Instructions to 2/21st Lond. R.

This Battalion will be holding R.1 Subsector at the time of the GAS INSTALLATION on nights of 11/12th, 12/13th and 13/14th. The duties of the Officer Commanding will be as under:-

1. To provide the necessary guides for carrying parties each night (found by the 2/24th Lond R.) See Appendix "A"

2. To effectively picquet all the trench junctions in R.1 Subsector North of the BOULEBOURT ROAD exclusive. See Appendix "B"

3. To arrange that all Vermorel Sprayers in the Subsector are ready for immediate use, together with the necessary personnel. Especial attention to be paid to those located on or near the Route to be followed by the carrying parties.

4. To give every assistance in his power to the Special Company R.E. billeted at ABRI CENTRALE and CHEMIN CREUX.

5. To ensure that between 7 p.m. and 5 a.m. during the three nights mentioned, no one, except officers on duty and carrying squads use any of the UP Communication Trenches mentioned in Appendix "A".

6. To block all Saps in that portion of his front over which GAS is discharged, so as to prevent backwash, and to make all necessary arrangements for same.

7. Special map attached, shewing position of Gas emplacements, Junction Picquets, and routes followed by Carrying Squads, and special division of Brigade Front into 5 portions for the purpose of installing the cylinders See Appendix "C".

8. Acknowledge.

Captain
Brigade Major
181st Infantry Bde.

Bde H.Q.
4-9-16

Cop No.1 to Division
2   2/21st Lond. R.
3   Q Company
4   Filed
5   War Diary
6   2/24th Lond. R.
7   Spare.

9. Special attention will be paid to all the points brought forward in Divl. letter S/S.249.3. This Officer G.S/92a 4 Runners will be detailed to report to the Officer of the 4th Bn. Special Brigade R.E. at 10 a.m. 13th Sept. at Bn. Headquarters.

SECRET   APPENDIX "A"

ORDERS FOR GUIDES
--o--

1. The O.C.2/21st Lond. R. will detail 24 men to act as guides to the Carrying Parties found by the 2/24th Lond. R. on nights 11/12th, 12/13th September, and 20 men on the night of 13/14th September. These men must be specially selected for their intelligence.

2. They will assemble to meet the Carrying Squads 2/24th Lond. R. at ANZIN CHURCH, under an officer to be detailed by O.C. 2/21st Lond. R., at 7.55 p.m. each evening. Each guide will carry a docket stating number of Squad that he is to guide, and the officer will be responsible that he leads off the correct squad. The same guide will lead the same numbered squad each night. (Dockets to be provided by O.C. 2/21st Lond. R. This will be shown to Officer or N.C.O. in charge of the Squad).

3. The Carrying Squads arrive at ANZIN at 10 minute intervals commencing about 8 p.m. each night. The O.C. Guides is responsible that the correct interval of time is maintained by Squads leaving ANZIN.

4. Route to be followed on night of 11/12th
    ROUTE UP - Overland alongside ANZIN Ave. to BETHUNE Road into ANZIN Ave - BARRICADE - ROCLINCOURT Road - CHEMIN CREUX - A Ave - BONNAL.
    ROUTE DOWN - G Ave - GRAND COLLECTEUR - CHEMIN CREUX - BLANCHARD - BIDOT Ave - FILATIERS Ave - GENIE Ave along BETHUNE Road overland alongside ANZIN Ave.
   Route to be followed on nights of 12/13th and 13/14th
    ROUTE UP - Overland along ANZIN Ave to BETHUNE Road - ANZIN Ave - BARRICADE - ROCLINCOURT Road - CHEMIN CREUX - A Ave - RIPPERT Ave - G Ave - BONNAL.
    ROUTE DOWN - CHEMIN CREUX - BLANCHARD - BIDOT Ave - FILATIERS Ave - GENIE Ave along BETHUNE Road overland alongside ANZIN Ave.

   Guides will lead Squads to Gas Emplacements in BONNAL as under :-

No. of Guide	No. of Squad	11/12	12/13	13/14
		No. of Emplacement		
1,2,3,4,	1,2,3,4,	30	36	41
5,6,7,8,	5,6,7,8,	29	35	40
9,10,11,12,	9,10,11,12,	28	34	39
13,14,15,16,	13,14,15,16,	27	33	38
17,18,19,20	17,18,19,20,	26	32	37
21,22,23,24	21,22,23,24	25	31	--

5. Squads on reaching the BONNAL will be met by an N.C.O. of the Special Company R.E. who will direct them to their particular bay.

6. On their return journey each night, after leading squads to overland track alongside ANZIN Ave west of BETHUNE Road guides will return to their Battalion via ANZIN Ave reporting to Battalion H.Q. on arrival.

7. The officer detailed in Para 2 will be responsible that all the above guides have a thorough knowledge of both the UP and DOWN Routes for both the night 11/12th and the nights 12/13th and 13/14th, and will be responsible that the route is walked at least twice beforehand by each guide, once to be by night.

Bde. H.Q.

                                                Captain
                                                Bde. Major.
                                                181st Infantry Bde.

SECRET   APPENDIX B

TRENCH PICQUETS

---o---

The O.C.2/21st Lond. R. will find Trench Picquets as under :-

Night 11/12th

No. of Picquet	Position	Duty
1.	Junction of BONNAL and G Ave.	To direct down squads down G Ave.
2.	" " " BIDOT	" " " " BIDOT
3.	" " G. COLLECTEUR and A Ave (2 posts)	" " UP " along A Ave to BONNAL
4.	" " G. COLLECTEUR and G Ave	" " DOWN squads to CHEMIN CREUX via G.COLLECTEUR
5.	" " G. COLLECTEUR and CHEMIN CREUX	" " DOWN squads to BLANCHARD
6.	" " G. COLLECTEUR and BIDOT	" " " " " ABRI CENTRALE & LOWER BIDOT
7.	" " CHEMIN CREUX and A Ave.	" " UP squads to G.COLLECTEUR
8.	" " A Ave and RIPPERT (2 posts)	" " " " " "
9.	" " CHEMIN CREUX and BLANCHARD	" " DOWN " " ABRI CENTRALE & BIDOT Ave.
10.	" " BLANCHARD & BIDOT (two posts, one at top of steps, one at bottom)	" " DOWN squads down LOWER BIDOT.

Nights of 12/13th and 13/14th

No. of Picquet	Position	Duty
1.	Junction of BONNAL and Chemin Creux	To direct down squads down CHEMIN CREUX
2.	" " " BIDOT	" " " " down BIDOT
3.	" " G.COLLECTEUR and RIPPERT & G Ave. (2 posts)	" " UP " from RIPPERT up G Ave.
4.	" " G.COLLECTEUR and BIDOT	" " DOWN " to ABRI CENTRALE
5.	" " A Ave and RIPPERT	" " UP " to GRAND COLLECTEUR. Via Rippert
6.	" " CHEMIN CREUX and A Ave.	" " " " to RIPPERT
7.	" " CHEMIN CREUX and BLANCHARD	" " DOWN " ABRI CENTRAL and BIDOT
8.	" " BLANCHARD & BIDOT (two posts, one at top of steps, one at bottom)	" " " " to LOWER BIDOT.

A special officer is to be detailed to post these picquets, he will be responsible that every man knows his duty thoroughly, and that they are withdrawn immediately on completion of the night's work.

Intelligent men should be selected.

They will be in position by 9 p.m. each night.

Bde. H.Q.
4-9-16

Captain
Brigade Major
181st Infantry Bde.

GAS INSTALLATION

Instructions to 2/24th.LOND.R.

During the installation on the nights 11/12th., 12/13th. and 13/14th. September the 2/24th. LOND. R. will be in DIVISIONAL Reserve at ETRUN.

1. The Battalion has been detailed to find the carrying parties required to complete the installation in sub sector "A" (see attached Map, App. "A").
The numbers required each night are as under:-

11/12th.	12/13th.	13/14th.
12 Officers	12 Officers	10 Officers
48 N.C.O's	48 N.C.O's	40 N.C.O's
480 men	480 Men	400 Men
12 Stretcher Bearers	12 Stretcher Bearers	10 Stretcher Bearers)

For all details see copy of G/S 949 and "Special Instructions for Carrying Parties" issued by 60th. Division (attached as Appendix "B").

These squads will move off from ETRUN at 10 minutes intervals, the first squad passing Brigade Headquarters at 7-30 p.m. They will be moved off under the orders of an Officer to be detailed by the O.C. 2/24th. LOND. R. This officer will be responsible that squads move off at correct intervals, and will hand to each Officer a docket, on which is stated the number of the two squads under his command, the gas emplacement in the BONNAL that the squads are to fill, and their Routes both up and down.

He will also hand to both N.C.O's of each squad a similar docket. These dockets will be provided by the Brigade. The Officer selected will report to the Brigade Major to receive instructions at 3 p.m. 11th. inst.

2. Each squad, on reaching ANZIN Church, will be met by a guide provided by the 2/21st. LOND. R., who will show the Officer, or N.C.O. i/c Squad, a docket with a corresponding number on it to that of the Squad. This man will guide the squad to the required emplacement and back as far as the BETHUNE Road (For all particulars of route, etc., see Instructions to 2/21st. LOND. R., attached as Appendix "C")

3. On reaching the BARRICADE, each squad will be met by CAPT.J.R. MACDONALD, 2/17th. Bn. L.R., who will direct the Officer or N.C.O. i/c Squad to the Officer of the 4th. Bn. Special Brigade R.E., to whom they will show their dockets (See paras. 3 & 4 Special Instructions, Appendix "B") and when the squad has taken over the cylinders, start them off down the ROCLINCOURT ROAD.

4. Officers or N.C.O's i/c Squads are responsible that the carriers are relieved periodically during the journey, and that a very slow pace is maintained throughout, whilst carrying the cylinders.

5. Squads will be directed to the entrance of the CHEMIN CREUX from ROCLINCOURT ROAD by an Officer of the 2/23rd. LOND. R., who will be on duty there.

6. Squads on completion of the work, will return direct to their Billets in ETRUN; handing over the poles to the Sapper in charge at 3/3rd. FIELD COY". R.E. Headquarters ANZIN, as they pass through. I/c each squad will be held responsible for this.

    NOTE. During the "UP" journey, the one spare pole per squad will be carried by the last man in front of the N.C.O. bringing up the rear of each squad.

7. The necessary sandbags will be drawn from Brigade Quartermasters Stores each day, at 3 p.m., and will be handed in to the same place by each squad on returning.
I.C. Squad to be responsible.
O.C. Battalion to be responsible for correct issue each day.

8. O.C. Battalion is responsible that every Officer, N.C.O, and man knows the number of his squad, and all other information that it may be necessary for them to know, contained in these instructions and appendices. Sufficient copies of "Special Instructions for Carrying Parties" are issued to enable every Officer Commanding Squads to possess one.

9. All ranks must be warned that the whole operation must be carried out as SILENTLY as possible, and all concerned, that, on no account whatever, are they to discuss the matter with anyone.

10. Acknowledge.

                                     Captain,
                                   Brigade Major,
                              181st. Inf. Brigade.

Copies to:-

1. Division
2. 4th.Bn.Special R.E.
3. Office
4. War Diary.
5. 2/24th. LOND. R.
6. 2/21st. LOND. R.
7. Spare.

App A   Special Map
"   B   Div Order G/S 2495
"   C   Instructions to 2/21 L.R.

SECRET.

ADDENDA. (To 2/22 Lond.R.)

The O.C. 2/22 Lond.R. will arrange for a Vermorel Sprayer and necessary personnel to be present during the whole of the operations each night at the MINOTAUR Dump. The N.C.O. in charge to report at 9.35 p.m. to the officer in charge guides.

APPENDICES ATTACHED.

APPENDIX A. Details as to guides.
    B. " " " trench picquets.
    C. Special Map.
    D. Divnl. letter G/S.249r.

Copy No. 1. Division.
    2. Special Bde. R.E.
    3. War Diary.
    4. File.
    5. 2/22 L.R.
    6. 2/23 L.R.
    7. 179th Inf.Bde.
    8. Spare.

5.9.16.

ABSOLUTE SILENCE MUST BE MAINTAINED THROUGHOUT.   COPY No. 3

SECRET.

181st INFANTRY BRIGADE.

GAS INSTALLATION.

GS/92e

Instructions to 2/22 Lond.R.

During the installation on the nights 11/12th, 12/13th, 13/14th Sept., the 2/22 Lond.R. will be holding RIGHT II Subsector. The duties of the O.C. will be as under:-

1. To provide the necessary guides for carrying parties (found by the 179 Inf.Bde). See APPENDIX A.

2. To effectively picquet all the trench junctions in RIGHT II Subsector (as detailed in APPENDIX B), to assist carrying parties in both B & C special subsectors.

3. To arrange that all Vermorel Sprayers in the Subsector are ready for immediate use, together with the necessary personnel. Especial attention is to be paid to those located on or near the route to be followed by the carrying parties.

4. To give every assistance in his power to any of the Special Co. R.E. that may be working in the subsector, and to furnish one man per emplacement to assist the men of the Special Bde. R.E. in putting back sandbags and closing the boxes. These men to be in position by 9 p.m. daily. "X" (See below)

5. To ensure that between 7 p.m. and 5 a.m. during the three nights mentioned, no one, except officers on duty and carrying squads use any of the "UP" Communication Trenches mentioned in Appendix A.

6. To block all Saps in that portion of his front over which Gas is discharged, so as to prevent backwash, and to make all necessary arrangements for same.

7. Special map attached, showing position of Gas Emplacements, Junction Picquets, routes followed by Carrying Squads, and special division of Brigade Front into 3 portions for the purpose of installing the cylinders. See APPENDIX C.

8. Special attention will be paid to all the points brought forward in Divnl. letter G.S.249.2. This Office G.S/92a. 4 Runners will be detailed to report to the Officer of the 4th Bn. Special Brigade R.E. at 10 a.m. 13th Sept. at Bn.H.Q.

9. Copy of Divnl. letter G/S.249r & "Special Instructions for Carrying Parties attached. See APPENDIX D.

10. Acknowledge.

                                                    Captain.
                                          Brigade Major.
                                181st Infantry Brigade.

"X"

4. Contd. - There will be one man at each of the following emplacements:-

Night of 11/12th.	Night of 12/13th.	Night of 13/14th.
52 - 53 - 54	58, 64 - 65.	56 - 57, 68.
55, 59 - 60.	66 - 67.	69 - 70 - 71.
61 - 62 - 63.		72.

SECRET.   APPENDIX "A".

ORDERS FOR GUIDES.

1. The 2/22 Lond.R. will detail 18 reliable men to act as guides to the Carrying Squads supplied by the 179th Inf. Bde. on the nights of 11/12th, 12/13th, 13/14th Sept.

2. These guides will assemble at MINOTAUR Dump each evening at 9.35 p.m. under an Officer to be detailed by O.C. 2/22 Lnd.R. Each guide will carry a docket stating number of squad that he is to guide and the route that he is to follow, this he will show to the Officer or N.C.O. in charge of the squad. The Officer will be responsible that each guide leads off the correct squad. The same guide will lead the same squad each night. The above-mentioned officer will work in conjunction with the Officer of the 179th Inf.Bde. posted at the same place for the purpose of starting off their Carrying Parties. Dockets for guides to be provided by O.C. 2/22 Lond.R. each night.

3. The first 4 Carrying Squads push up the Cylinders along the 40 cm. Tramway to the MINOTAUR Dump, the first squad leaving with Cylinders at 10 p.m. The remaining 14 Squads arrive via VASE AVENUE. Each Squad, after taking over the Cylinders from No. 4 Special Bn. R.E. moves off at 10 minute intervals.

4. The same route will be followed each night, viz.-
   ROUTE UP - MINOTAUR AVENUE - ANNIVERSAIRE AVENUE - SUTHERLAND AVENUE - BOYAU.
   ROUTE DOWN - BOYAU - WICK AVENUE - GRAND COLLECTEUR - VICTOIRE AVENUE.

   Guides will lead Squads to Gas Emplacements in BOYAU in accordance with attachment to Divnl.Letter G/S.249r.of the 1st inst. headed "C" Sub-sector, No. 1. Guide leading No. 1 Squad and so on.

5. Squads on reaching the BOYAU, will be met by an N.C.O. of the Special Brigade, R.E. who will direct men to their particular Bay.

6. Guides on reaching VICTOIRE AVENUE will leave the squad and return to Bn. H.Q. via VASE and MINOTAUR AVENUES.

7. The Officer detailed in para. 2. will be responsible that all the above guides have a thorough knowledge of both the UP and DOWN Routes for both the night 11/12th and the nights 12/13th and 13/14th, and will be responsible that the route is walked at least twice beforehand by each guide, once to be by night. Spare guides should be trained to replace possible casualties.

                                                    Captain.
                                                 Brigade Major.
                                              161st Infantry Brigade.

5.9.16.

SECRET. APPENDIX "B".

TRENCH PICQUETS.

The O.C. 2/22 Lond.R. will find Trench Picquets as under:-

Each Night.

No. of Picquet.	Position.	Duty.
1.	Junction of NEW FANTOME & BONNAL.	(a) To direct UP Squads to Gas emplacements required. Squads for Nos. 55-59 emplacements northwards. *along BONNAL* Squads for No. 54 emplacement (first night only) southwards along BONNAL. (b) To direct DOWN Squads along BONNAL southwards to BIDON.
2.	Junction of BONNAL & INTERMEDIATE.	To direct Squads along BONNAL northwards.
3.	" " BONNAL & ORR AVENUE.	" " " " "
4.	" " BONNAL & WICK AVENUE.	To direct DOWN Squads down WICK AVENUE.
5.	" " BONNAL & OLD FANTOME.	To prevent DOWN Squads from turning down OLD FANTOME.
6.	" " OLD FANTOME & PLACE D'ARMES.	To direct UP Squads to BONNAL.
x 7.	" " OLD & NEW FANTOME.	Officers post, details as under.
8.	" " G.COLLECTEUR & FANTOME (2 Posts).	To direct UP Squads to BONNAL.
9.	" " G.COLLECTEUR & SUTHERLAND AVENUE (F.13).	To direct UP Squads to BONNAL.
10.	" " G.COLLECTEUR & SUTHERLAND AVENUE (F.14).	" " " " " "
11.	" " G.COLLECTEUR & WICK AV.	To direct DOWN Squads along G.COLLECTEUR northwards.
12.	Brigade Left Boundary.	" " " " "
13.	All Other necessary points along Route up to BONNAL from MINOTAUR Dump.	

x The Duty of this Officer will be to find out the number of each Squad as it reaches him and direct it up the OLD or NEW FANTOME according to the Table given below.

Night 11/12th.		Night 12/13th.		Night 13/14th.	
No.of Squad.	Trench.	No.of Squad.	Trench.	No.of Squad.	Trench.
1 to 4.	NEW FANTOME.	1 to 4.	NEW FANTOME.	1 to 4.	NEW FANTOME
5 to 16.	OLD FANTOME.	5 - 24.	OLD FANTOME.	5 to 20.	OLD FANTOME
17 to 24.	NEW FANTOME.			21 to 24.	NEW FANTOME

A special officer is to be detailed to post these picquets, he will be responsible that every man knows his duty thoroughly, and that they are withdrawn immediately on completion of the night's work.

Intelligent men should be selected.

They will be in position by 9 p.m. each night.

5.9.16.

Copy No. 1. Division.
2. War Diary.
3. File.
4. R.E.
5. 2/23 L.R.
6.   "   "
7. 180th Inf.Bde.
8. Spare.

ABSOLUTE SILENCE MUST BE MAINTAINED THROUGHOUT.

Copy No 2

SECRET.

65/928

181st INFANTRY BRIGADE.

GAS INSTALLATION.

Instructions to 2/23 Lond.R.

During the installation on the nights 11/12th, 12/13th, 13/14th Sept., the 2/23 Lond.R. will be in Brigade Reserve. The duties of the Officer Commanding will be as under:-

1. To find on each of the above nights a party as under:-
   - 4 Officers
   - 16 N.C.Os.
   - 160 Men.
   - 4 Stretcher bearers.

   For all details see Divnl. letter G/S 249r. and "Special Instructions for Carrying parties attached as APPENDIX A.

   It will be best if the bulk of the above party are drawn from ABRI CENTRALE. The O.C.Bn. will make his own arrangements, both as to marching the party to the ROCLINCOURT AVE. prior to drawing the cylinders and as to moving those not billeted at ABRI CENTRALE back to their own dugouts. He will, however, be responsible that no block is caused to Carrying parties moving up, by these troops returning.

2. By 8.55 p.m. each evening, this party will be in position in ROCLINCOURT AVE. with the head of No. 1 Squad opposite the entrance to the FANTOME AVE. Before leaving their dugouts each evening, the O.C. will arrange to issue each officer with a docket on which is stated the Nos. of the two squads he commands, the Number of the Gas Implacement the squads are to fill, and the ROUTE UP and DOWN. He will issue a similar docket to each of the two N.C.Os. of each squad, and will arrange, as far as possible, that the same squads keep to the same numbers each night. These dockets will be supplied by the Brigade.

3. An officer of the 180th Infantry Bde. will be stationed at the junction of the FANTOME AVE. and ROCLINCOURT AVE. It will be his duty to direct i/c Squads to the officer of the Special Brigade R.E. who will, having inspected their dockets, hand over the cylinders to them. He will then, observing the proper intervals, start squads off up the FANTOME at 10 minute intervals.

4. The Squads will move up, deliver the cylinders, and return by the Routes mentioned in APPENDIX B to ABRI CENTRALE, where they will at once enter their dugouts and clear the trenches, handing over the poles on arrival to a sapper of the Special Bde. R.E. there. I/c Squads will be responsible for the correct handing over.

   NOTE.- During the "UP" journey, the one spare pole per squad will be carried by the last man in front of the N.C.O. bringing up the rear of each squad.

5. To arrange that all the officers and at least one N.C.O. per squad walks the Route "UP" and "DOWN" at least twice (once by night) beforehand. No extra guides will be provided (for Route, see APPENDIX B).

6. An officer, 2/22 Lond.R., will be stationed at the junction of the NEW and OLD FANTOME; he will direct squads up one or other, according to their numbers.

7. To indent for the necessary sandbags (see APPENDIX A, "Special Instructions, para. 3"), and arrange for issue each day

-2-

and for collection and storage on completion of each day's work.

8. Officers and N.C.Os. i/c squads are responsible that the carriers are relieved periodically during the journey and that a very slow pace is maintained throughout whilst carrying the cylinders.

9. To find Trench Picquets as shown in APPENDIX C (Attached).

10. Copy of instructions to O.C. 2/22 Lond.R. for information. (APPENDIX D).

11. Special map attached, showing position of Gas emplacements, junction picquets, routes followed by Carrying Squads and special division of Brigade Front into 3 Subsectors for the purpose of installing the cylinders (Appendix E attached).

12. To detail 16 men to act as guides to Carrying Squads found by the 180th Inf.Bde. (APPENDIX F).

13. O.C. Battalion is responsible that every Officer, N.C.O. and man knows the number of his squad, and all other information that it may be necessary for them to know, contained in these instructions and appendices. Sufficient copies of "Special Instructions for Carrying Parties" are issued to enable every Officer Commanding Squads to possess one.

14. All ranks must be warned that the whole operation must be carried out as SILENTLY as possible, and all concerned, that on no account whatever, are they to discuss the matter with anyone.

15. To arrange for a Vermorel Sprayer and the necessary personnel to be on duty at the BARRICADE. The senior N.C.O. will report to Capt. J.H.MACDONALD at 8.50 p.m. each night there.

16. Special attention to be paid to all instructions contained in Divnl. letter G/S. 249s., this office G.S./92a.

17. ACKNOWLEDGE.

APPENDIX A - Divnl. Letter.
" B - Routes.
" C - Trench Picquets.
" D - Orders to 2/22 L.R.
" E - Map.
" F - Guides to 180 Inf.Bde.

Captain.
Brigade Major.
181st Infantry Brigade.

6.9.16.

SECRET   APPENDIX B

ROUTES FOR CARRYING PARTIES

---oOo---

The Routes to be followed by the 8 carrying parties found by the 2/23rd Lond. R. are as under:-

NIGHT of 11/12th

No. of Squad	Route Up	Gas Emplacement	Route Down
1,2,3,4,	FANTOME – NEW FANTOME turn left up BONNAL	59	return along BONNAL – BIDOT – ABRI CENTRALE
5,6,7,8,	FANTOME – OLD FANTOME turn right down BONNAL	51	ditto

NIGHT OF 12/13th

1,2,3,4.	FANTOME – NEW FANTOME turn left up BONNAL	58	ditto
5,6,7,8.	FANTOME – OLD FANTOME turn right down BONNAL	46	return along BONNAL – CHEMIN CREUX – ABRI – CENTRALE.

NIGHT OF 13/14th

1,2,3,4.	FANTOME – NEW FANTOME turn left up BONNAL	57	return along BONNAL BIDOT – ABRI CENTRALE
5,6,7,8.	FANTOME – OLD FANTOME turn right down BONNAL	42	return along BONNAL – CHEMIN CREUX – ABRI CENTRALE.

A VERY SLOW PACE is to be maintained throughout when carrying cylinders.

APPENDIX C

TRENCH PICQUETS

The O.C. 2/23rd Lond. R. will find Trench Picquets as under :-

No. of Picquet	POSITION	DUTY
No. 1	Junction of CHEMIN CREUX and ROCLINCOURT Road.	This Post will consist of 1 Officer & 4 O.R. & the officer will be responsible for directing squads from ROCLINCOURT Road into CHEMIN CREUX & preventing any blockages that might occur on the Road.
No. 2	Junction of BIDOT and ROCLINCOURT Ave (2 posts)	To direct DOWN squads into TUNNEL under ROCLINCOURT Road.
No. 3	Junction of BIDOT and FILATIERS Avenue	To direct DOWN squads along FILATIERS.
No. 4	At entrance to BLANCHARD at BARRICADE	To prevent any traffic up BLANCHARD & if shelling occurs direct carrying squads of 2/24 L.R. "A" Subsector down ROCLINCOURT Avenue.

APPENDIX C

contd.

No. of Picquet	Position	DUTY
Nos. 6.6.7.	At trench junction from FILATIERS Tunnel under LILLE Road into main GENIE Avenue.	To direct DOWN squads straight through into GENIE Ave.
No. 8	At point where ANZIN Ave breaks into two.	To direct UP squads to BARRICADE.
No. 9	At point where steps from Tramway lead down into Village Street.	To turn UP squads 180 Infy. Bde. from open into Trench
No.10	Requisite number between VILLAGE STREET and ROCLINCOURT Ave.	To direct UP squads 180th Inf. Bde. to BARRICADE.

   A special officer is to be detailed to post these picquets, he will be responsible that every man knows his duty thoroughly, and that they are withdrawn immediately on completion of the night's work.

        Intelligent men should be selected

        They will be in position by 8 p.m. each night.

   xxxxxxxx   xxxxxxx

SECRET.   APPENDIX "F".

INSTRUCTIONS FOR GUIDES FOR
180th Infantry Brigade.

1. The O.C. 2/23 Lond.R. will detail 16 men to act as guides to the Carrying Parties found by the 180 Inf.Bde. on nights 11/12th, 12/13th, 13/14th Sept. These men must be specially selected for their intelligence.

2. These guides will assemble to meet the above squads at 9 p.m. daily at 3/3rd Field Coy. R.E.H.Q., ANZIN, under an officer to be detailed by O.C. 3/3rd Field Coy.R.E. Each guide will carry a docket stating number of squad that he is to guide and route to be followed. The officer will be responsible that he leads off the correct squad. The same guide will lead the same numbered squad each night. (Above dockets will be provided by O.C. 2/23 L.R. and will be shown to the officer or N.C.O. i/c Squad). There will be an officer of the 180th Inf.Bde. there with whom this officer will co-operate.

    [margin note: O.C. 2/23 L.R.]

3. As to position of Carrying Squads, see Page 3, para. 8, Divnl. Letter G/S.249r., APPENDIX A.

4. Routes to be followed as under. Guides will have the same numbers as the squads which they are selected to guide.

Night of 11/12th.

No. of Squad.	ROUTE UP.	Gas Emplacement.	ROUTE DOWN.
9 - 12	Overland from ANZIN along 40 cm. tramway past MADAGASCAR - enter VILLAGE STREET-SOLE STREET-ROCLINCOURT AVE.-FANTOME - OLD FANTOME - turn right down BOURAL.	52	Along BOURAL - BIDOT - FILATIERS AVE. - GENIE - up BETHUNE ROAD - overland alongside ANZIN AVE. west of BETHUNE ROAD.
13 - 16	ditto.	53	ditto.
17 - 20	As above to FANTOME then - NEW FANTOME - turn right down BOURAL.	54	ditto.
21 - 24	As above to FANTOME - NEW FANTOME - turn left up BOURAL.	55	ditto.

Night of 12/13th.

No. of Squad.	ROUTE UP.	Gas Emplacement.	ROUTE DOWN.
9 - 12	Route as for night 11/12th.	47	Along BOURAL - CHEMIN CREUX - BLANCHARD - BIDOT - FILATIERS, then as above.
13 - 16	ditto.	48	ditto.
17 - 20	ditto.	49	Route as for 9-12 Squads night 11/12th.
21 - 24	ditto.	50	ditto.

Night of 13/14th.

No. of Squad.	ROUTE UP.	Gas Emplacement.	ROUTE DOWN.
9 - 12	ditto.	43	Route as for 9-12 Squads night 12/13th.
13 - 16	ditto.	44	ditto.
17 - 20	ditto.	45	ditto.
21 - 24	Route as for 21 - 24 Squads night 11/12th.	56	Route as for 21-24 Squads night 11/12th.

5. Guides will lead squads back to ANZIN, returning to Bn. H.Q. and reporting on arrival.

6. The officer detailed in para. 2 will be responsible that all the above guides have a thorough knowledge of both the "UP" and "DOWN" Routes for each night and will be responsible that the route is walked at least twice beforehand by each guide (once by night) Spare guides should be trained.

SECRET.   APPENDIX IV.

                        181st INFANTRY BRIGADE

                        W A R   D I A R Y.

                        1st - 30th September, 1916.

                        RAID BY 2/21 LONDON REGT.

                        Vol. I.   No. 4.
                        ---------------oOo---------------

SECRET.　　　　　　　　　　　　　　　　　　　　　Copy No. 3

R A I D   B Y
2/21 Lond. Regt. on night of
22/23rd Sept. 1916.
(23/24 handwritten correction)

Order No. R.1.

Ref. Sketch Map attached.
----

1. **OBJECT.** To obtain prisoners and cause damage to enemy.

2. **JUMPING OFF POINTS.** "T" Heads of SAPS 23 and 24.

3. **POINTS OF INGRESS & EGRESS.** A.22.b.90.30 and A.23.a.02.35.

4. **DISTRIBUTION.** Party of about 50 under command of Sec.Lieut. SOUTHIN with Sec.Lieut. TOWNEND second in command, divided into -
   - (1) Right Group   23 men under Sec.Lieut. SOUTHIN
   - (2) Left Group   23 men under   "   " TOWNEND
   - (3) Centre Group   12 men under   "   " HAMILTON

   Further support, if required, will be found from the Sap Garrison of Saps 23 and 24.

   Right and Left Groups will each be told off into 3 Sections -
   - (a) Blocking Party   1 N.C.O. and 5 men.
   - (b) Blocking Party   1 N.C.O. and 5 men.
   - (c) Attacking Party   1 Off., 1 Sgt. & 10 men.

   Centre Group will act as covering party to Right and Left Groups.

5. **OBJECTIVE.** Communication Trench marked X on attacked sketch.

6. **ACTION.** At ZERO, Right and Left Groups will enter enemy's lines at "d" and "a" respectively, leave blocks at "d" and "a", work on to "c" and "b" respectively, leave blocks at "c" and "b", and work up C.T. marked X until recall is signalled.

   At the same time Centre Group will endeavour to get a footing in trench between "a" and "d".

7. **COUNTERSIGN.** SUTTON-VENY.

8. **CODE WORD FOR WITHDRAWAL.** BLIGHTY.

9. **EQUIPMENT.** Steel Helmets - Service dress with puttees - no belts.

10. **ARMS.**

Blocking Party	2 Bayonet men - 10 rounds in magazine - 2 clips in pocket. 4 bombers each to carry a knobkerry and 8 bombs.
Attacking Party	3 Bayonet men - 10 rounds loaded - 2 clips in pocket. 6 Bombers, each to carry a knobkerry and 8 bombs. 1 Officer) Revolver and 1 Sergt.) 8 bombs each.
Centre Group	10 Bayonet men - 10 rounds loaded - 2 clips in pocket and 2 bombs. 2 Carriers each with 2 buckets of 20 bombs each.

/Contd.

- 2 -

10.	ARMS (Contd.)	Each Section will further carry -

                                    2 yards of rope.
                                    2 wire cutters.
                                    1 electric torch. (If obtainable).

11. **STORES REQUIRED.**   284 Bombs.
                                    28 Knobkerries.
                                    12 wire cutters.
                                    18 yards light rope.
                                    Electric Torches.

12. **ADVANCE STRETCHER BEARING PARTY.**   To be in waiting at L.23/4 BONNAL.

13. **WATCHES.**   Will be synchronised by all concerned.

14. **SIGNALS.**   For Recall (at plus 20) - Ratatat by M.Gs.

                Failing (For Artillery Barrage - Red, Green, Red,
               Telephone(Green. alter.
                         (For cease fire - Red, Red, Red.

                        For Direction - Very Lights from ROCADE
                                 at 1 minute intervals from
                                 plus 22.

                        For drawing Enemy fire - 2 fixed lights
                                 at flank.

15. **COMMUNICATION.**   Wires will be laid from Advanced Coy. Headquarters to Sapheads.

16. **IDENTITY DISCS.**   Special Discs will be issued.

17. **RECOGNITION MARKS.**   Splash of whitewash on tunic, back & front.

18. **MACHINE GUNS.**   (1) Will keep up normal fire until plus 15.
                                        (2) Will give recall signal.

19. **STOKES GUNS.**   Will stand by with a view to counter hostile M.G. fire.

20. **ARTILLERY.**   Will break wire beforehand and stand by for orders at ZERO.

                                                                    Lieut.Col.
                                              Cmdng. 2/21 London Regt.

NOTES.   ZERO will be notified to all concerned later.

             Any telephone reference to above raid will be referred to as BILLIKEN.

            ACKNOWLEDGE.

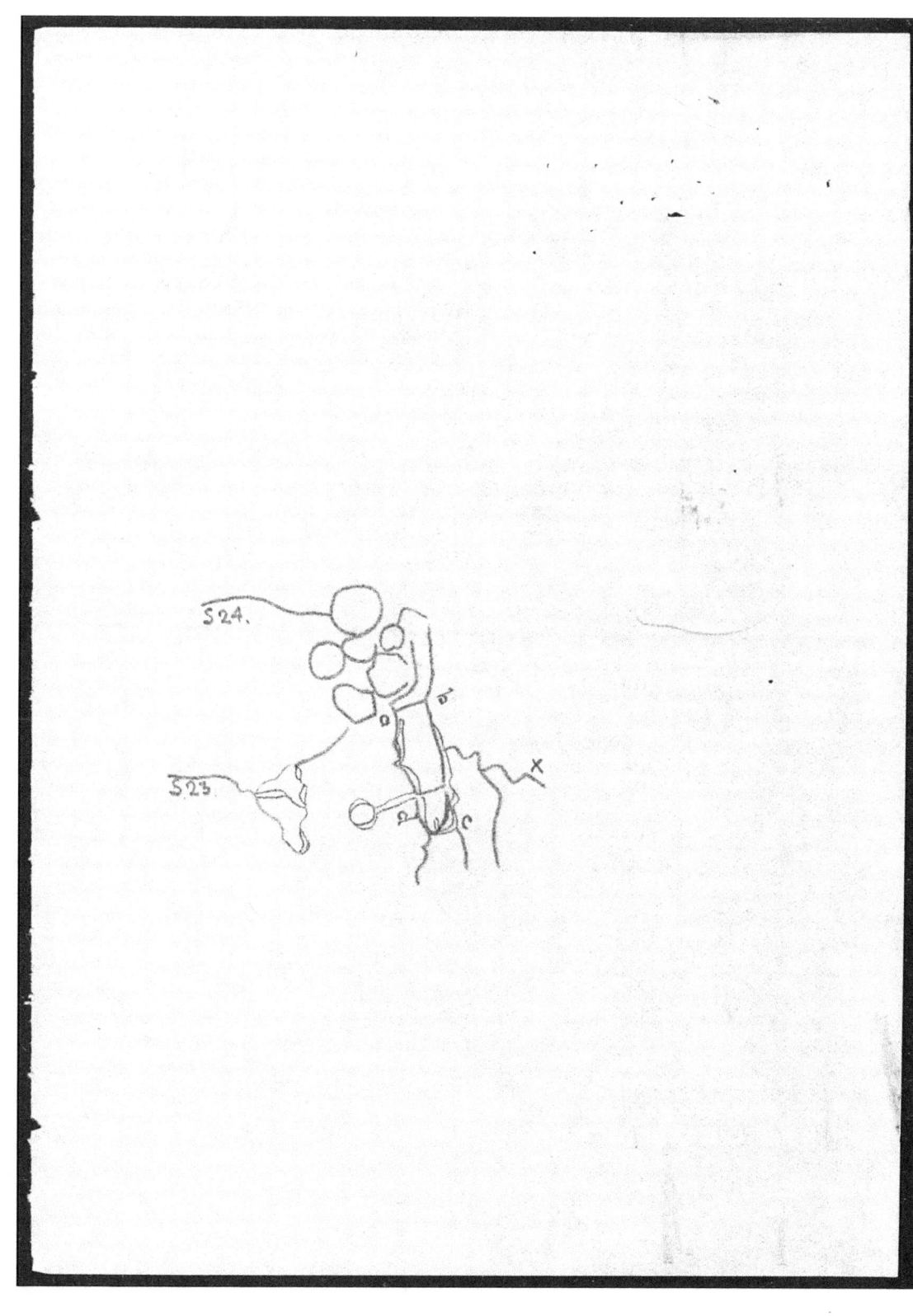

SECRET.

Headquarters,
    60th (London) Divn. "G".

The following is the Report by the O.C. 2/21 London Regt. of the Special Operations carried out by the 2/21 L.R. last night:-

> "Preliminary reconnaissance at 8 p.m. under Sec.Lieuts. SOUTHIN and TOWNEND showed that only one gap was passable in the enemy's wire and tracing tapes were laid from near that point to Sap 23.
> Wire cutting party went out under Sec.Lieut. Hamilton from Sap 23 at 10.20, followed by the two attacking parties, all parties being clear of Sap by 10.45 p.m.
> The attacking parties were ready in position to rush the gap at 11.15 p.m. awaiting ZERO time. At 11.20 p.m. the enemy evidently being prepared, a shower of bombs was thrown among our men and Sec.Lieut. SOUTHIN ordered the gap to be rushed. The enemy bombs, however, were directed on the gap which was enveloped in smoke and the party was driven back returning through covering party to Sap 23. Covering party threw all their bombs into the enemy's lines and retired.
> On the roll being called, Sec.Lieut. TOWNEND and Sergt. Line were found missing. A search party immediately went out and in about half an hour, two bodies were reported on the enemy side of their wire.
> Wire cutters were used and Sec.Lieut. TOWNEND, who was alive, was carried to a shell hole some 20 yards back, where he was taken over by a stretcher bearer party who brought him in.
> Three attempts were then made to recover the body of Sergt. Line lying in a small shell hole, which the enemy continued to bomb. Sec.Lieut. TIDDY was wounded and the parties were forced to give up further attempts.
> During these three attempts, Sergt. HESSEY undoubtedly saved further casualties by picking up an enemy bomb which fell among the party and throwing it into the next shell hole where it exploded.
>
>   (signed) B. FLETCHER.
>   Lieut.Col.
> 24.9.16.   Cmdng. 2/21 London Regt."

I consider that the operation failed chiefly owing to the want of dash and resolution amongst the men of the raiding party, though I do not think they were conscious of having left a wounded officer and N.C.O. behind them, owing to the pitch black darkness of the night. The officers and some of the N.C.O's behaved with courage, as did also the covering party.

The latter, although they retired a few yards after their bombs were expended, still maintained a position just out of

contd.

reach of enemy bombs, and the officer in command assisted the search parties.

The search parties did their duty well, although they were unable to ~~murex~~ remove the body of the dead Sergeant owing to its position in the hostile wire.

I have informed the O.C. Battalion of my opinion, and instructed him to inform the raiding party of it, in very definite terms.

[signature]
Brig-General
Cmdg. 181st Infantry Brigade

24-9-16

HQ 1/1 Infey Bde
Vol 5

On His Majesty's Service.

Confidential

D.A.G.
2nd Echelon
Base

SECRET.

181st INFANTRY BRIGADE.

WAR DIARY.

From 1st October, 1916.
To 31st October, 1916.

VOL. I.   No. 5.

------------oOo------------

Army Form C. 2118.

WAR DIARY
or
INTELLIGENCE SUMMARY.
of 181st INFANTRY BRIGADE.

(Erase heading not required.)

Hour, Date, Place	Summary of Events and Information	Remarks and references to Appendices
ETRUN 1-10-16	A nice day. Bright morning, very little wind. E.S.E. Time was altered to winter time at 11 a.m. the clock being put back to 12.1 a.m. At 12.30am old time the 2/23 Lond R. carried out a Seuve. shaft with 2" and S Stokes TMs on the GERMAN Support and front lines opposite their right front. No less than 715 Stokes Shells were fired in two bursts of 3 minutes each and considerable damage was done to the hostile trenches. Throughout the day our TMs and artillery shewed intermittent activity. Our M. G's fired during the afternoon at a suspected O.P. in a haystack near THELUS. The enemy shewed slightly more activity with his TMs during the day but did no damage. He not patrols out, nothing special to report. The enemy about sunset fired a series of different coloured rockets from THELUS Southwards towards ARRAS. Aircraft active, our planes were heavily shelled about 6 a.m. Several hostile working parties dispersed by LEWIS gun fire during the night. 1 officer 4 OR 1/6¹ LR to FREVIN CAPELLE for M.G gas Course. 3 OR 2/21 LR to PCQ for Sniping Course. 2 OR from each battalion to 3rd ARMY SCHOOL of TRENCH MORTARS. LIGNY ST FLOCHEL.	[signature]
ETRUN 2-10-16.	A damp morning, very wet afternoon & evening. Wind mild South. A demonstration was given in the method of firing Smoke bombs from TMs in a field W of MAROEUIL it was attended by representatives from all Bns in the DIVISION. A quiet day on the whole front. Intermittent artillery and TM activity on our part. our TMs did considerable damage. The enemy were again extraordinarily quiet. Patrols out had considerable difficulty owing to the sodden state of the ground. Patrols working hard at the BENTAL. 20 Hrs 8 men 2/21 LR to AGNIERES for Crater consolidation.	[signature]

Forms/C. 2118/10

WAR DIARY or INTELLIGENCE SUMMARY

Army Form C. 2118.

of 181st INFANTRY BRIGADE.

Hour, Date, Place	Summary of Events and Information	Remarks and references to Appendices
ETRUN 3-10-16	A fairly fine day, practically no wind, wind there was S.W. by W. Our artillery were considerably more active during the day. Heavy gun shelling vicinity of NINE ELMS. Our TM's were active during the day. One 4.5 hows registered during the afternoon on several different targets. From 3-5 pm our Medium TM's attempted to cut the wire opposite the left of our subsector so as to enable a raid organized in 6 pm by 1/24 LR to take place. They made such amazingly bad shooting that the raid had to be postponed. The enemy put over several hundreds of Stokes during the afternoon & was very uneasy throughout the night. Q. Lott M.G. made accurate shooting during the evening at the MILLE Road DUMP. A most unfortunate incident occurred during the early hours of the morning. Lt McBIRNEY & LT McBIRNEY out on patrol with 2/LT HUNT 1/23 L.R. and 4 men were shot at by sentry of 18th H.L.I. belonging to 106th Bde on our right. Lt McBIRNEY was dangerously wounded in the stomach. Work still progressing.	[initial]
ETRUN 4-10-16	A very wet morning with heavy showers in the afternoon. Fairly strong S.W. wind. The 1/4th B⁴ relief was duly carried out during the day without incident. The day was fairly quiet owing to the Relief. The enemy were also fairly quiet until between 8 p.m. 10.30 p.m. when the enemy's heavy TM's bombarded our front line causing 6 casualties. This is an unwelcome relief of two weapons which she had not fired on our front for over a fortnight. A hostile MG again fires with great accuracy on the MILLE road DUMP. All available men working on the firing line.	APPENDIX I [initial]

WAR DIARY
or INTELLIGENCE SUMMARY.

of 181st Infantry Brigade

Army Form C. 2118.

(Erase heading not required.)

Instructions regarding War Diaries and Intelligence Summaries are contained in F.S. Regs, Part II. and the Staff Manual respectively. Title pages will be prepared in manuscript.

Hour, Date, Place	Summary of Events and Information	Remarks and references to Appendices
ETRUN 5-10-16	A wet morning, clearing up about 11.30 a.m., fine afternoon. Fresh WEST wind. 50 men commenced work on the light railway to be laid up the CHEMIN CREUX. 14 men from each of the three Battalions in the line commenced on the cleaning of the BOYAU. Our artillery was quieter than usual. One T.M. fired intermittently during the day. In retaliation to the hostile MG which has been firing on the LILLE road, 8 of our Vickers concentrated on the enemy's dump on the LILLE road with apparent effect. Enemy quieter. Enemy fired a few heavy minenwerfer during the evening. A nil casualty went returned.	[signature]
ETRUN 6-10-16	A quiet day, wind appeared to hold off the rain. Bursts of heavy firing again from the SOMME. Wind Strong S.W. Our T.M's fired on the enemy front line and area throughout the day. Our medium gunning on O.P. to collapse, a quantity of stakes etc to be thrown up. The enemy was very quiet again, firing a few Canal Infram rifle grenades & whizz bangs. A great deal of work was carried at during the day on the BOYAUS & communication trenches. Progressing on dugouts. The fortification of the discharge of the GAS installed in the 186 BRIGADE sector on our right was sent twice during the last moment. NCO's once for 1.0 a.m. On each occasion Troops arrived at the last moment. NCO's H. 3 Bay R to CAMIERS for a musketry course. Lt/cn & NCO's of 2/24 LOND R & MONTENEES for Cradle Consolidation.	[signature]

Army Form C. 2118.

WAR DIARY
— OR —
INTELLIGENCE SUMMARY.
of 1st INFANTRY BRIGADE

(Erase heading not required.)

Instructions regarding War Diaries and Intelligence Summaries are contained in F.S. Regs., Part II. and the Staff Manual respectively. Title pages will be prepared in manuscript.

Hour, Date, Place	Summary of Events and Information	Remarks and references to Appendices
ETRUN 7-10-16.	A nice morning. Heavy shower about 5 pm. Wind strong SW. The GAS discharge was again timed for 6.30pm & again cancelled. 2" Mortars fired with great effect on hostile wire opposite 500 Crater cutting wire in 3 places. Enemy T.Ms in afternoon considerably damaged the enemy support trench. Enemy guns quiet on the gate in the wire during the night. The enemy was slightly more active though only in retaliation. Our GS active during the night. Patrols out but the enemy was very nervous & not much could be done. Bde Major & OC 2/3 F.C., R.E. inspected the Berrah with a view to its drainage. Work progressing on Berrah communication trench; light railway up CHEMIN CREUX dugouts & B.1 & T.H. emplacement.	fntz
ETRUN 8-10-16.	A damp muggy day with a certain amount of rain. Wind fresh SW. Enemy trenches bombarded throughout the day by T.M's & rifle grenades with considerable effect. A most successful raid was carried out near 500 Crater at 6 pm by 1/21st Lond R. 4 prisoners being secured. See APP. At 6.45 pm the 106? Infy Bde discharged GAS accompanying it with a fairly heavy bombardment: retaliation came onto our line, in the centre of Right 2 Subsector which had already suffered from the effects of the raid. Ab 10.45 pm a second bombardment in connection with the GAS was started & again our trenches suffered. A German wire toggle by one of our snipers. Losses for 7th: One officer 4.6.R 2/24 L.R. to TREVIN CHAPELLE for mild Gas Cause. 1 OR. 5 men 1/23 & 6 men 1/21 L.R. to LE TOUQUET for heavy gun comm.	APPENDIX II fntz

Army Form C. 2118.

WAR DIARY
of 181st INFANTRY BRIGADE
INTELLIGENCE SUMMARY.

(Erase heading not required.)

Instructions regarding War Diaries and Intelligence Summaries are contained in F. S. Regs., Part II. and the Staff Manual respectively. Title pages will be prepared in manuscript.

Hour, Date, Place	Summary of Events and Information	Remarks and references to Appendices
ETRUN 9-10-16	A much nicer day. wind fresh SW. Infantry the tactical side of the war DIARY who operate with attacks. Daily Intelligence Summary. 2 Offrs 6 OR 2/24 Lord R to AGNIERES Crater Consolidation Course.	APP II.
ETRUN 10-10-16	A beautiful day. wind strong SW. Relief carried out between Battalions without incident. 3 OR 1/4th R to M.G.Q. Sniping Course.	APP I.
ETRUN 11-10-16	A damp cold day. rain in morning. wind strong SW. 1 Officer 2 OR 2/21 } LR to LIGNY ST FLOCHEL for TM course " " 2/22 " 2 " 2/24	
ETRUN 12-10-16	A cold rough day very strong SW wind. The DIV'NL General inspected a portion of the right subsector	
ETRUN 13-10-16	Autumn windy day. Strong SSW wind. 2 Officers 20 R to AGNIERES Crater Consolidation. 3 OR 2/20 LR to ACQ Sniping course. By D.LTCOL E.C. DA COSTA EAST LANCASHIRE REGT. cdg 9th LANCASHIRE FUSILIERS arrived to take over command of the BRIGADE vice BRIG-GEN C.M.B.M PARSONS. C.B.	

Army Form C. 2118.

WAR DIARY
or
INTELLIGENCE SUMMARY.
(Erase heading not required.)

of 181 INFANTRY BRIGADE.

Instructions regarding War Diaries and Intelligence Summaries are contained in F.S. Regs., Part II. and the Staff Manual respectively. Title pages will be prepared in manuscript.

Hour, Date, Place	Summary of Events and Information	Remarks and references to Appendices
ETRUN 14-10-16	A cold dull day. Very strong SSW wind	JMB
ETRUN 15-10-16	A cold day. Some rain in the morning & again in the afternoon. Strong NSW wind. At midnight 14/15 BRIG GEN EC DA COSTA took over command of the BRIGADE. BRIG GEN GMcN PARSONS CB left for ENGLAND at 8.30 a.m. For details as to raid carried out by 2/23rd LONDR See App IV	APPENDIX IV JMB
ETRUN 16-10-16	A very cold bright day fresh NNW wind. Stavinges arrived by DIV Artillery. BIG & MEDIUM TMS bombarded the enemy's TM emplacements apparently with some success. The BIG TM fired for the first time. The relief of BDE was postponed owing to the bombardment & did not take place until 4.30 p.m. Information the 2/21 LR relieving ETRUN at 4.30 p.m. Orders at 12.30 p.m. Information received that the DIVISION to be shortly relieved by the 3rd CANADIAN DIVISION	APPENDIX I JMB
ETRUN 17-10-16	A nasty day cold & overcast. Showers in daytime & heavy rain at night. Wind W. 2 Officers & 8 men to PONNIERES for Crater Consolidation 2/23 LR	JMB

Army Form C. 2118.

WAR DIARY
of 8th 181st INFANTRY BRIGADE
INTELLIGENCE SUMMARY.
(Erase heading not required.)

Instructions regarding War Diaries and Intelligence Summaries are contained in F. S. Regs., Part II. and the Staff Manual respectively. Title pages will be prepared in manuscript.

Hour, Date, Place	Summary of Events and Information	Remarks and references to Appendices
ETRUN 18-10-16	A cold damp day. Several showers of rain. Wind N.W. 30 R=/R3 L.R. WACQ to SNIPING COURSE. GEN RUDKIN visited BDE HQ during the morning.	
ETRUN 19-10-16	A sunnier day. heavy rain fell nearly all day. very cold wind N.W. light. Orders from DIV received re relief of DIVISION by 3rd CANADIAN DIVISION.	See APP V
ETRUN 20-10-16	A Beautiful Sunny day. very cold. fresh N.E. wind. MAJOR MORRISSEY DSO Bde Major 8th CANADIAN INF BDE visited the Trenches prior to taking over. Arrangements made in connection with same.	
ETRUN 21-10-16	A Beautiful Sunny day. very cold very sharp frost on night 20/21. Wind light N.E. Staff Captain goes to NEW AREA to arrange for billets. Orders issued re relief.	
ETRUY 22-10-16	A Beautiful day. cold. wind N.E. Tremendous gunfire heard from the SOMME. Representative of CANADIAN BN visit their opposite numbers in the line. STAFF CAPT. 8 CDN INF BDE visits BDE HQ. MAJ GEN LIPSETT CB a CANADIAN DIV went round BOMMY Trench. Orders issued r.e. move to back area. 4th PPCMR arrives MAROEUIL	

Forms/C. 2118/10

Army Form C. 2118.

WAR DIARY or INTELLIGENCE SUMMARY.

of 181st INFANTRY BRIGADE

(Erase heading not required.)

Instructions regarding War Diaries and Intelligence Summaries are contained in F.S. Regs., Part II. and the Staff Manual respectively. Title pages will be prepared in manuscript.

Hour, Date, Place	Summary of Events and Information	Remarks and references to Appendices
ETRUN 23-10-16	A misty dull day much warmer, wind very slight SW. Staff Capt 8th Can Inf Bde visits trenches re Company with 51st Capt 181st Bn Repts of 1st CMR to Right I. 1st Bn CMR arrives ETRUN. 4/23rd Lond R marches from ETRUN to 12E7.LE7.HHHEAO. Bde Area. Allied fresh instructions issued.	
ETRUN 24-10-16	A wet day clearing up a bit in the afternoon. Wind very slight SW. 4th CMR Commence relieving 4/24 Lond R in Bde Reserve at 7.30 am. relief complete by 10.30 am. 2/24 Lond R have hot meal at AMBROEUIL and march at 2.30 pm to 12E1.LE2.HHH617. 1st CMR Commence relieving 2/22 L R at 9.30 am. relief complete by 12.30 pm. 2/22 Lond R return to ETRUN in afternoon. 181st TM Batty relieved by 6.10 pm. 181 MG Coy by 8.45 pm both return to ETRUN. 2/2nd Can MR arrive AMBROEUIL. 2/23 Lond R to IVERGNY. 2/6 F Amb to Sus-ST-LEGER. 520th Coy DSC. HQN FARM to LA FONTAINE. 2/2 FE Coy RE on relief to FERME DOFFINE. Orders received re move on 25th Oct and acknowledged.	APPENDIX I
ETRUN & IVERGNY 25-10-16	A wet day fine evening. Wind S. 2nd CMR relieve 2/21 Lond R in Right I. relief complete by 1 pm. 2/21 to MAROEUIL. 2/22 4 Lond R 181 MG Coy, 181 TM Batty march from ETRUN to 12E1 LE2 HHH617 for all other move see APPENDIX I. 3rd CMR move into Div Reserve at ETRUN GOC 181 INF BDE hands over Command of RIGHT SECTOR to OC 8th CAN INF BDs at 2 pm. Repot Centre opens at IVERGNY 2 pm. 2/23 L.R route march & clean up afternoon.	

Army Form C. 2118.

WAR DIARY
of 181 INF BDE
INTELLIGENCE SUMMARY.
(Erase heading not required.)

Instructions regarding War Diaries and Intelligence Summaries are contained in F. S. Regs., Part II. and the Staff Manual respectively. Title pages will be prepared in manuscript.

Hour, Date, Place		Summary of Events and Information	Remarks and references to Appendices
IVERGNY.	26-10-16	A windy day. South wind, fine night. See Appendix V for all moves. Brigade H.Qrs. established. 2/23. 2/24 LOND R start training in new Billets. Orders issued for march on 28th and Billeting arrangements for night 28/29. COLONEL F.D WATNEY 2/4 WEST SURREY REGT reports to take over command of 2/21 LOND R. vice LT COL B FLETCHER. DIV GEN visits Bde HQ. Route Marches on 28th inst recommended by BRIGADE MAJOR	App V.
IVERGNY	27-10-16	Brigging in morning & blowing a Southerly gale. 2/21 L R moved up to ETREE WAMIN on arrival of the 13th Div. COL WATNEY took over the command. Other units marching & training. BRIGADIER & RDE MAJOR attended Conference at DIV HQ at 3.30 p.m. re BATTLE STANDING ORDERS. GEN HORN Comg 1ST ARMY sends DIV HQ at 4 pm & seen Brigadier	App V.
IVERGNY OCCOCHES	28-10-16	A fine morning, dark very still, strong S wind. Brigade marches to new area. see Appendix V. Div orders for move & billets for 29th not received 2.30 pm. Billets finally settled 7.30 pm. Orders issued to units 8.30 pm. All units marched well & very few men fell out.	APPENDIX V App V.

WAR DIARY
INTELLIGENCE SUMMARY.

(Erase heading not required.)

of 181st INFANTRY BRIGADE

Army Form C. 2118.

Instructions regarding War Diaries and Intelligence Summaries are contained in F. S. Regs., Part II. and the Staff Manual respectively. Title pages will be prepared in manuscript.

Hour, Date, Place		Summary of Events and Information	Remarks and references to Appendices
OEUF-ETS FIENVILLERS	29-10-16	A really horrible day, clearing towards evening. Strong S. wind. Rain fell during the whole of the march of the Brigade South to the new Area in spite of the Northern mackerel sky. Great trouble was experienced with the Transport in the hill between BOISBERGUES and AUTHEUX. Many of the mules fitting badly. For all details of move see APPENDIX V. At 8 a.m. information was received that the 3/3 2d Coy RE were to march East to join VIIIth CORPS. The Coy was clear of OEUF-ETS at 9.45 a.m.	APPENDIX V.
FIENVILLERS	30-10-16	A terrible day, heavy rain, very strong S. wind. The 2/23 LR marched into billets in CANDAS from OUTREBOIS arriving about noon. Conference of CO's at Bde HQ. Bombs Lewis Gns & various points & methods of training. Div: Battle Stadium B'res' & various points as to the method of carrying Captain items of equipment. June 3 p.m.	
FIENVILLERS	31-10-16	Heavy storms of rain in morning, beautiful afternoon. West wind. All units engaged in training. Brigadier watched the training of the 2/22 & 2/23 LR. Staff Captain visits Division during afternoon. Information received that the 3/3 2d Coy RE are to return to the Bde Area.	

Mitchell Capt.
for Brigade Major

BRIG - GENL
Comdg 181st INFANTRY BRIGADE

SECRET.   APPENDIX I.

181st INFANTRY BRIGADE.

W A R   D I A R Y.

1st - 31st October, 1916.

I N T E R - B A T T A L I O N   R E L I E F S.

VOL. I.   No. 5.

----------------oOo--------------

SECRET. Copy No. 13

181st INFANTRY BRIGADE ORDER No. 22.

Reference – Maps 51 B & C. Monday,
Trench Map. 2nd October, 1916.

1. Battalions in the front line will be relieved by Bns in reserve on the afternoon of the 4th inst. according to Table below, under arrangements to be made by Os.C. concerned. The leading platoon of 2/21 L.R. to reach ANZIN Communication Trench by 1 p.m.

2. The 2/24 L.R. will take over Control Posts by 12 noon on 4th inst from the 2/21 L.R.

3. The O.C. 2/23 L.R. will take over command of the ECURIE Defences from the O.C. 2/22 L.R.

4. Completion of relief will be reported to Brigade H.Q. as per attached Code.

5. Acknowledge.

UNIT.	FROM.	TO.	IN RELIEF OF
2/21 Lond.R.	Divnl. Reserve.	R I.	2/23 Lond.R.
2/22 " "	Brigade Reserve.	R II.	2/24 " "
2/23 " "	R I.	Brigade Reserve.	2/22 " "
2/24 " "	R II.	Divnl. Reserve.	2/21 " "

The 2/21 L.R. will move up from ETRUN to ANZIN by platoons at 5 minute intervals.

Captain.
Brigade Major.
181st Infantry Brigade.

Issued at 7.30 p.m.

Copy No. 1. 2/21. 8. 179th Inf.Bde.
2. 2/22. 9. O.C.Art.Group.
3. 2/23. 10. 181 T.M.Battery.
4. 2/24. 11. Pioneer Coy. ECURIE.
5. 181 M.G.Coy. 12. File.
6. 3/3rd Fld.Coy.R.E. 13. War Diary.
7. 106th Inf.Bde.

SECRET.   Copy No. 13.

181st INFANTRY BRIGADE No. 23.

Reference – Maps 51 B & C   Sunday,
            Trench Map.   8th October, 1916.

1. Battalions in the front line will be relieved by Bns. in reserve on the afternoon of the 10th inst. according to Table below, under arrangements to be made by Os.C. concerned. The leading platoon 2/24 L.R. to reach ANZIN Communication trench by 3 p.m.

2. The 2/22 L.R. will take over Control Posts by 12 noon on 10th inst. from the 2/24 L.R.

3. The O.C. 2/21 L.R. will take over command of the ECURIE Defences from the O.C. 2/23 L.R.

4. Os.C. 2/21 and 2/23 L.R. will arrange their relief so that it is completed by 3.45 p.m.

5. Completion of the relief will be reported to Brigade H.Q. as per attached Code.

6. Acknowledge.

UNIT.	FROM.	TO.	IN RELIEF OF.
2/21 Lond.R.	R I.	Brigade Reserve.	2/23 Lond.R.
2/22 " "	R II.	Divnl. Reserve.	2/24 " "
2/23 " "	Brigade Reserve.	R I.	2/21 " "
2/24 " "	Divnl. Reserve.	R II.	2/22 " "

The 2/24 L.R. will move up from ETRUN to ANZIN by platoons at 5 minute intervals.

                                              K. Antill.
                                              Captain.
                                              Brigade Major.
                                              181st Infantry Brigade.

Issued at 7.30 p.m.

Copy No. 1. 2/21.   8. 179th Inf.Bde.
         2. 2/22.   9. O.C.Art.Group.
         3. 2/23.   10. 181 T.M.Battery.
         4. 2/24.   11. Pioneer Coy. ECURIE.
         5. 181 M.G.Coy.   12. File.
         6. 3/3rd Field Coy. 13. War Diary.
         7. 106th Inf.Bde.

SECRET.   Copy No. 13.

181st INFANTRY BRIGADE ORDER No. 24.

Reference – Maps 51 B & C.   Saturday,
            Trench Map.   14th October, 1916.

---

1. Battalions in the front line will be relieved by Bns. in reserve on the afternoon of the 16th inst. according to Table below, under arrangements to be made by Os.C.concerned. The leading platoon 2/22 L.R. to reach ANZIN Communication Trench by 1 p.m.

2. The 2/23 L.R. will take over Control Posts by 12 noon on 16th inst. from the 2/22 L.R.

3. The O.C. 2/24 L.R. will take over command of the ECURIE Defences from the O.C. 2/21 L.R.

4. Completion of the relief will be reported to Brigade H.Q. as per attached Code.

5. Acknowledge.

UNIT.	FROM.	TO.	IN RELIEF OF.
2/21 Lond.R.	Brigade Reserve.	R I.	2/23 Lond.R.
2/22 " "	Divnl. Reserve.	R II.	2/24 " "
2/23 " "	R I.	Divnl. Reserve.	2/22 " "
2/24 " "	R II.	Bde. Reserve.	2/21 " "

The 2/22 Lond.R. will move up from ETRUN to ANZIN by platoons at 5 minute intervals.

                                    (signed)   J.N.HORLICK.
                                                    Captain.
                                               Brigade Major.
                                          181st Infantry Brigade.

Issued at 7.30 p.m.

Copy No. 1. 2/21 L.R.   8. 179th Inf.Bde.
         2. 2/22 L.R.   9. O.C.Art.Group.
         3. 2/23 L.R.   10. 181 T.M.Battery.
         4. 2/24 L.R.   11. Pioneer Coy.ECURIE.
         5. 181 M.G.Coy.   12. File.
         6. 3/3rd Field Coy.R.E.   13. War Diary.
         7. 106th Inf.Bde.

SECRET.   APPENDIX II.

181st INFANTRY BRIGADE.

W A R   D I A R Y.

1st - 31st October, 1916.

RAID BY 2/22 LONDON REGT.

VOL. I.   No. 5.

------------- --------oOo---------------------

2/22 London Regiment.

OPERATION ORDER
No. 1.
---

1. INFORMATION. The Battalion will raid the hostile front line between A & B including the Sap leading therefrom.

2. OBJECTS.
   (i) To obtain a living prisoner.
   (ii) To establish identification.
   (iii) To do the greatest damage possible.

3. ZERO. Time and date to be notified later.

4. HOSTILE WIRE. Hostile wire on raid sector and on A.22.b.05.70 (approximate) is being dealt with by T.Ms. see Appendix B.

5. OUR OWN WIRE. The necessary gaps in our own wire are in preparation. Lieut. HUNTINGTON is responsible for this.

6. COMMAND. Capt. COLMER will be in command and will establish himself at the eastern end of tunnel at - 1 hr.

7. STRENGTH. Raiding party composed as under:-
   Left party Sec.Lieut. BRASSEY, 1 N.C.O. & 6 men.
   Centre   " Lieut. HAYFORD, 1 N.C.O. & 8 men.
   Right   " Sec.Lieut. WESTON, 1 N.C.O. & 6 men.
   Blanket & Ladder Party 1 N.C.O. & 6 men) Under
   Left Bombing Block 1 N.C.O. & 6 men   ) Sec.Lt.
   Right Bombing Block, 1 N.C.O. & 6 men.   ) CRONHELM.
   Rear Party, 2 N.C.Os. & 6 men.
   Total strength - 4 Officers, 8 N.C.Os. & 44 men.

8. ASSEMBLY POINT. Mine Shaft near Left Company's advanced Headquarters, Five Hundred Avenue.
   Parties will proceed to French Trench via the tunnel at - 1 hr. in the following order:-

   Right Party.
   Centre Party.
   Left Party.
   Right Bombing Block.
   Blanket & Ladder Men.
   Left Bombing Block.
   Rear Party.

9. ADVANCE & ASSAULT. At Zero, the entire raiding party, less Rear Party, will advance. The Blanket Party covered by Right and Left Block parties must reach the enemy wire slightly in advance of remainder. The Blanket men will bridge any part of enemy's wire still remaining uncut and remainder of raiding party will go through them. No local hostile bombing is to be allowed to interfere with the advance through the wire. The Blanket men and Bombing Blocks will be under the immediate command of Sec.Lieut. CRONHELM who will subsequently establish a report centre at junction of Trench D and German front line. He will be responsible for the passing back to the rear, of any prisoners or our own wounded and will also see that passages through the wire are marked and improved prior to the Recall Signal. To assist him, he will have 2 men as runners in addition to the Blanket men. The Right Blocking Party will move straight to junction of Trench E and Enemy front line. They will establish Bombing Posts at ee. The Left Blocking Party will move straight to junction of Trench C

/ and

and Enemy front line. They will establish similar Bombing posts at cc. Right and Left Raiding parties search and clean up front line from junction of Trench D to ee and cc respectively. Centre party will work up Trench D, clean out dugouts found, killing or capturing occupants. O.C. this party will use his discretion in selecting a place for a Bombing Block to cover his operations.

10. RECALL. At plus 20 minutes, Officers and N.C.Os. in charge of parties will withdraw their parties, reporting to Sec.Lt. CRONHEIM at Report Centre en route. They will then make their way to the Point of Assembly by the shortest possible routes, using their own discretion as to the safety of their men. Should there be a heavy barrage at BONNAL Trench, temporary shelter may be taken in the French Trench. On arrival at Assembly position a roll will be called and any description of booty will be handed over to Lieut. HUNTINGTON.

11. COMMUNICATION. A telephone will be installed in the old French Trench and will be in communication with Battalion and Company Headquarters. Additional communication by runners throughout.

12. DRESS. Skeleton equipment and pouches; rifles charged, 9 rounds in magazine, 20 in pouches, one bomb in each pocket. 2 men in each bombing group will carry canvas buckets full of bombs. These men will carry a life preserver instead of a rifle. Shorts are not to be worn. For the purpose of recognition all ranks will wear a piece of white tape round the left shoulder strap. No regimental badges or buttons to be worn, and no papers carried which could possibly lead to identification by the enemy. Identity discs will not be worn. Companies will be responsible that the men's pay books are collected before going to the Point of Assembly.

13. ADVANCED DRESSING STATION. An advanced Dressing Station will be established by Capt. ASTBURY who will be responsible for all arrangements of evacuating casualties from that station.

14. DISCIPLINE. All ranks to be thoroughly warned that indiscriminate and undirected bombing will hinder and not assist the advance. Also that casualties cannot be attended to during the advance, but every will be made to collect and bring in casualties after the Recall. All ranks are further warned that our own barrage fire may appear very close but there will be no danger from it. In the event of their being taken prisoner, no information beyond their rank and name need be given.

15. FEINT ATTACK. A feint attack will take place on the Right Company's front at approximately A.22.b.05.75, see Appendices C & D.
Capt. A.McCOMAS will be in general command of these operations.

16. SIGNAL OF RECALL. At plus 20, Machine Guns will fire their usual rat-a-tat and "Very" lights will be sent up from the SAUSAGE REDOUBT at ECURIE.

17. ACKNOWLEDGE.

Note.- All N.C.Os. in charge of parties will be supplied with luminous watches, and will be synchronised at the Assembly Position.

Copies to all concerned.   (signed) A.D.BORTON. Major.
7.10.16.   Cmdng. 2/22 London Regt.

SECRET.
PRELIMINARY REPORT of the 2/22 Lond.R. Raid on 8th Oct/16.

Punctually at 6.3 p.m. the feint bombardment started the basis of which was Smoke Bombs, immediately whistles and horns were distinctly heard in the German lines. This excitement was probably caused by the smoke bombs being mistaken for gas.

At 6.5 p.m. the Artillery Barrage opened and the raiding party left the OLD FRENCH Trench, all were clear by 6.8 p.m.

They moved across right up to and in fact almost in the barrage, picking up two prisoners in a saphead en route.

The wire was found to be beautifully cut and there was no necessity to use the blankets. A gap of about 20 yards having been made with only one or two gooseberries and bits of loose wire remaining.

Sec.Lieut.CRONHELM and 6 men moved straight along the sap and entered the German trench at junction of sap and front line where he established his report centre. He then waited for the right and left bombing blocks who came up immediately.

RIGHT PARTY.

The right bombing block turned right handed down the German front line followed immediately by Sec.Lieut. WESTON's party. They reached their objectives without any difficulties, about 7 or 8 dugouts were bombed. A German was shot and another unwounded German captured. On the recall signal the whole party withdrew. Sec.Lieut.WESTON was apparently hit whilst in the trench, an artery near the groin being severed. On withdrawing the whole party reported to Sec.Lieut.CRONHELM.

LEFT PARTY.

The left blocking party was sent along the trench left handed by Sec.Lieut. CRONHELM but got into the open as the trench was so flattened as to be unrecognisable. Here they were joined by Sec.Lieut. BRASSEY's party who had also crossed the Trench. Both parties went on till some fairly thick wire was encountered and from there bombed the support German trench. On returning, a wounded German was picked up in the front trench. The party then, having bombed 2 or 3 dugouts in front line trench, returned on recall signal to the OLD FRENCH Trench.

CENTRE PARTY.

The Centre party under Lieut. HAYFORD moved straight up past their objective to the support line which they found to be a deep, well-duck-boarded trench. They did not go down it but retired about 10 yards and made a block. Here the Germans made a bombing attack on them, wounding Lieut. HAYFORD slightly in the head and 2 other men. On the recall they retired. Whilst moving up they had bombed a dugout, presumably occupied, as a bomb was thrown out. Lieut. HAYFORD, knowing prisoners had been taken, contented himself with bombing it and did not allow his party to go in, much as they wanted to.

At 6.25 p.m. (recall) Sec.Lieut. CRONHELM, having had Lieut. HAYFORD's and WESTON's parties report to him on their way back, went in search of Lieut. BRASSEY's party and to see if there were any others left behind. Finding no one and seeing no activity except German bombs being thrown, he retired to the OLD FRENCH Trench with his runners, who were, with the greatest difficulty, persuaded to leave the German trenches.

Contd.

Captain COLMER who was established in the OLD FRENCH Trench with an advanced telephone station, was wounded and two men killed, in fact the majority of the casualties appear to have occurred in or near this trench on the return of the party.

ACTION BY THE ENEMY.

Extremely slight opposition to the raiding party in the German trenches.

S.O.S. fired at 6.23, no action until 6.35 p.m. when a 77 mm. barrage was placed on 500 Crater all along the BONNAL, 500 AVENUE and COLLECTEUR, Aerial torpedoes on SUTHERLAND AVENUE. "Oilcans" on CENTRE 1 front, Rifle grenades on OLD FRENCH trench. Barrage ceased at 7.10 p.m. when the only M.G. heard on raid sector opened apparently from Crater XXXlll.

GERMAN TRENCHES.

Front line trench extraordinarily knocked about, not duckboarded, but dry.

Communication trench not duckboarded, very wide, from 6-8 ft. deep, dry.

SUPPORT TRENCH.

From what could be seen duckboarded, deep and in good condition.

CASUALTIES.

Officers: Capt COLMER wounded in thigh by rifle grenade.
Lieut. HAYFORD wounded slightly by bomb splinter in the head.
Sec.Lieut. WESTON badly wounded in thigh.

Other Ranks: 2 men killed by shell fire, 5 men wounded, 10 men slightly wounded, 1 man missing (apparently this man, who had been previously wounded in the German communication trench, had to be left by the man who was helping him out, who, whilst doing so, was himself badly wounded.
This information was not obtained for some considerable time afterwards.

GENERAL.

The whole operation went through without a check, all parties moving straight to their objective without any hesitation. The men behaved extremely well and in fact had to be restrained from trying to push on to the second line. The Smoke bombs from the Trench Mortars were most accurate and were invaluable in drawing the main volume of Artillery, Trench Mortar, and Machine Gun fire well away from the scene of the main operation, for certainly the first 20 minutes.

(signed) A.D.BORTON.
Major.
Cmdng. 2/22 London Regt.

SUPPLEMENTARY TO PRELIMINARY REPORT
of the 2/22 Lond.R's. raid 8.10.16.

Sergt. SNELL - RIGHT BLOCK.

When we got to our position, 8 Germans who had apparently been lying in a hole just behind the Trench, got up and tried to run back to their support line. They were bombed and at least 4 dropped. A Bosche was found with his head in a hole and was pulled out by the feet and taken back and made a prisoner. I kept my position until the order of Recall was given.

Sergt. NICHOLLS & CORPL. PULLEN - LEFT BLOCK.

On our way to the left post we came on 3 dugouts in darkness and there were cries of "Kamerade" from all 3, but we could not get them to come out. We chucked about 30 bombs down and took one prisoner who we had to knock on the head as he refused to come.

Pte. BROAD with Centre Party advanced up the Centre Trench. They took one prisoner at once, 2 dugouts were bombed as they could not get the Germans to come out; one of these dugouts was connected underground with a sniper's post from which we were fired at, so we pushed a bomb down each loophole and waited to hear it explode.

(signed) A.D.BORTON.

Major.
Cmdng. 2/22 Lond.R.

9.10.16.

SECRET.   R.D.8/5.

Headquarters,
   60th (London) Divn. "G".

1.   The raid by the 2/22 Lond.R. was very well planned
and carried out with great determination and rapidity.
Most of the casualties were occasioned during the retirement of the raiders after plus 20 minutes, the hostile
barrage before that time being put on to our front line
trench opposite the point where our feint smoke attack was
made.   Undoubtedly fewer casualties would have occurred
had not Capt. COLMER (who was mainly responsible for the
organisation of the raid) been wounded by an unlucky shot
from a rifle grenade just before the hostile barrage was
placed on at about the OLD FRENCH Trench.

2.   v Although the feint attack with Smoke Bombs drew fire
for about 20 minutes, it is a question whether such a
heavy hostile barrage would have been put up in the absence
of a Smoke Bomb demonstration.

3.   I consider it would be advisable not to utilise
Smoke Bombs in future but to request to employ heavy guns
for counter-battery work a few minutes before Zero to
neutralise any barrage. A feint could be made with the
field gun group.

4.   The time allowed for the raiders was 20 minutes,
which according to them was all too short to deal effectively with all the enemy they saw.

                                                Brig.-General.
9.10.16.   Cmdng. 181st Infantry Brigade.

2/22 London Regiment.

APPENDIX "A".

ARTILLERY.

TIME TABLE.   Zero an intense bombardment of enemy's front line A B for 25 seconds.
Plus 20 minutes - bombardment until "Cease Fire" on co-ordinates selected by O.C. Right Group.

APPENDIX "B".

2" TRENCH MORTAR.

Previous to the raid both Trench Mortar guns employed in cutting wire in front of A B.

APPENDIX "C".

3" TRENCH MORTARS.   6 Guns.

A & B Guns approx. A.22.b.05.15. — Commence firing at - 2 and will fire gunfire for 3 minutes. Target Crater XX and front line behind this crater. 120 rounds.

C Gun A.22.a.50.65. — At Zero will fire gunfire for 30 secs. on Crater XXXlll. 10 rounds. At plus 20 will fire gunfire for 3 minutes traversing on enemy's front line between A.16.c.90.15 to A.16.c.93.07. 60 rounds.

D & E Guns in BONNAL between GREEN AVENUE & ORR AVENUE. — At Zero both will fire for 3 minutes gunfire (traversing searching fire) between A.16.c.85.20 and A.16.c.93.07. 120 rounds.

F Gun in BONNAL just to left of E Gun. — From plus 3 will fire at a slow rate of fire till the Recall Signal is given. Target same as for D & E guns. 180 rounds.

APPENDIX "D".

SMOKE TRENCH MORTARS.

Same target and rate of fire as A & B 3" Mortars.

SECRET.   APPENDIX III.

181st INFANTRY BRIGADE.

WAR DIARY.
(TACTICAL).

1st - 31st October, 1916.

VOL. I.   No. 5.

----------------oOo----------------

CONFIDENTIAL. W.S.13.

WEEKLY INTELLIGENCE SUMMARY
of
181st INFANTRY BRIGADE.

From 10 a.m. 3.10.16   To 10 a.m. 10.10.16.

During the past week there has been nothing of special importance to report. On the 8th inst. the enemy front line between A.16.c.70.48 and A.16.c.76.30 was raided by the 2/22 Lond.R., four prisoners were taken and a number of dugouts bombed: in conjunction with this Raid, a feint was made with Smoke Bombs against A.22.b.20.80 which caused great excitement in the enemy lines, the smoke being apparently mistaken for gas.

Enemy works in the vicinity of Nine Elms have received considerable attention from our Artillery during the week.

T.Ms. in conjunction with field artillery daily fired on the enemy wire and front line, considerable damage being done. The gaps cut in the wire have been maintained throughout the night by Lewis Guns.

The attitude of the enemy during the past week has been quiet though slightly more activity was evinced during the last two or three days. On the night of the raid, heavy T.Ms. did considerable damage to the centre of R II Subsector, and on the early morning of the 10th Mortars considerably damaged the BONNAT in R I Subsector between L.24 and L.25. Hostile fire, however, is well in hand, and is always successfully silenced.

The general condition of the trenches has suffered severely from the adverse weather conditions, there has, however, been a marked improvement in this direction during the last few days.

H.Q. 181 Inf.Bde.,
10.10.16.

Captain.
Brigade Major.

CONFIDENTIAL.

DAILY INTELLIGENCE SUMMARY
of
181st INFANTRY BRIGADE.

From 10 a.m. 9.10.16   To 10 a.m. 10.10.16.

1. **OPERATIONS.**
   (a) Throughout the day our T.Ms. bombarded the enemy lines, paying special attention to A.22.b.35.40, A.22.b.85.27 A.23.a.35.40, considerable damage being done at each of these points.
   From 3 p.m. to 3.15 p.m. artillery carried out a bombardment of suspected Minnenwerfer positions. Howitzers also bombarded the vicinity of Nine Elms, A.17.a.55.30.
   Throughout the night, Stokes and Lewis guns kept the gaps cut in the enemy wire under fire.
   M.Gs. fired last night in accordance with prearranged scheme.
   (b) The enemy was very active with his T.Ms. yesterday, the BONNAL being rather badly damaged between L.24 and L.25, the winch chamber of the Mine Shaft was also blown in.(L.24)
   At 8.15 p.m. following a bombardment some distance to the left, the enemy fired some "Whizz-bangs" against our front line.
   A hostile M.G. fired on the LILLE Road Dump without effect.
   (c) Patrols sent out last night had nothing of importance to report.

2. **INTELLIGENCE.**
   The heavy T.Ms. were firing from the suspected T.M. emplacement at A.17.c.15.20 and A.22.b.38.95. The enemy opposite R II Subsector were extremely nervous last night, bombs being aimlessly thrown over their wire at dusk and at intervals between 1.45 a.m. and 4.15 a.m.

3. **GENERAL.**
   (a) Two Germans were seen at A.23.a.5.6, they were fired at and one was shot through the arm.
   (b) Owing to better weather, there was considerably more aerial activity yesterday. At about 11.30 p.m. last night, an aeroplane carrying a light flew over our lines.

4. **WORK DONE.**
   (a) General repairs to BONNAL where damaged by hostile bombardment. Rebuilding the traverses in left Collecteur repairing damage done to wire between M.33 and 500 AVENUE

                                            Captain.
H.Q. 181 Inf.Bde.,   Brigade Major.
   10.10.16.

1. OPERATIONS Contd.
   (b) At 3 p.m. yesterday, the enemy secured a direct hit on the M.G. emplacement at A.22.a.55.20 with a T.M. completely destroying same. There were no casualties but sundry spare parts were damaged.

CONFIDENTIAL.   I.S. 90.

DAILY INTELLIGENCE SUMMARY
of
181st INFANTRY BRIGADE.

From 10 a.m. 10.10.16   To 10 a.m. 11.10.16.

1. **OPERATIONS.**

    (a) Our artillery and T.Ms. were fairly active yesterday, shelling the enemy's front and second lines with good results, quantities of debris being thrown up in places. A number of rifle grenades were fired with good effect. Between 11 and 11.50 a.m. and again at 5.35 p.m., our heavy guns bombarded THELUS.
    Between 2 a.m. and 3 a.m. we bombarded enemy trenches in reply to enemy's heavy T.M. fire on our left.
    Lewis guns fired throughout the night on gaps cut in enemy's wire. M.Gs. carried out a prearranged indirect fire scheme.

    (b) The enemy was very active with T.Ms. throughout the morning, particularly against the centre of this Sector, doing considerable damage to the BONNAL between L.24 and L.26. With the exception of a few rifle grenades in the afternoon, the enemy was quiet.
    During the night, the enemy badly damaged our wire for about 30 to 40^x to the right of L.21. Enemy M.G. firing from about 100^x to the left of LILLE ROAD swept our DUMP between 8 and 9 p.m.

2. **INTELLIGENCE.**

    At 3 p.m. three of the enemy were seen behind the Wrecked Aeroplane (A.23.a.5.7) in a trench: they were fired on and disappeared.

3. **GENERAL.**

    (a) The inter-Battalion relief was successfully carried out yesterday afternoon.
    (b) Our aircraft were very active throughout the day: they were heavily fired on but, as far as could be seen, all returned safely.
    An enemy aeroplane was observed at 6.40 a.m. today approaching from THELUS: it circled over our lines and returned in a S.E. direction.

4. **WORK DONE.**

    (a) General repairs to trenches, paying special attention to BONNAL where damaged by rain and enemy T.M. fire.

                                                    Captain.
                                                    Brigade Major.

H.Q. 181 Inf.Bde,
11-10-16.

CONFIDENTIAL.   I.S.91.

DAILY INTELLIGENCE SUMMARY
of
181st INFANTRY BRIGADE.

From 10 a.m. 11.10.16   To 10 a.m. 12.10.16.

1. **OPERATIONS.**
   (a) There was intermittent activity on the part of our artillery against the enemy front and support lines, suspected T.M. positions were bombarded, one heavy Mortar was silenced and it is believed the emplacement was destroyed. From 11.30 p.m. to 12.30 p.m. our T.Ms. were active in reply to hostile T.Ms. which were effectively silenced. During the afternoon T.Ms. fired on the enemy wire opposite R I Subsector and later bombarded the enemy front and second lines. Gaps cut in the enemy wire were maintained during the night by Stokes and Lewis guns; this fire apparently did a considerable amount of damage to the enemy trenches opposite R II Subsector, where large quantities of debris were thrown up and big gaps made in the parapet.
   M.Gs. carried out a prearranged indirect fire scheme.
   (b) The enemy were considerably more agressive yesterday. During the morning heavy T.Ms. bombarded our front line, Sap 24 being badly damaged. Hostile artillery also fired a number of rounds which did but little damage. During the afternoon the enemy bombarded R I Subsector with A.Ts. and rifle grenades but without effect.
   (c) A number of patrols were sent out last night but these had nothing of importance to report.

2. **INTELLIGENCE.**
   There was considerable activity in the enemy trenches opposite R I Subsector yesterday, the tops of caps being several times seen for a second.
   The trench behind the Wrecked Aeroplane (A.23.a.5.7) was again occupied yesterday.

3. **GENERAL.**
   (a) The weather was very changeable yesterday and observation was much hampered thereby.
   (b) There was but little aerial activity yesterday.

4. **WORK DONE.**
   (a) Continuation of repairs to damage caused in BONNAL by hostile bombardment; repairs to wire between Saps 20 and 21; traverses revetted in COLLECTEUR and duckboarding.

                                                   Captain.
                                               Brigade Major.

H.Q. 181 Inf.Bde.,
      12.10.16.

CONFIDENTIAL.   I.S.92.

DAILY INTELLIGENCE SUMMARY
of
181st INFANTRY BRIGADE.

From 10 a.m. 12.10.16   To 10 a.m. 13.10.16.

1. **OPERATIONS.**
   (a) There was considerable artillery activity yesterday. During the morning the guns fired on haystacks in the vicinity of BOIS CARRE and on the enemy works round THELUS. At midday, the guns bombarded the enemy lines, considerable damage was done, wood and other debris being thrown up and parapets demolished at several points. T.Ms. continued wire-cutting yesterday, fire being concentrated on the enemy wire opposite Saps 21, 23 and 29 with good effect.
   Throughout the day there was intermittent activity on our part with rifle grenades.
   (b) Yesterday the enemy were very active with T.Ms. and A.Ts. especially against R I Subsector. In the afternoon they hit and damaged a Stokes gun at the L.20 emplacement. At about 6.30 a.m. the BIDOT was blown in about 70x from BONNAL.
   During the night the enemy bombarded our saps with rifle greandes.
   (c) Five patrols were sent out last night but there was nothing of special importance to report.

2. **INTELLIGENCE.**
   Two Germans, thought to be officers, were seen looking over their parapet opposite Sap 21. They wore light blue caps with shiny black peaks.
   Three of the shells fire from the heavy German T.M. yesterday were blind (only four were fired); they are in all respect identical with the blind T.M. shell reported yesterday, the fuzes being set at 15 seconds.
   A Red Cross wagon was seen proceeding in the direction of BOIS CARRE from THELUS yesterday afternoon.
   One green light was seen on our extreme right at 10.50 p.m.
   Our 2" T.M. disclosed a steel structure at A.23.c.9.9.

3. **GENERAL.**
   (a) Snipers fired on enemy loopholes where movement had been observed with K.A.P. bullets.

4. **WORK DONE.**
   (a) Revetting and sandbagging in BONNAL: Revetting in COLLECTEUR: sumping and clearing saps: duckboarding in COLLECTEUR and AVENUE RIPPERT.
   (b) Lewis guns dispersed a hostile working party to the right of Crater at A.22.b.2.5.

H.Q. 181 Inf.Bde.,   Captain.
13.10.16.   Brigade Major.

CONFIDENTIAL.   I.S.93.

DAILY INTELLIGENCE SUMMARY
of
181st INFANTRY BRIGADE.

From 10 a.m. 13.10.16   To 10 a.m. 14.10.16.

1. **OPERATIONS.**
   (a) Yesterday was quieter. At midday, 18-pdrs. fired a few rounds against the enemy lines, some of which appeared to be duds. Throughout the day, T.Ms. fired intermittently on enemy wire and front line. Numerous rifle grenades were fired at "Stand To" yesterday. Between 8 p.m. and 1.30 a.m. M.Gs. carried out a prearranged 'strafe' on the enemy's communications and trench railways; at 10 p.m. light and medium T.Ms. participated firing principally against A.16.c.90.25.
   (b) The enemy were considerably more active yesterday; a large number of rifle grenades were fired while T.Ms. did considerable damage to our wire in R I Subsector. At 12.15 p.m. an enemy howitzer blew in the entrance to Mine Shaft at L.26. About midday, two or three "Whizz-bangs" fell in the vicinity of the Left COLLECTEUR but no damage was done. At 10.10 p.m. a party of the enemy were sighted approaching our lines between the LILLE ROAD and BIDOT; they were successfully repulsed by rifle fire (vide separate report already rendered).
   Opposite R II Subsector the enemy replied to our 'strafe' with heavy T.Ms. and rifle grenades, no damage was done.
   (c) Patrols sent out last night examined the wire between Saps 23 and 26; they reported it to be badly damaged with several unexploded enemy T.M. bombs lying amongst the wire.

2. **INTELLIGENCE.**
   A T.M. emplacement has been located at A.23.a.85.45, the artillery have registered on this point. From 9.30 p.m. to 10.10 p.m. the enemy fired no Very lights opposite R I Subsector. Three rockets were fired between 10.2 p.m. and 10.10 p.m. which burst into two red lights.

3. **GENERAL.**
   (b) There was but little aerial activity yesterday, at 8 a.m. two of our 'planes flew over the enemy lines, being heavily fired on with M.Gs..

4. **WORK DONE.**
   (a) Repairs to BONNAL where damaged by hostile bombardment especially in R I Subsector: repairs to BIDOT: clearing entrance to Mine Shaft (L.26): revetting in COLLECTEUR; duckboarding and sumping in various saps.
   (b) At 11.50 a.m. and 7 a.m. parties of the enemy were seen working on the ridge at the north edge of THELUS.
   New earth has been thrown up in the vicinity of the Wrecked Aeroplane (A.23.a.5.7).

Captain,
Brigade Major.

H.Q. 181 Inf.Bde.,
14.10.16,

SECRET.   Copy No. 13

181st INFANTRY BRIGADE ORDER No. 24.

Reference - Maps 51 B & C.
Trench Map.

Saturday,
14th October, 1916.

1. Battalions in the front line will be relieved by Bns. in reserve on the afternoon of the 16th inst. according to Table below, under arrangements to be made by Os.C. concerned. The leading platoon 2/22 L.R. to reach ANZIN Communication Trench by 1 p.m.

2. The 2/23 L.R. will take over Control Posts by 12 noon on 16th inst. from the 2/22 L.R.

3. The O.C. 2/24 L.R. will take over command of the ECURIE Defences from the O.C. 2/21 L.R.

4. Completion of the relief will be reported to Brigade H.Q. as per attached Code.

5. Acknowledge.

UNIT.	FROM.	TO.	IN RELIEF OF.
2/21 Lond.R.	Brigade Reserve.	R I.	2/23 Lond.R.
2/22 " "	Divnl. Reserve.	R II.	2/24 " "
2/23 " "	R I.	Divnl. Reserve.	2/22 " "
2/24 " "	R II.	Brigade Reserve.	2/21 " "

The 2/22 Lond.R. will move up from ETRUN to ANZIN by platoons at 5 minute intervals.

Captain,
Brigade Major,
181st Infantry Brigade.

Issued at 7.30 p.m.

Copy No. 1. 2/21.
2. 2/22.
3. 2/23.
4. 2/24.
5. 181 M.G.Coy.
6. 3/2rd Field Coy.
7. 106th Inf.Bde.
8. 179th Inf.Bde.
9. O.C.Art.Group.
10. 181 T.M.Battery.
11. Pioneer Coy. ECURIE.
12. File.
13. War Diary.

CONFIDENTIAL.   I.S.94.

DAILY INTELLIGENCE SUMMARY
of
181st INFANTRY BRIGADE.

From 10 a.m. 14.10.16   To 10 a.m. 15.10.16.

1. OPERATIONS.
   (a) Throughout the day there was considerable artillery activity, the guns were apparently being directed by aircraft. During the afternoon a number of rounds were fired into the enemy second line opposite R I Subsector. There was intermittent T.M. activity, special attention being paid to the enemy's wire opposite Saps 21 and 23. T.Ms. did considerable damage to the enemy lines opposite R II Subsector, a number of sandbags being thrown up.
   At 11 p.m. light T.Ms. bombarded the enemy front line opposite Sap 21, 600 bombs being fired in a few minutes.
   At 3 a.m. the 2/23 Lond.R. raided the enemy lines "A.23. c.98.87. The enemy's front line was successfully entered. The Left Raiding party proceeded for about 80x along the trench without meeting with any opposition. The Right party met with some opposition from hostile bombers; no prisoners were taken (a separate report has been rendered regarding this).
   At 3.10 a.m. the enemy lines opposite R I Subsector were bombarded by T.Ms. and heavies.
   M.Gs. searched the enemy's second line, communication trenches and trench railways in A.17., later co-operating in the 2/23 Lond.R's. raid.
   (b) The enemy were moderately active yesterday. Shortly after 10 a.m. R I Subsector was bombarded with T.Ms., A.Ts. and rifle grenades, particularly with the latter, the BONNAL being damaged in five places. Opposite R II Sub-sector a heavy T.M. severely damaged the BONNAL between L.29 and M.30. The enemy replied to our bombardment of 11 p.m. with "oil-cans" and rifle grenades and to that of 3.10 a.m. with rifle grenades, A.Ts. and T.Ms. During the night a M.G. fired on the GRAND COLLECTEUR.
   (c) Patrols sent out last night had nothing of importance to report.

2. INTELLIGENCE.
   There were a great number of blinds, both of T.M. and artillery shells fired by the enemy yesterday; 10 out of 12 shells fired against R II Subsector being blind.
   At 8 p.m. last night a large fire was seen to be burning in a ruined house behind the lines held by the 35th Division.
   During the raid, the enemy sent up a number of rockets which burst into two red lights, upon which hostile T.Ms. and artillery opened fire.
   At 7.15 p.m. four pairs of red lights were sent up which were followed by heavy bombardment to our left.
   Soon after 3 a.m. the enemy sent up a green rocket upon which their fire slackened; another one was sent up shortly afterwards and their fire ceased.

3. GENERAL.
   (b) Our aircraft were active yesterday.

4. WORK DONE.
   (a) Repairs to BONNAL where damaged by hostile bombardment: duckboarding and revetting in the BONNAL and COLLECTEUR.

H.Q. 181 Inf.Bde.,
15.10.16.

                                                    Captain.
                                               Brigade Major.

CONFIDENTIAL.   I.S.95.

DAILY INTELLIGENCE SUMMARY
of
181st Infantry Brigade

From 10 a.m. 15.10.16   To 10 a.m. 16.10.16.

1. **OPERATIONS.**
    (a) Yesterday morning, howitzers bombarded the enemy lines and suspected T.M. emplacements, considerable damage being done to the enemy wire. During the afternoon the bombardment was carried on with 18-pdrs. and T.Ms. Throughout the night Lewis Guns kept under fire the gaps cut in the enemy wire. M.Gs. fired during the night on enemy communication trenches and trench railways.
    (b) At 10.20 a.m. the enemy sent over a few rifle grenades from opposite R I Subsector. From 11 a.m. to 5 p.m. the enemy intermittently bombarded the Sector with heavy T.Ms., six heavy T.M. shells which struck Sap 24 failed to explode: these were found to be 10". At 4 p.m. GREEN AVENUE was somewhat damaged by 4 heavy T.M. shells which burst in the vicinity. At 9.15 p.m. the enemy replied to T.M. activity on our left with artillery, T.Ms. and Minnenwerfers, bombarding for about 10 minutes. Opposite R I Subsector, a few 'oil-cans' were sent over.
    (c) The three patrols sent out last night had nothing to report.

2. **INTELLIGENCE.**
    The enemy are apparently in a very "nervy" condition, upon our troops in R II Subsector firing 5 rounds rapid at 5 a.m. this morning, the enemy immediately sent up a large number of flares and heavily bombed their own wire. After our artillery had bombarded a suspected T.M. position at 4.35 p.m. yesterday a large volume of flame and much smoke arose, apparently a store of some nature was set on fire. During the bombardment on our left last night, the enemy sent up two red and one green rocket, accompanied by green lights further to the right.
    A double red rocket, fired by the enemy at 9.15 p.m. was apparently the signal for artillery and T.Ms. to open fire; at 9.35 p.m. when artillery had ceased fire, one green rocket was sent up.
    A wooden cross with a flag nailed on to it was shown opposite R II Subsector yesterday (co-ordinate is being obtained).
    At 1 p.m. a wooden disc on a pole was put up above the parapet of trench immediately in front of the Wrecked Aeroplane (A.23.a.5.7). At 2.10 p.m. a pigeon was seen to fly from German Support line in a northerly direction.

3. **GENERAL.**
    (b) There was little aerial activity yesterday.

4. **WORK DONE.**
    (a) Repairs to BONNAT where damaged by hostile fire: wiring at L.22: repairs to GREEN AVENUE: revetting junction of COLLECTEUR and SUTHERLAND AVENUES.
    (b) A hostile working party opposite R I Subsector was dispersed by Lewis Gun fire at 12.30 a.m.

                                                       Captain.
H.Q. 181 Inf. Bde.   Brigade Major.
16.10.16.

CONFIDENTIAL.   W.S.14.

WEEKLY INTELLIGENCE SUMMARY
of
181st INFANTRY BRIGADE.

[Stamp: HEADQUARTERS 17 OCT. 1916 181st INFANTRY BDE.]

From 10 a.m. 10.10.16 To 17.10.16.

    The past week has been marked by increased enemy activity, this has been especially so with heavy T.Ms., which, in spite of an exceptionally large number of blinds, succeeded in doing considerable damage to the BONNAL at various points. The enemy fire was, however, effectively kept down by howitzers which, in co-operation with T.Ms. daily fired on the enemy wire, front and support lines, paying special attention to suspected T.M. positions, while heavier guns fired on enemy works in the vicinity of THELUS and BOIS CARRE.

    On the night of the 15th inst. a party of the enemy, who approached our line between BIDOT and the LILLE ROAD, were successfully repulsed by rifle fire.

    On Monday, 16th inst., the Corps heavy artillery in conjunction with the 60th Divnl. Artillery and T.Ms., carried out a pre-arranged strafe of suspected T.M. positions. A great deal of damage was apparently done, debris of all sorts being thrown about, and, at 10.34 a.m., a T.M. shell caused a big explosion.

    During the early hours of the 15th inst. the 2/23 Lond.R. raided the enemy trenches at A.23.c.98.87. The trenches were entered without opposition: the left party penetrated along the trench for a distance of about 30^x without meeting any of the enemy. The right party reached their objective but suffered some casualties from hostile bombers during the retirement. The raiding party reported that the trench had been absolutely demolished by the fire of our T.Ms. Since this date the enemy has, apparently, suffered considerably from "nerves", having thrown bombs into his own wire during the last two nights.

    A T.M. emplacement has been located at A.23.a.85.45.

                                                        [signature]

                                                           Captain.
                                                    Brigade Major.

H.Q. 181 Inf.Bde.,
17.10.16.

CONFIDENTIAL.

DAILY INTELLIGENCE SUMMARY
of
181st INFANTRY BRIGADE.

From 10 a.m. 16.10.16   To 10 a.m. 17.10.16.

1. **OPERATIONS.**
   (a) Throughout the day the Corps Heavy Artillery in conjunction with the 60th Divnl. Artillery and Trench Mortars heavily bombarded suspected T.M. positions, observation being carried out by aircraft. The shooting appeared to be good, large quantities of debris being thrown up.
   During the night, Lewis Guns fired on Gaps in the enemy wire, while M.Gs. fired indirect fire on enemy trench junctions and railways.
   (b) The enemy did not reply to our bombardment. There was slight T.M. activity during the latter part of the day and a few rifle grenades were sent over about 9 p.m. from opposite R I Subsector.
   (c) Patrols sent out last night had nothing of importance to report.

2. **INTELLIGENCE.**
   For the second night in succession the enemy bombed his own wire opposite R II Subsector, several bombs being thrown into the wire near Crater 500 about 3 a.m..
   Shortly after 11 p.m. the enemy showed red lights opposite both R I and R II Subsectors: no action followed.

3. **GENERAL.**
   (a) Aircraft were very active all day carrying out observation work in connection with our bombardment.
   (b) Hostile aircraft were more active than they have been for some time, several hostile 'planes were over ETRUN during the course of the day, meeting with heavy fire from anti-aircraft guns.
   (a) Contd. The inter-Battalion relief by night was successfully accomplished: the relief commenced at 5 p.m. finishing shortly after 1 a.m.

4. **WORK DONE.**
   (a) But little work was possible last night owing to the relief, a few minor repairs were however made in the BONNAL.
   (b) New chalk has been thrown up at A.22.b.35.35.

J.R. Macdonald
Captain.
Brigade Major.

H.Q. 181 Inf.Bde.,
17.10.16.

CONFIDENTIAL.

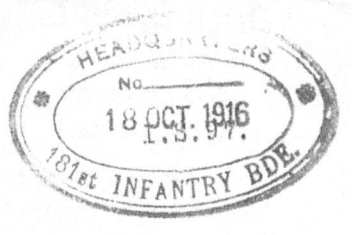

DAILY INTELLIGENCE SUMMARY of 181st INFANTRY BRIGADE.

From 10 a.m. 17.10.16   To 10 a.m. 18.10.16.

1. OPERATIONS.
   (a) During the morning artillery fired on A.16.b and A.16.d., later 4.5s. bombarded the enemy lines opposite R II Subsector, while a suspected M.T. emplacement at A.22.a.85.45 was also fired on.
   Throughout the day, T.Ms. intermittently bombarded the enemy lines. M.Gs. fired indirect fire on LES TILLEULS during the evening.
   (b) Hostile T.Ms. were more agressive yesterday, the BONNAL being badly damaged at its junction with Sap 24, while in R II Subsector, the BONNAL was badly damaged at its junction with GREEN AVENUE. A number of rifle grenades were sent over which did no damage.
   Between 7 a.m. and 7.35 a.m. the enemy bombarded our extreme left with rifle grenades and T.Ms. of every kind: but little damage was done, the bulk of the missiles falling in the centre sector.
   During the night, enemy M.Gs. swept the parapets of R I Subsector.
   (c) The three patrols sent out last night found nothing of special importance to report.

2. INTELLIGENCE.
   A T.M. was definitely located at A.22.b.44.63.
   It is possible that the enemy expected a raid last night opposite R I Subsector as, between 3 a.m. and 4 a.m. an exceptionally large number of flares were sent up while our parapets were kept under continual M.G. fire.
   A M.G. emplacement is suspected at A.22.b.40.90.
   Presumably blasting operations of some kind are still in progress behind the enemy's lines, several explosions being heard during the day.

3. GENERAL.
   (a) There was but little aerial activity yesterday.
   (b) At 11.30 a.m. four hostile aeroplanes were over our lines flying very high.

4. WORK DONE.
   (a) Repairs to trenches where damaged by hostile bombardment, wiring in front of Sap 31A, repairs to wire between Sap 32B and Crater 500.

                                                Captain.
                                           Brigade Major.

H.Q. 181 Inf.Bde.
     18.10.16.

1. OPERATIONS. (Contd.)
   (b) A lucky shot from a heavy Mortar, falling in the vicinity of one of our 3" Mortars, blew in the ammunition recess, a number of rounds being destroyed.

CONFIDENTIAL.   I.S. 98.

DAILY INTELLIGENCE SUMMARY
of
181st INFANTRY BRIGADE.

From 10 a.m. 18.10.16   To 10.a.m. 19.10.16.

---

1. **OPERATIONS.**

   (a) At midday our T.Ms., which had been bombarding the enemy lines throughout the morning, heavily bombarded the enemy, his trenches being badly damaged at A.23.a.9.0. and A.23.a.05.40, while a lucky shot fired against the enemy wire behind Crater 500 produced a big sheet of flame and smoke.

   During the day, our artillery were quiet, but from 11 p.m. onwards, 4.5s. fired about 6 shells every half-hour for the greater part of the night.

   Lewis Guns fired on gaps cut in the enemy wire throughout the night.

   As the enemy has lately used a lot of indirect M.G. fire against our dumps during the night, our M.Gs. last night paid special attention to the enemy dumps in addition to sweeping the LILLE ROAD.

   (b) In a desultory manner, hostile artillery was active throughout the day with but meagre success; our sentry post at F.1. in the GRAND COLLECTEUR was somewhat damaged by a "Whizz-bang", while during the afternoon, the vicinity of the LILLE BARRICADE was shelled by 4.2s.

   The enemy fired about the normal number of rifle grenades yesterday.

   (c) One of the patrols sent out last night to reconnoitre the small sap running out from enemy line to the right of Crater 500 were bombed from the enemy front line when within 10^X of the wire. There was no fire from the sap which probably is not held by the enemy.

2. **INTELLIGENCE.**

   Roughly 30% of the "Whizz-bangs" fired by the enemy yesterday were blinds.

   The enemy is apparently still in a state of considerable nervous tension. For the fourth time in succession he bombed his own wire at regular intervals during the night opposite Saps 24 and 26.

   At 8.30 p.m. a flash was seen from a tree on the LILLE ROAD. This was thought to be a signal that waggons were approaching our dumps as enemy M.Gs. immediately commenced sweeping the road.

   It was noticed yesterday that the marked diminution in hostile T.M. fire resulted in a correspondingly increased amount of "Whizz-bang" activity.

3. **GENERAL.**

   (h) Mist and rain prevalent yesterday made observation difficult and there was but little aerial activity.

4. **WORK DONE.**

   (a) General repairs to trenches with special attention to revetting: wiring from Sap 32B to Crater 500.
   Sumping and duckboarding Saps 30A, 32A and 32B.

   (b) The enemy has started rebuilding O.P. at A.22.b.35.40 which was destroyed some days ago. At A.16.d.65.12, the enemy appears to be deepening his trench.

                                                    Captain.
                                                    Brigade Major.

H.Q. 181 Inf.Bde.
19.10.16.

CONFIDENTIAL.   I.S.99.

DAILY INTELLIGENCE SUMMARY.
181st INFANTRY BRIGADE.

From 10 a.m. 19.10.16   To 10 a.m. 20.10.16.

1. OPERATIONS.
   (a) Yesterday was quieter. Throughout the day T.Ms. in conjunction with Field Guns fired on the enemy wire and lines, a number of direct hits being obtained.
   At 1 p.m. 4.5s. shelled a T.M. emplacement at A.22.b.45.63.
   At 7.30 p.m. and again at 10 p.m. M.Gs. fired on the Cross Roads at LES TILLEULS, while at 11.30 p.m. M.GS. fired on the enemy Trench Railway junctions.
   Throughout the night, Lewis Guns maintained gaps cut in the enemy wire.
   (b) Hostile artillery again shelled the BARRICADE and vicinity. The enemy artillery, though quieter, was, nevertheless fairly active. Opposite R I Subsector, the enemy were active with T.Ms. and rifle grenades, no damage was done.
   (c) Patrols sent out last night found nothing of importance to report.

2. INTELLIGENCE.
   At 1.15 p.m. a German battery fired four shells ("Whizz-bangs"): the first burst in their front line and the remaining three just in front.
   An aerial grenade fired into the BONNAL yesterday which failed to explode, as the pin had not been withdrawn, was dated 23.8.16.
   Upon a single rifle shot being fired from an O.P. opposite R II Subsector, hostile M.Gs. immediately opened fire.

3. GENERAL.
   (b) There was but little aerial activity yesterday.

4. WORK DONE.
   (a) Every available man on revetting and clearing trenches throughout the Sector, paying special attention to BONNAL.

H.Q. 181 Inf.Bds.
20.10.16.

                                                    Captain.
                                            for Brigade Major.

CONFIDENTIAL.   I.S.100.

DAILY INTELLIGENCE SUMMARY
of
181st INFANTRY BRIGADE.

From 10 a.m. 20.10.16   To 10 a.m. 21.10.16.

1. OPERATIONS.
   (a) Artillery were active at intervals during the day, firing on the works in the vicinity of THELUS and on the enemy lines.
   T.Ms. were quieter yesterday, especially so in R I Sub-sector. In R II, T.Ms. fired a number of rounds for the purpose of silencing hostile Mortars.
   A Lewis Gun opened fire at 750^X on a working party at A.17.a.85.20; two men were seen to fall and party dispersed. Later they reassembled and were dispersed by the 18-pdrs.
   Throughout the night Lewis Guns maintained the gaps cut in the enemy wire.
   Six rifle grenades were fired into a suspected sniping post at A.22.b.5.4 with the desired result.
   (b) The enemy was rather more active yesterday with T.Ms. and rifle grenades, but very little damage was done. Hostile artillery was also active: a large number of 5.9s. burst near SABLIERE, evidently searching for the light railway below CHEMIN CREUX.
   (c) Patrols sent out last night found nothing of importance to report.

2. INTELLIGENCE.
   The working party referred to in para. a of OPERATIONS, were apparently working on a Trench Railway. The head and shoulders of a man wearing a chocolate-coloured cap with a shiny peak was seen yesterday.
   Very few lights were sent up during the night.

3. GENERAL.
   (a) There were three Observation Balloons up yesterday, while the enemy had one up over THELUS.
   There was considerable aerial activity yesterday. At 10.45 a.m. a hostile L.V.G. type aeroplane approached our lines but was driven off by anti-aircraft guns.

4. WORK DONE.
   (a) Revetting trenches throughout the sector where they had fallen in: clearing and sumping 500 AVENUE: strengthening wire between Sap 32B and Crater 500.

H.Q. 181 Inf.Bde.
21.10.16.

Captain.
Brigade Major.

CONFIDENTIAL.   I.S.101.

DAILY INTELLIGENCE SUMMARY.
of
181st INFANTRY BRIGADE.

From 10 a.m. 21.10.16   To 10 a.m. 22.10.16.

---

1. OPERATIONS.
    (a) Artillery were again active firing on the enemy's lines and works in the vicinity of THELUS throughout the day.
    Light and Medium T.Ms. from time to time bombarded the enemy lines paying special attention to A.22.b.55.37 opposite R I Subsector and A.16.c.95.40 opposite R II Subsector, where emplacements were suspected. At A.16.c.95.40 a number of posts and other debris were thrown up.
    At 5.15 p.m. Lewis Guns fired on a working party at A.17.c.85.20, but it was too dark to observe results.
    Machine Guns fired during the night on enemy second line and trench junctions, while at 9 p.m. and 3 a.m. one gun fired long bursts at the enemy's dumps.
    (b) The enemy were rather more aggressive yesterday, activity with Aerial Torpedoes being especially marked. Heavy T.Ms. were active against R I but no damage was done.
    Hostile artillery fired a large number of 5.9s. into ECURIE during the afternoon, without doing much damage: later the MINOTAUR Dump was shelled, causing some casualties.
    M.Gs. again subjected our Dumps to indirect fire during the night.
    (c) Patrols sent out last night had nothing of importance to report.

2. INTELLIGENCE.
    It is suspected that a relief took place last night opposite this Sector, owing to the fact that scarcely any lights were put up, while none of the enemy sentries fired single shots as is their custom throughout the night.
    At 5 a.m. a gong was sounded in the enemy lines.

3. GENERAL.
    (b) Hostile observation balloons were up yesterday. There was a considerable amount of aerial activity during the day.

4. WORK DONE.
    (a) Owing to the better weather the trenches have considerably improved and good progress has been made with revetting. Wiring between Saps 23 and 24: clearing BONNAL at different points where it had fallen in.

                                                    Captain.
                                                 Brigade Major.

H.Q. 181 Inf.Bde.
    22.10.16.

CONFIDENTIAL.   I.S.102.

DAILY INTELLIGENCE SUMMARY
of
181st INFANTRY BRIGADE.

From 10 a.m. 22.10.16   To 10 a.m. 23.10.16.

1. OPERATIONS.
   (a) During the last 24 hours there has been considerable artillery activity our guns shelled FARBUS and the vicinity throughout the day and night, while field guns fired on suspected T.M. positions. T.Ms. were fairly active throughout the day firing on the enemy support lines.
   Lewis Guns maintained gaps cut in the enemy wire throughout the night.
   M.Gs. carried out an indirect fire scheme.
   (b) Enemy T.M. were active yesterday, particularly so against R I Subsector, but no damage was done, except for one shell which struck the BONNAL C.L.24, levelling it for about 3 yds. The enemy also put over a number of A.Ts.
   (c) Patrols sent out last night found nothing of importance to report.

2. INTELLIGENCE.
   At A.17.c.85.20 the enemy are carrying on some work which is apparently of an important nature, as although the working party has been dispersed time after time during the last three nights, they have persistently reassembled upon the termination of our fire.

3. GENERAL.
   (b) There was considerable aerial activity yesterday, hostile aeroplanes being over BERUM several times during the day, while soon after 4 p.m. a fight took place between five of our 'planes and four of the enemy in which one hostile aeroplane was driven to earth in the neighbourhood of ROCLINCOURT while one of our 'planes alighted near the BETHUNE Road with a damaged propeller.

4. WORK DONE.
   (a) General repairs throughout the Sector with special attention to revetting.

H.Q. 181 Inf.Bde.
23.10.16.

J.R.Macdonald
Captain,
Brigade Major.

CONFIDENTIAL.   I.S. 103.

DAILY INTELLIGENCE SUMMARY
of
181st Infantry Brigade.

From 10 a.m. 23.10.16   To 10 a.m. 24.10.16.

---

1. **OPERATIONS.**
    (a) Our T.Ms. were considerably more active yesterday: this was especially so against R I Subsector where our fire was concentrated on L.29.b.95.30 - 95.35 and A.23.a.05.35 where T.M. emplacements were suspected. Our 4.5s. fired three rounds on a hostile heavy T.M. firing from L.16.d.4.3 effectively silencing it.
    Throughout the night our Lewis Guns swept the enemy wire and parapets.
    M.Gs. fired last night on the hostile dump reported to be in the vicinity of Nine Elms.
    (b) Hostile activity yesterday was chiefly confined to replies to our T.M. fire. Hostile snipers were very active yesterday. Hostile M.Gs. were somewhat active during the early part of the day.

2. **INTELLIGENCE.**
    During the last two days there has been a big deterioration in the accuracy of the enemy T.M. fire. This, it is thought, supports the theory that a relief took place opposite this sector on the night of the 21st. A patrol which approached our line near L.28 was dispersed by Lewis Gun fire.

3. **GENERAL.**
    (b) Yesterday was a bad day for observation and there was but little aerial activity.

4. **WORK DONE.**
    (a) General repairs to trenches throughout the Sector, firebays 5, 6, and 7 at L.29 reconstructed.
    (b) The enemy has erected new wire at A.23.a.6.2.

                                                    Captain.
                                                Brigade Major.

H.Q. 181 Inf.Bde.
   24.10.16.

SECRET. APPENDIX IV.

181st INFANTRY BRIGADE.

WAR DIARY.

1st - 31st October, 1916.

RAID BY 2/23 LONDON REGT.

VOL. I. No. 5.

---------------o0o---------------

SECRET. APPENDIX IV.

SECRET.

2/23 London Regiment.

Order No. 1.

No 3

Reference — $\frac{1}{10,000}$ Roclincourt and Trench Maps.

RD 9/1

1. A raid on the German Trenches at point A.23.c.98.87 will be carried out by a party of the 2/23 Lond. Regt.

2. OBJECTS.
   (i) To obtain identification.
   (ii) To cause all possible damage.

3. ZERO. Time and date to be notified later.

4. RAIDING PARTY. as under:-
   O.C. Lieut. G.H. BAKER.

   Right Blocking Party....1 N.C.O. & 5 men) under 2/Lt.H.E.
   Right Raiding Party ....1 N.C.O. & 7 men)   DAVIS.

   Left Blocking Party ....1 N.C.O. & 5 men) Under Lieut.G.H.
   Left Raiding Party .....1 N.C.O. & 7 men)   BAKER.

   Blanket men & Orderlies 1 N.C.O. & 4 men) Under 2/Lt. A.L.
   Rear Party   ....2 N.C.Os.& 10 men) SEABROOK.

   TOTAL ... 3 Officers, 7 N.C.Os. and 38 men.

5. ASSEMBLY POINT.
   The whole raiding party will assemble in dugouts in the CHEMIN CREUX at – 30 minutes. The party will leave in the order laid down in paragraph 7 for the jumping-off point, moving by AVENUE "G" and Sap 21. They will be counted out by the O.C. Raiding Party.

6. JUMPING OFF POINT.
   The Jumping-off point will be to the right of and at the head of Sap 21. The party will be counted out here by 2/Lt. H.G.D. SAYERS.

7. ADVANCE AND ASSAULT.
   At Zero entire raiding party will advance in the following order:-

      Blanket Party and Orderlies.
      Right and Left Blocking Parties.
      Right and Left Raiding Parties.
      Rear Party.

   The Blanket party must reach the wire slightly in advance of the Right and Left Blocking parties. The two Blanket men will throw their blankets on to the wire and withdraw to the sides, 2/Lt.SEABROOK, his two orderlies and the raiding party, less rear party, passing over. If the blankets are not required the Blanket men will pass through the gap and remain as Orderlies, with 2/Lt.SEABROOK.
   2/Lt.SEABROOK will establish his report centre at the point of entry. He will remain there throughout the raid, and will be responsible for the passing back of prisoners, wounded etc. and for the improvement of the passage through the wire. (This is to be done by the blanket men). At the Recall Signal he will count out the two raiding parties. The O.C. of each raiding party will report to him as they leave the trench. When all are out he will withdraw on the rear party, bringing them in with him and covering the retirement of the

-2-

raiding parties. In case of emergency he will be responsible for utilising the rear party to the best advantage. The N.C.O. will assist him in his duties. The two Orderlies will, during the advance, each lay a thick trail of paper from sandbags which they will carry.

The right and left blocking parties will closely follow the blanket party, being led by their respective officers they will immediately follow 2/Lt.SEABROOK through or over the wire and leap into the trench at the point reached by him. Right party to the right and left party to the left. They will be seen into the trench by their respective officers down the German trench. The Right blocking party will proceed to the trench junction at A.23.d.95.83, where they will form a block. The left blocking party will proceed down the German trench to the trench junction at A.23.c.98.98 and there form a block. Any prisoners taken by the blocking parties will be immediately passed back to the raiding parties. These blocking parties must get to their objectives with as little delay as possible, it is not their duty to bomb dugouts etc. en route. Immediately behind the blocking parties will move the raiding parties led by their N.C.Os. They will enter the trench at the same point as the blocking parties, and headed by their Officers will work down the trench right and left, cleaning it up, bombing dugouts, and doing all possible damage until either the Recall Signal is given or the bombing block is reached.

The rear party will follow raiding parties, the junior N.C.O. leading, the senior N.C.O. in rear. The senior N.C.O. will be responsible for dropping two men as connecting files each 20 yards, the last two being within easy range of the gap in the enemy's wire. This party will be responsible for keeping connection between the raiding party and the Officer's post in Sap 21, for passing back prisoners and wounded, and for covering the retirement of the raiding party. In case of emergency they will act under 2/Lt.SEABROOK's orders. The N.C.Os. in charge, however, will take immediate action on their own initiative in case of any flanking move on the part of the enemy. They will report any action which they have taken immediately to the officer's post in Sap 21 after the raid.

8. RECALL.
At plus 15 minutes officers and N.C.Os. in charge of blocking and raiding parties will withdraw their respective parties leaving by the point of entry and reporting to Sec.Lt. SEABROOK en route. Officers will be the last of their parties to leave the trench. Blocking parties will cover the retirement of the raiding parties to the point of exit. They will make their way as rapidly as possible to the jumping-off point (head of Sap 21) being directed by the connecting files of the rear party. On reaching this point they will be counted in by the Officer posted there, and moved down the sap to the BONNAL, thence via AVENUE "G" to the assembly dugouts in CHEMIN CREUX, where the final count will be made. When all the above are clear, 2/Lt.SEABROOK will withdraw the blanket and rear parties in the manner laid down in para. 7, via the same routes as above. These parties being also counted in, in same manner as above.
Signal of Recall:- Rat-a-tat-tat from Machine Guns.

9. ARTILLERY.
(a) The XVII Corps Heavy Howitzers intend carrying out counter-battery work commencing at - 2 minutes.
(b) C.C. Right Group will co-operate as under:-
(1) Feint bombardment from plus 2 to plus 2.20 minutes. Bombardment on German front line on each side of point A.23.a.00.35.
From plus 2.20 to plus 2.40 minutes box barrage on German lines in rear and on each side of point A.23.a.00.35.
The above will be carried out by Field Guns.

(ii) From plus 15 minutes to "Cease Fire" bombardment of Trench Junctions A.23.b.50.20, A.23.b.00.50, A.23.a.55.90, and selected T.M.Emplacements by 4.5 howitzers and 2" T.Ms.

10. STOKES GUNS.
(a) From - 4 hours to - 3.50 hours dummy bombardment on German front line between points A.23.c.98.98 and A.23.d.05.83 by 4 guns. 600 rounds.
(b) From plus 10 to plus 15 minutes bombardment of German trench junctions between A.23.a.00.85 and A.23.a.40.40 by 4 guns. 300 rounds.

Dugouts for teams will be provided in the BONNAL trench. The O.C. 181 T.M.Battery to arrange to deal with any emergency that may arise.

11. LEWIS GUNS.
Lieut. L.J.OPPENHEIMER will arrange that both flanks of the raiding party are protected by Lewis Gun fire in case of need.

12. The O.C. 181 Machine Gun Coy. will co-operate by bursts of fire from zero to plus 10 minutes on usual trench junctions. From plus 10 minutes to plus 15 minutes he will cease fire. From plus 15 minutes to cease fire he will fire his rat-a-tat-tat, which will act as "Recall Signal".

13. Major A.G.PEMBERTON, O.C. "A" Company will make all necessary arrangements for dealing with any serious counter offensive on the part of the enemy.

14. The remainder of the Battalion and "D" Company, 2/21 L.R. at ABRI CENTRALE will stand to in their dugouts with a sentry posted over each.

15. COMMUNICATIONS.
An advanced telephone station will be installed at the head of Sap 21. Here 2/Lt.SAYERS will be stationed and will be responsible for the reporting of progress of "A" Coy.H.Q., who will transmit it to Bn. H.Q. Two runners will be attached to him there. It is an absolute necessity that information, even of a negative character, should be forwarded to Bn.H.Q. every 5 minutes. 2/Lt.SAYERS will, in addition, be responsible for both the counting out and in of the entire raiding party.
Os.C.Companies are responsible that no messages except those of a tactical nature are sent over the telephone from - 30 minutes to the receipt of the "Normal conditions" message.

16. CONTROL POSTS.
A control post will be established by O.C. "A" Coy. in the BONNAL 40 yds. either side of the junction of Sap 21, and no traffic will be allowed between these points from - 30 minutes to "Normal conditions". Between the above times, there will be no movement in the trenches except of men on special duty, and all down traffic will give way to up traffic.

17. An ADVANCED DRESSING STATION will be established in the BONNAL. All necessary arrangements as to extra personnel and stretchers to be made by the M.O. direct with the Advanced Dressing Station, ANZIN.

18. DRESS.
All men of the raid party, except blanket men, will wear steel helmets and Service Dress with puttees, but will not wear equipment. All articles and marks on clothing that
/might

might lead to identification will be removed and no personal letters or effects to be carried. Lieut. BAKER will be responsible for this. Special identity discs will be issued to each Officer and man. Faces will be blackened, and empty bandoliers worn round the chest passing over the right shoulder, and white tape round both shoulder straps.

19. ARMS etc. CARRIED BY RAIDING PARTY.

Each N.C.O. and man who carries a rifle will have a round in the chamber, 4 in the magazine and 10 rounds in the right hand side pocket of his tunic.

2/Lt. SEABROOK .... Rifle and Fixed Bayonet.

Blanket Party.
N.C.O. .... Rifle & Fixed Bayonet & Wire cutters.
2 Blanket men .... Slung rifle, belt with bayonet, wire blanket, wire cutters.
2 Orderlies .... Rifle & Bayonet, wire cutters, sandbags filled with papers.

Right & Left Blocking parties.
N.C.Os. .... Rifle & fixed Bayonet, two bombs in left side pocket.
2 Bayonet men .... - do -
1 Bomber .... Life preserver, bucket of 10 bombs.
2 Carriers .... Life preserver, bucket of 10 bombs.

Raiding parties.
Officers .... Revolver, two bombs in left side pocket.
N.C.Os. .... Revolver, two bombs in left side pocket, one Very Pistol each, one cartridge in breech 3 in right breast pocket.
Other Ranks .... Rifle & bayonet, two bombs in left side pocket.

Rear Party .... Rifle & Bayonet, 20 rounds in right hand side pocket.

20. Watches of all concerned will be synchronised at Bn.H.Q. at 5 p.m. the afternoon before the raid is to take place.

21. PRISONERS.
Men will be detailed from each raiding party whose duty it will be to take any prisoners captured to 2/Lt. SEABROOK who will pass them back to BONNAL via Sap 21, whence they will be brought direct to Bn.H.Q. O.C. "A" Coy. will provide necessary escorts. Route via AVENUE "G" and COLLECTEUR.

22. The code "MESSAGE RECEIVED" will be issued from Bn. H.Q. when normal conditions may be resumed.

23. All ranks must understand the absolute necessity of pushing straight through to their objective without being diverted by any flanking bombing attack or rifle fire.

24. Silence must be maintained throughout the entire operation.

25. All ranks will be warned that, in the event of their being captured by the enemy, they will on no account give the name of their regiment, Brigade or Division, but state their number, name and initials only.

26. A hot meal will be served to the raiding party on return.
27. ACKNOWLEDGE.

14.10.16.

(Signed)

Major.
Cmdng. 2/23 Lond.R.

Copy No. 1. Divn.
       2. File.
       3. War Diary.
       4. Right Group Art.
       5. 106th Brigade.
       6. 2/24 Lond.R.
       7. 181 Inf.Bde.
       8. 181 Inf.Bde.
       9. 181 T.M.Battery.

Report of Raid made by the

2/23rd Battalion The London Regt

on night of 14/15th October 1916 on enemy's lines.

The scheme as laid down in orders issued by me was rigidly adhered to. At - 4 hours on the 14/10/16, 6 Stokes Guns opened fire on that part of the enemy's lines which it was intended to raid. The fire from these guns was very accurate, and did considerable damage to the enemy's front line. In all, 650 rounds were fired. The result of this was retaliation of a very heavy nature, which lasted for about one hour. During this period the enemy threw over all classes of shells and Trench Mortars. Up to this time we suffered no casualties.

The Heavy artillery opened punctually at - 2 minutes on counter battery work.

The Right Group opened a feint bombardment from plus 2 to plus 2.20 minutes, bombarding the enemy's front on each side of A.23.a.00.35. From plus 2.20 to plus 2.40 mins. the artillery opened a feint box barrage at the same point. The firing of these guns was most effective, and was well directed. 4 Stokes Guns also co-operated in this feint bombardment from plus 4 minutes, firing in all about 450 shells. There is no doubt that this feint bombardment had the effect of drawing, at that time, the whole of the enemy retaliation, as the sector opposite was subjected to fire of every description.

While this was in progress our raiding party, which left the jumping off point at minus 2 minutes, were successfully enabled to cross No man's land with no casualties. The Raiding party carried out the programme exactly, proceeding across no man's land in perfect order. The wire was found to be well cut, and was easily negotiated with the aid of the blankets. Upon 2/Lt SEABROOK, who was leading the party, reaching the German Trench he was met by 2 sentries, at whom he fired. They immediately ran away. The whole party as arranged entered the trench, dispersing to the right and left. The Left blocking party proceeded down the trench followed by the Left Raiding Party under Lieut. Baker, for a distance of about 60 yards. This party did not encounter or see any Germans. They however bombed one dug-out on the parapet side. All of the left party returned. The party going to the right preceded by the bombing block encountered one German who was shot dead. This man's cap and rifle were brought back. The Blocking party proceeded about 40 or 50 yards where they came to a communication trench and established a block. This party on their way were bombed and shot at from a dug-out. The raiding party called down the dug-out for the occupants to come out but they received no reply, and therefore bombed the dugout. The next dugout was also bombed. On the return journey this party encountered no opposition, but Germans were closely following the Blocking Party, throwing bombs at them all the way. I regret to say that during this return journey of the Blocking Party one bomber was killed, one had his leg blown to pieces, and another one was injured. This party now consisted of above three officers and included one unwounded Corporal. Every effort was made by the two latter to bring back the dead man and the severely wounded man, but without avail, the unwounded Corporal having eventually to bring in the third man (wounded). These two left the trench before arriving at the point of entry, and had to creep

- 2 -

through the German wire, hence their delay in arriving back. Mr. SEABROOK, the Officer at the point of entry, was the last to leave his point, and was attacked by several Germans while he was awaiting the last of the party. After a fight, during which he bayonetted one, he was compelled to leave.

The total number of casualties are as follows:-

    1 Officer slightly wounded
    1 man missing, believed killed.
    1 man missing and severely wounded.
    7 men wounded.

Of the above 7, one was wounded in the German Trench, and the remaining 6 sustained their injuries through enemy barbed wire and shrapnel on the return journey through no man's land.

The information received with regard to the condition of the German Trenches was that they were very wide, and very badly knocked about. With the exception of there being a few dugouts and trench boards, one would hardly have known they were trenches.

The following booty was brought back:-

    1 Cap (which has been sent to Headquarters)
    2 rifles.

I have made most careful enquiries, and it is satisfactory to note that the duties allotted to the several members of this raiding party were all carried out exactly as laid down.

                                      Major
Commanding 2/23rd Battalion The London Regt.

15/10/16.

SECRET.   APPENDIX V.

181st INFANTRY BRIGADE.

WAR   DIARY.

1st - 31st October, 1916.

DIVISIONAL RELIEF.

VOL. I.   No. 5.
and move to back area

------oOo------

SECRET.   Copy No.

181st INFANTRY BRIGADE ORDER No. 25.

Reference Maps:- LENS II, Scale -   Headquarters,
              1/100,000. Trench Maps.   21st October, 1916.

1.   The 60th (London) Divn. (less Artillery) is to be relieved by the 3rd Canadian Divn. (less Artillery).
      The 181st Infantry Brigade will be relieved by the 8th Canadian Infantry Brigade in the line on 23rd - 26th October, as shown in Table A.
      The 181st Infantry Brigade is to be concentrated in the new area by midnight 27th/28th October, and will move as shown in Table B. (This Table will be issued later).

2.   Battalion Commanders will hand over command of their Subsectors on completion of relief. Completion of relief of each Unit to be reported to this office by the code word "DIXIES".

3.   The 181 Machine Gun Company will be relieved by the 8th Canadian Brigade Machine Gun Company during evening of 24th October, under arrangements to be made by Os.C. Companies concerned, relief to be complete by midnight 24th/25th October.
      The 8th Canadian Brigade Machine Gun Company will be billeted prior to relief in ANZIN, billeting party reporting to TOWN MAJOR who will make all arrangements. The Company will arrive at ANZIN about 2 p.m. on 23rd inst. Separate instructions as to disposal of their transport will be issued by Staff Captain.
      The 181 Machine Gun Company on relief will be billeted for the night of 24th/25th October at their Rear Headquarters, ETRUN. The Company will march on 25th October, under orders to be issued by O.C. 2/22 London R. and remain under his orders until arrival in New Area.

4.   The 181 Trench Mortar Battery will be relieved by the 8th Canadian Trench Mortar Battery during the evening of 24th October under arrangements to be made by O.C. Batteries concerned, relief to be complete by midnight 24th/25th October. The 8th Canadian Trench Mortar Battery will be billeted, prior to relief, ANZIN billeting party reporting to TOWN MAJOR who will make all arrangements. The Battery will arrive at ANZIN about 2.30 p.m. on 23rd inst.
      The 181 Trench Mortar Battery on relief will be billeted for night 24th/25th October at their Rear H.Q. ETRUN.
      A motor lorry will be provided on 25th October to transfer the Mortars and stores to the New Area (instructions as to same will be issued by the Staff Captain). The personnel, accompanied by handcarts, will march on 25th October under orders to be issued by O.C. 2/22 London R. and remain under his orders until arrival in new area.

5.   For time and place for guides to meet incoming Battalions, see Table A.
      Battalions will provide at least one guide per platoon and one per Lewis Gun Team, if any further guides are required, Officers Commanding concerned will make their own arrangements.
      The 181 Machine Gun Coy. and 181 Trench Mortar Battery will each find one guide per gun team and one for Headquarters.
      An officer will be in charge of the guides of each Unit.

6.   The following personnel will remain with the relieving Unit. They will report to the Staff Captain, 8th Canadian Infantry Brigade at Brigade Headquarters, ETRUN, at 10 a.m. on 27th inst., whence they will proceed in lorries to rejoin their Units.
      The Brigade Signal Section will leave 3 linesmen and two guides with the 8th Canadian Brigade Section, Signal Coy.
      The 2/21, 2/22 and 2/24 London R. will each leave 1 Officer and 6 N.C.Os.
      The 181 Trench Mortar Battery will leave 1 Officer and 2 N.C.Os.
      The 181 Machine Gun Coy. will leave 1 Officer, and 1 man per gun in the line :

                                                                            /Contd.

The above will be rationed and quartered by the Unit to which they are attached, but will have with them rations for the day following the relief.

7. Advance parties will come to this area on 22nd inst. Instructions as to same will be issued soperately.

8. Separate instructions as to relief of Control Posts, Light Railway Party and other details, also as to Transport, will be issued by the Staff Captain.

9. The 179th Infantry Brigade is to be relieved on the same dates by the 9th Canadian Infantry Brigade. The 2/14th London R. (London Scottish) holding Centre 1, being relieved on the 25th October.

10. All Defence Schemes, Maps, Air Photos, & (up to the scale of and including 1/20,000) are to be handed over to relieving Units. Receipts will be taken.

11. The greatest care must be taken to ensure that all Trench and other stores are handed over correctly and receipts obtained. Instructions on this subject are being issued.

12. Billets will be handed over clean and the usual certificates rendered.

13. Refilling Points will be notified later.

14. On completion of the relief on the 25th inst. the command of the Right Sector will pass to the G.O.C. 8th Canadian Infantry Brigade and the 181st Infantry Brigade Headquarters at ETRUN will be closed.
A Brigade Report Centre will be opened at BERLENCOURT at 2 p.m. on 25th inst.

15. Acknowledge.

J.M.Horlick
Captain.
Brigade Major.

H.Q. 181 Inf.Bde.
21.10.16.

Issued at 7.30 p.m.

Copy No.			
1.	File.	13.	2/23 Lond.R.
2.	War Diary.	14.	2/24 Lond.R.
3.	60th Division.	15.	181 M.G.Coy.
4.	179th Inf.Brigade.	16.	181 T.M.Battery.
5.	8th Can.Inf.Brigade.	17.	3/3rd Field Coy.R.E.
6.	106th Inf.Brigade.	18.	520th Divnl. Train.
7.	A.D.M.S.	19.	2/6th Field Ambulance.
8.	C.R.E	20.	Staff Captain.
9.	O.C. 60th Divnl.Train.	21.	Brigade Signal Section.
10.	Right Group Artillery.	22.	TOWN MAJOR, MAROEUIL.
11.	2/21 Lond.R.	23.	TOWN MAJOR, ANZIN.
12.	2/22 " "	24 & 25.	Spare.

RELIEF OF 181st INFANTRY BRIGADE by 8th CANADIAN INFANTRY BRIGADE.   TABLE A.

Date. OCT.	UNIT.	From.	To.	Relieved by.	GUIDES. From.	GUIDES. Time.	GUIDES. Place.	REMARKS.
23rd.	2/23rd Lond.R.	Divnl.Reserve, ETRUN.	IZEL LES HAMEAU	1st CANADIAN MTD. RIFLES.	BACK AREA	-	-	See Table B.
24th.	2/24th Lond.R.	Bde.Reserve.	M.ROEUIL, then IZEL LES HAMEAU.	4th CANADIAN MTD. RIFLES.	M.ROEUIL.	7.20 a.m.	ANZIN CHURCH	Billeting parties/report TO M.ROEUIL at 8 a.m. 1/24 L.R. platoon 4th C.M.R. to reach ANZIN CH. at 7.30 a.m. 1st platoon-1st C.M.R. to reach ANZIN CHURCH at 9.30 a.m.
25th.	2/22nd Lond.R.	RIGHT II.	ETRUN.	1st CANADIAN MTD. RIFLES.	ETRUN.	9.20 a.m.	ANZIN CHURCH	
25th.	2/21st Lond.R.	RIGHT I.	M.ROEUIL	2nd CANADIAN MTD. RIFLES.	M.ROEUIL.	9.30 a.m.	ANZIN CHURCH	Billeting parties/report TOWN MAJOR M.ROEUIL at 9.30 a.m. 2/21 L.R. 1st platoon 2nd C.M.R to reach ANZIN CH. at 9.30 a.m.
26th.	2/22nd Lond.R.	DIVNL.RESERVE, ETRUN.	IZEL LES HAMEAU.	5th CANADIAN MTD. RIFLES.	BACK AREA.	-	-	See Table B.
26th.	2/21st Lond.R.	M.ROEUIL.	IZEL LES HAMEAU.	-	-	-	-	See Table B.

NOTES.

Oct. 24th. (i) ROUTES UP FOR 4th CANADIAN MTD.RIFLES.- M.ROEUIL-LOUEZ-ANZIN (meet guides) - (a) Coy.relieving Coy. 2/24 L.R. at ABRI CENTRALE. ANZIN AVE.-BARRICADE-BLANCHARD AVE. (b) Coy.relieving Coy. 2/24 L.R. at ABRI MOUTON. ANZIN AVE.-ROCLINCOURT AVE.-VENUE MOUTON. (c) Coy.relieving Coy. 2/24 L.R. at SUNKEN ROAD. ANZIN AVE.-ROCADE AVE. -HIGH STREET-LABYRINTHE AVE.-FISH AVE.-ANNIVERSAIRE AVE. (d) Coy.relieving Coy. 2/24 L.R. at ECURIE. ANZIN AVE.-ROCADE AVE.

Oct. 24th. ROUTES DOWN FOR 2/24 LOND.R. (a) From ABRI CENTRALE, BLANCHARD AVE.-GENIE AVE.-ANZIN-LOUEZ-M.ROEUIL. (b) From ABRI MOUTON, AVE.MOUTON-GENIE AVE.-ANZIN-LOUEZ-M.ROEUIL. (c) From SUNKEN ROAD-ANNIVERSAIRE AVE.-BETHUNE AVE.-ANZIN-LOUEZ-M.ROEUIL. (d) From ECURIE.MADAGASCAR AVE.-ANZIN-LOUEZ-M.ROEUIL.

Oct. 24th. (ii) ROUTES UP FOR 1st CANADIAN MTD.RIFLES.- ETRUN-LOUEZ-ANZIN (meet guides) (a) Coy.relieving Right Coy.2/22 LR ANZIN AVE.-ROCLINCOURT AVE.-ANTOINE AVE. (b) Other 3 Coys. ANZIN AVE.-ROCADE AVE.-HIGH STREET-LABYRINTHE AV.

Oct. 24th. ROUTES DOWN FOR 2/22 LOND.R.- (a) Right Coy. FANTOME AVE.-GENIL AVE.-ANZIN-ETRUN. (b) Other 3 Coys. LABYRINTHE AVE.-HIGH STREET-ROCADE AVE.-ANZIN AVE.-ANZIN-ETRUN.

Oct. 25th. (iii) Bns. will move to and from ECURIE and ROUTE DOWN for 2/21 L.R. as for normal inter-Battalion Relief. ROUTE UP for 2nd CAN.MTD.RIFLES and ROUTE DOWN for 2/21 L.R. as for normal inter-Battalion Relief.

(iv) No platoon or other unit is to leave its position in the line until properly relieved. (v) All down parties will give way to Up parties. (vi) all units 181 Inf.Bde. on reaching billets after relief will report time east of ANZIN CHURCH. of arrival of last platoon by runner to this office. (vii) All details regarding relief will be arranged by Os.C.Units concerned.

SECRET.

The following amendments will be made to 181st Infantry Brigade Order No. 25:-

1. **Page 2, para. 14.** For "BERLENCOURT" read "CHATEAU LIENCOURT".

2. **Table B.**
    Against date 24th Oct. 2/23 Lond.R. in column "TO" erase "BERLENCOURT" and substitute "H.Q. and 3 Companies to BERLENCOURT, 1 Coy. and 4 Officers to SARS-LEZ-BOIS.

3. **Table B.** Note at bottom of page reference Brigade H.Q. erase "BERLENCOURT" substitute "LIENCOURT".

4. **Table B.** Note at bottom of page reference 2/6th Field Ambce. and 520th Coy. A.S.C. This note to be erased and following substituted:-
    "2/6th Field Ambulance will move to BERLENCOURT on 24th Oct. under orders from A.D.M.S."
    "520th Coy. A.S.C. will move to SARS-LEZ-BOIS on 24th Oct. under orders from O.C. 60th Divnl. Train. The O.C.Coy. will make his own Billeting arrangements."

5. **TABLE.B.**
    Add following Notes:-
    (a) "Refilling point will open at 9 a.m. 24th Oct. at point H.18.c.8.4. on SARS-LEZ-BOIS - MAIZIERES Road".
    (b) "A temporary receiving station for sick will be opened by 2/6th Field Ambce. at BERLENCOURT immediately on their arrival there."

6. **Appendix to Table B.**
    (a) Against Tuesday 24th Oct. 2/23 Lond.R. in Column "Moves to Billets in", to the word "BERLENCOURT" add "and SARS-LEZ-BOIS."
    (b) Against Tuesday 24th Oct. add "2/6th Field Ambce. to BERLENCOURT: billets arranged by M.GIRAUD, who will meet 2/6 Fld.A.billeting party at CHURCH, BERLENCOURT at 10 a.m."
    (c) Insert in Column of Remarks of 24th Oct.- "The Billeting arrangements at BERLENCOURT will be under the O.C. 2/23 Lond.R.
    (d) Against "NOTE" - erase all matter dealing with 2/6th Field Ambce. and in Column of Remarks substitute for present note "O.C. 520th Coy. A.S.C. will make his own billeting arrangements in SARS-LEZ-BOIS".

Captain.
Brigade Major.

H.Q. 181 Inf.Bde.
22.10.16.

Reference:- LENS II 1/100,000
ARRAS 51C 1/40,000

Move of 181st INFANTRY BRIGADE to NEW AREA

TABLE "B"

DATE Octr.	UNIT	FROM.	TO.	ROUTE.	STARTING TIME.	REMARKS.
23	2/23 Lond.R.	BERRUN	IZEL LES HAMEAU.	Via HABARCQ.	On relief by 1st C.M.R. Timed for 1 p.m.	1. By day all units on leaving either BERRUN or MAROEUIL for New area will move by single platoons and vehicles at 200 intervals until south of ARRAS -ST.POL road. They will then be formed up and move as a unit. Units will march independently (except 181 M.G.Coy. and 181 T.M.Battery who will march under orders of O.C. 2/22 Lond.R.
24	2/23 Lond.R.	IZEL LES HAMEAU.	BERLEN-COURT.	Roads south of IZEL LES HAM-EAU-MANIN-GIV-ENCHY le NOBLE -LIGNEREUIL.	To be clear of IZEL LES HAMEAU by 10.30 a.m.	2. Attention is drawn to paras. 6 and 7 Divnl.Standing Orders.
	2/24 Lond.R.	Brigade Reserve.	IZEL LES HAMEAU.	Via MAROEUIL & HABARCQ.	On relief by 2nd C.M.R.	3. The Brigade Band will play the 2/23.Lond.R. and will move under O.C. 2/23 L.R. orders. He will arrange billets for them at both IZEL LES HAMEAU and BERLINCOURT.
	3/3rd Field Coy. R.E.	ANZIN.	FERME DUFRINE.	March under orders from C.R.E.		4. O.C. 2/24 L.R. will arrange for a hot meal to be served during rest halt at MAROEUIL.
25.	3/3rd Field Coy. R.E.	FERME DUFRINE.	MAIZIERLS.	Via PENIN.	To be clear of FERME DUFRINE by 10.15 a.m.	5. For billeting arrangements see APPENDIX attached.
	2/24 Lond.R.	IZEL LES HAMEAU.	MAIZIERES.	Via PENIN.	To pass road junction J.2.a.J.5. at 11 a.m.	6. Instructions as to lorries issued separately.
26.	2/22 Lond.R. } 181 M.G.Coy. } 181 T.M.Bty. }	BERRUN.	IZEL LES HAMEAU.	Via HABARCQ.	To be clear of BERRUN by 10.30 a.m.	
	2/22 Lond.R. } 181 M.G.Coy. } 181 T.M.Bty. }	IZEL LES HAMEAU.	GOUY-EN-TERMOIS.	PENIN-MAIZIERES.	To be clear of IZEL LES HAMEAU by 10.30 a.m.	
	2/21 Lond.R.	MAROEUIL.	IZEL LES HAMEAU.	Via HABARCQ.	To be clear of MAROEUIL by 10.30 a.m.	
27.	2/21 Lond.R.	IZEL LES HAMEAU.	DENIER.	Roads W. of IZEL LES HAMEAU-MANIN -GIVENCHY le NOBLE-TINCHEBRAY IL	To be clear of IZEL LES HAMEAU by 10.30 a.m.	

Bde.H.Q. move under separate orders, arriving BERLENCOURT on afternoon 25th inst.
1/5 Field Ambulance & 520th Coy. A.S.C. move to SARS-LEZ-BOIS under orders from A.D.M.S. & O.C.60th Div.Tr. in respectively

APPENDIX to TABLE B.

BILLETING ARRANGEMENTS.

Date. October.	UNIT.	Moves to Billets in.	Interpreter arranging Billets.	Interpreter meets Billeting Party.		REMARKS.
				Time.	Place.	
Monday 23rd.	2/23 Lond.R.	IZEL LES HAMEAU.	M.GIRAUD.			Billeting party must be sent on well in advance accompanied by Interpreter.
Tuesday 24th.	2/23 Lond.R. 2/24 "	BERLENCOURT. IZEL LES HAMEAU.	M.GIRAUD. M.FORNE.			do. do.
Wednesday 25th.	2/22 Lond.R.) 181 M.G.Coy.) 181 T.M.Bty.)	IZEL LES HAMEAU.	M.FORNE.	10 a.m.	CHURCH.	
	2/24 Lond.R.) 3/3rd Fld.Co.)	MAIZIERES.	M.GIRAUD.	9 a.m.	CHURCH.	The billeting arrangements at MAIZIERES will be under the O.C. 2/24 Lond.R.
Thursday 26th.	2/22 Lond.R.) 181 M.G.Coy.) 181 T.M.Bty.)	GOUY EN TERNOIS.	M.GIRAUD.	10 a.m.	CHURCH.	
	2/21 Lond.R.	IZEL LES HAMEAU.	M.FORNE.	10 a.m.	CHURCH.	
Friday 27th.	2/21 Lond.R.	DENIER.	M.FORNE.			Billeting party must be sent on well in advance accompanied by interpreter.

NOTE:-

| Tuesday 24th. ? | 520th Coy. A.S.C. 2/6th Field Ambulance. | SARS LES BOIS. SARS LES BOIS. | | | | Os.C. 520th Coy. A.S.C. and 2/6th Field Amb. will mutually arrange their billets in SARS LES BOIS. |

SECRET.   G.S./392/14.

H.Q.179th.Inf.Bde.   H.Q. 1/12th.L.N.Lancs.R.
   180th. ,,   ,,   Div. Train.
   181st. ,,   ,,   Div. Supply Column.
C.R.A.   A.D.V.S.
C.R.E.   Camp Commandant.
A.D.M.S.   XVII Corps.
60th.Div.Signals.   "A".

Ref.Map. LENS Sheet. 11.

(1) Table D issued from this office on the 21st.Oct. giving the allotment of areas in the New Area is cancelled and the following substituted:-

HOUVIN HOUVIGNEUL.   Div. H. Q.

179th.Inf.Bde.Area.   Troops.
SERICOURT   ....   Bde.H.Q.   )
SIBIVILLE.   )   179th.Inf.Bde.
BUNEVILLE.   )   2/4th.Fd.Co.R.E.
MONTS EN TERNOIS.   )   2/4th.Fd.Amb.
MONCHEAUX.   )   Det. Train.
MONVAL.   )
Routes HAUTE AVESNES - TILLOY - AMBRINES.

180th.Inf.Bde. Area.   Troops.
HOUVIN HOUVIGNEUL...Bde.H.Q.   )
HOUVIGNEUL.   )   180th.Inf.Bde.
CABETTEMONT.   )   1/6th.Fd.Co.R.E.
MAGNICOURT.   )   2/5th.Fd.Amb.
)   Det.Train.
REBREUVE and PETIT BOURET are added to this area on the 26th.
Route ACQ - Road junction on ARRAS - St.POL road at HAUTE AVESNES - BERLES - PENIN.

181st. Inf. Bde. Area.   Troops.
BEAUDRICOURT.   ...   Bde. H.Q.   )
IVERGNY.   )   181st. Inf. Bde.
)   3/3rd. Fd.Co. R.E.
)   2/6th.Fd.Amb.
)   Det. Train.
REBREUVIETTE - ROZIERE - WAMIN - ETREE WAMIN and OPPY will be added to this area on the 26th.
Route HERMAVILLE - IZEL LES HAMEAU - MANIN - LIENCOURT.

GOUY EN TERNOIS   ...   ...   )   1/12 L.N.Lancs R.

HOUVIN HOUVIGNEUL.   ...   ...   )   60th.Div.Supply Column.
)   Det.Train.
)   60th.San. Sec.

BROUILLY.   ...   ...   )   60th.Mob.Vet.Sec.

(2) Acknowledge.

   23rd.October.1916.
   Issued at Oppin.
                                              Lieut.Col.
                                              General Staff.

Brigade Major.

       Herewith amended copy of Schedule attached to this office A.1189/17 dated 29-10-16.

                          BM Edward
                                   Captain,
                                   Staff Captain,
                                   181st. Inf. Bde.

33-10-16

USE OF LORRIES

Date	Time & place to report	Destination	Load	Remarks
23rd.	Q.M.Stores 2/23rd.LOND. R. 8 a.m.	IVERGNY	Blankets surplus Offrs.kit &c.& Band music, stands & rifles	A Guard to accompany the Lorries, consisting of 1 officer, & a minimum of men who cannot march, with rations for that & the 2 following days.
24th.	1 Lorry Q.M. Stores 2/24th. 1 Lorry Q.M. Stores 2/22nd. 7 a.m.	BEAUDRICOURT Report for orders at MAIRIE REBREUVIETTE	Blankets surplus Officers' kit &c.	Do. -do- Lorries can make a second journey if necessary
25th.	1 Lorry Bde. Q.M.Stores 7 a.m. 1 lorry near 181 T.M.B. Rear H.Q.& thence rear H.Q.181 M.G. Coy.7 a.m.	BEAUDRICOURT Report for orders at MAIRIE REBREUVIETTE	Blankets, Stores &c. -Do-	Do. -do-
26th.	Q.M.Stores 2/21st.Bn. 8 a.m.	ETREE - WAMIN or WAMIN	-Do-	Do. -doN
27th.	Bde.H.Q. 10 a.m.	2/21st. ETREE - WAMIN 2/22nd. REBREUVIETTE 2/23rd. IVERGNY 2/24th. BEAUDRICOURT 181 M.G.COY) REBREUVIETTE 181 T.M.BTY)	)To convey)personnel)of Bde.)left in)trenches)to hand over to incoming Brigade.	To report to Bde. H.Q. at BEAUDRICOURT on completion of duty.

NOTE:- The lorry for Brigade H.Q. on 25th. will report back at ETRUN as soon as possible, to convey Bde. H.Q. office stationery, and personnel to BEAUDRICOURT. A 3rd. lorry from Division will report at 7 a.m. on 25th. xxxxxxxxxxxxxxxxxxxxxx to be at the disposal of the M.G.COY. to take forage or xxxxx rations to IZEL LES HAMEAU, and report back here at 2 p.m, or as soon after as possible, to convey the remainder of Brigade H.Q. to BEAUDRICOURT.

B W Edwards Captain,
Staff Captain,
181st. Inf. Bde.

23-10-16

Brigade Major.

Brigade Major

---

1. With reference to the move of the Brigade to the new area, 8 lorries will be attached to the Brigade from the 22nd. to the 27th. inclusive.

2. They will be used for the purpose of moving to the new area all xxx surplus Officers' kit, blankets, Trench Mortars, and additional stores, which have been authorised, but for which no additional transport is provided.

3. The route to the new area will be as follows:-
ARRAS - ST.POL road as far as LE QUESNET or LIGNY ST.FLOCHEL roads where the lorries will turn South to the new area.

Return via PENIN - TINCQUES - ARRAS - ST.POL road.

4. Great care must be taken that the lorries do not interfere with the troops marching.

5. No stores of any nature are to be taken by lorry to the intermediate area where troops halt for the night only, i.e. IZEL LES HAMEAU.

6. These lorries will report here by noon to-day the 22nd. inst., and the Drivers will be rationed and accommodated by Q.M.S.HARRISON.

7. The Officer in charge of the Guard referred to in the "Remarks" column of attached will select a Quartermaster's Stores in the place stated, unload the stores at once, and post a guard over same till arrival of his unit. He will assist the Interpreter and billeting party of his unit on arrival, by having previously reconnoitred the village.

8. Owing to these lorries being provided, the first line transport will march only with its authorised equipment and loads, all surplus being carried by the lorries.

B.Bildwood
Captain,
Staff Captain,
181st. Inf. Brigade.

22-10-16

Brigade Major

USE OF LORRIES

Date	Time & place to report	Destination	Load	Remarks
23rd.	Q.M.Stores 2/23rd.LOND.R. 8 a.m.	BERLENCOURT	Blankets surplus Offrs. kit &c. & Band music, stands & rifles.	A Guard to accompany the lorries, consisting of 1 Officer, & a minimum of men who cannot march, with rations for that & the 2 following days.
24th.	1 Lorry Q.M. Stores 2/24th. 1 Lorry Q.M. Stores 2/22nd 7 a.m.	MAIZIERES GOUY-EN-TERNOIS	Blankets surplus Officers' kit &c.	Do. -do- Lorries can make a second journey if necessary
25th.	1 Lorry Bde. Q.M.Stores 7 a.m. 1 lorry near 121 T.M.B. Rear H.Q. & thence rear H.Q.121 M.G. Coy. 7 a.m.	BERLENCOURT GOUY-EN-TERNOIS	Blankets, Stores &c -Do-	Do. -do-
26th.	Q.M.Stores 2/21st.Bn. 8 a.m.	DENIER	-Do-	Do. -do-
27th.	Bde.H.Q. 10 a.m.	2/21st.DENIER 2/22nd.GOUY-EN-TERNOIS 2/23rd.BERLENCOURT 2/24th.MAIZIERES 121 M.G.COY) GOUY-EN- 121 T.M.Bty) TERNOIS	) to convey) personnel) of Bde.) left in) trenches) to hand over to incoming Brigade.	To report to Bde.H.Q. at BERLENCOURT on completion of duty.

NOTE:- The lorry for Brigade H.Q. on 25th. will report back at ETRUN as soon as possible, to convey Bde.H.Q. office stationery, and personnel to BERLENCOURT. A 3rd. lorry has been asked for from Division to report at 2 p.m. on 25th. for the same purpose.

Captain,
Staff Captain,
181st. Inf. Brigade.

Attention is directed to the last paragraph of Divnl. Standing
Order No. 7.

SECRET.   Copy No. 15

181st INFANTRY BRIGADE.

ORDER No. 26.

Headquarters,
26th October, 1916.

Reference - LENS II (1/100.000).

1. The 60th (London) Division (less Artillery) is to move south on the 28th inst.

2. The 181 Infantry Brigade and attached troops will march that day and halt for the night 28/29th as shown in TABLE "A".

3. Echelons A & B Transport and Baggage wagons will accompany Units. Supply wagons will move from Refilling Point and march under orders of O.C. 520th Coy., A.S.C.

4. Orders for billeting parties as shown in TABLE "B".

5. Refilling Point 29th inst. on DOULLENS-AUXI-LE-CHATEAU Road between FROHEN-LE-GRAND and road junction about 2 miles west of that place. Time will be notified later.

6. Brigade Headquarters will close at IVERGNY at 11 a.m. and reopen at OCCOCHES at the same hour.

7. Acknowledge.

                                        Captain.
                                    Brigade Major,
                                181st Infantry Brigade.

Issued at 6 a.m. 27th inst.

Copy No. 1. 60th Divn.   9. 2/6th Field Amb.
        2. 2/21 L.R.   10. 520th Coy. A.S.C.
        3. 2/22 L.R.   11. A.D.M.S.
        4. 2/23 L.R.   12. C.R.E.
        5. 2/24 L.R.   13. Staff Captain.
        6. 181 M.G.Coy.   14. Brigade Signal Officer.
        7. 181 T.M.Battery.   15. War Diary.
        8. 3/3rd R.E.   16. File.

MARCH TABLE - 181st INFANTRY BRIGADE.

TABLE "A".

UNIT.	ROUTE TO STARTING POINT.	STARTING POINT.	TIME.	DESTINATION.	ROUTE.
Brigade Hd.Qrs.		Cross roads at southern end of IVERGNY.	9.30 a.m.	OCCOCHES.	Le SOUICH - BOUQUEMAISON - NEUVILLETTE - ¼ of LA CLOSERIE FM.
2/23 L.R.		do.	9.30 a.m.	BARLY.	Le SOUICH - BOUQUEMAISON - NEUVILLETTE.
2/24 L.R.		do.	9.40 a.m.	BARLY.	do.
2/22 L.R.	Via road passing through second R of REBREUVIETTE.	do.	9.47 a.m.	NEUVILLETTE.	do.
2/21 L.R.	Via road junction ¼-mile N. of N in WARLIN. + BEAU-DRICOURT.	do.	9.55 a.m.	NEUVILLETTE.	do.
181 M.G.Co.) 181 T.M.By.)	Via road passing through Z of RUZIRRE.	do.	10.5 a.m.	RANSART.	Le SOUICH - BOUQUEMAISON - M of LA CLOSERIE FM.
3/3rd Fld. Coy. R.E.	Will keep road clear in IVERGNY until passage of 181 M.G.Coy.	do.	10.10 a.m.	OCCOCHES.	Le SOUICH - BOUQUEMAISON - NEUVILLETTE - ¼ of LA CLOSERIE FM.
2/6th Fld. Amb.		do.	10.15 a.m.	NEUVILLETTE.	Le SOUICH - BOUQUEMAISON.
520th Coy. A.S.C.		do.	10.20 a.m.	FROHEN-LE-PETIT.	Le SOUICH - BOUQUEMAISON - NEUVILLETTE - BARLY - REBER-OTHS.

All Units will be clear of the DOULLENS - FREVENT - ST.POL Road by 12 noon 28th inst.

TABLE "B".

BILLETING TABLE - 181st INFANTRY BRIGADE.

Date.	Unit.	Moves to Billets. in -	Billeting Party to meet.	Time.	Place.	Remarks.
Saturday, 28th October.	Brigade H.Q.	OCCOCHES.	Mons. SARTIGE. (Brigade Interpreter.)	9.30 a.m.	Chateau.	
	5/3rd R.E.	do.	do.	10 a.m.	Church.	
do.	2/23 Lond.R.	BARLY (and if necessary 1 Coy.at OCCOCHES)	Mons. GIRAUD.	9 a.m.	Mairie.	
do.	2/24 Lond.R.	do.	do.	9 a.m.	do.	Billeting to be under O.C. 2/24 L.R.
do.	2/22 Lond.R.	NEUVILLETTE.	Staff Captain or representative.	9 a.m.	Mairie.	
	2/21 Lond.R.	do.	do.	9 a.m.	do.	
	2/8th Fld.Amb.	do.	do.	9 a.m.	do.	
do.	181 M.G.Coy.	RANSART.	Information re billets to be obtained from Mons. TRITIEZ's house. Billeting parties to be under O.C. 181 M.G.Coy.		M.TRITIEZ's house, RANSART.	
	181 T.M.Bty.	do.	do.		do.	
do.	520 Coy.A.S.C.	Arrangements to be under O.C. 60th (London) Divisional Train.				

To O.C. 3/3 Field Co RE.
The 3/3 & 1/6 Field Co RE will move today to FAMECHON 5 miles East of DOULLENS. On arrival at FAMECHON they will come under orders of XIII Corps.
The above 2 coys will concentrate at BEAUREPAIRE at noon today where further orders will be issued them by a staff officer of the Division.
BEAUREPAIRE is 3 miles EAST of DOULLENS

You will be clear of OCCOCHES by 9.45 AM
acknowledge

P. Bradshaw
Captain
J. Bde Major
1st Infantry Bde

SECRET.   Copy No. 15

181st INFANTRY BRIGADE ORDER No. 27.

Reference - LENS II (1/100,000)   Headquarters,
                                                    28th October, 1916.

1. The 60th (London) Division (less Artillery) is to continue its move south on the 29th inst.

2. The 181st Infantry Brigade, and attached troops, will march that day and halt for the night 29/30th inst. as shown in Table "A".

3. Echelons A & B Transport and Baggage wagons will accompany Units.

4. Orders for Billeting parties as shown in Table "B".

5. Brigade Hd.qrs. will close at OCCOCHES at 10 a.m. and reopen at FIENVILLERS at the same hour.

6. Refilling point Domst - ROAD between BERNAVILLE and FIENVILLERS

7. Acknowledge.

                                                    Captain.
                                                    Brigade Major.
                                                    181st Infantry Brigade.

Issued at 7 p.m. 28.10.16.

Copy No.				
1.	60th Divn.		10.	520th Coy.A.S.C.
2.	2/21 L.R.		11.	A.D.M.S.
3.	2/22 "		12.	C.R.E.
4.	2/23 "		13.	Staff Captain.
5.	2/24 "		14.	Brigade Signal Officer.
6.	181 M.G.Coy.		15.	War Diary.
7.	181 T.M.Bty.		16.	File.
8.	3/3rd Field Co.R.E.		17.	1/12 D.N.L.
9.	2/6th Field Ambce.			

MARCH TABLE - 181st INFANTRY BRIGADE.

TABLE "A".

UNIT.	ROUTE TO STARTING POINT.	STARTING POINT.	TIME.	DESTINATION.	ROUTE.
Bde.H.Q.		Road junction south-ern end of OUTREBOIS.	9 a.m.	FIENVILLERS.	Le QUESNEL FARM - BOIS BERGUES.
2/24 L.R.		Cross roads about one mile S.S.W. of B of BARLY.	8.20 a.m.	FIENVILLERS.	OUTREBOIS - Le QUESNEL F.RM - BOIS BERGUES.
2/22 I.R.	Road running through R of BARLY.	do.	8.27 a.m.	CANDAS.	OUTREBOIS - Le QUESNEL FARM - BOIS BERGUES - FIENVILLERS.
2/21 L.R.	do.	do.	8.35 a.m.	LUTHEUX.	OUTREBOIS - Le QUESNEL FARM.
2/6th Fld.Amb.	do.	do.	8.43 a.m.	MONTPLAISIR and MACFER.	OUTREBOIS - road passing through second E of Le QUESNEL FARM.
2/23 L.R.	-	do.	8.48 a.m.	OUTREBOIS.	-
181 M.G.Coy.) 181 T.M.Bty.)	To be clear of RANSART by 9 a.m.			OUTREBOIS.	H.te. VISEE - RISQUETOUT - OCCOCHES.
1/12 L.N.L. Pioneers.	-	CANTELEUX X roads.	9.30 a.m.	BOIS BERGUES.	Route as per 60th Div. Order No.5.
520th Coy. A.S.C.	as ordered by O.C. 60th Divnl. Train.			Le QUESNEL FARM.	Route as ordered by O.C. 60th Divnl. Train.
3/3rd Field Co. R.E.	Remain in their present billets.				

TABLE "B"

Date	Unit	To be billeted at	Time for billeting party	To be at	To meet
29th.	Brigade H.Q.	FIENVILLERS	10 a.m.	--	--
	2/21 LOND. R.	AUTHEUX	To make their own billeting arrangements		
	2/22 -Do-	CANDAS	9-30 a.m.	Town Major's office CANDAS	To get all information from Town Major
	2/23 -Do-	OUTREBOIS	8 a.m.	MAIRIE	To meet Staff Captain
	2/24 -Do-	FIENVILLERS	9 a.m.	Town Major's office CANDAS	To get all necessary information re billets in FIENVILLERS
	181 M.G.COY.) 181 T?M.BATT)	OUTREBOIS	8 a.m.	MAIRIE	To meet Staff Captain
	5/3rd.R.E.	Remain in present billets at OCCOCHES			
	2/6 FLD.AMBCE.	(MONPLAISIR (MACFER LE QUESNEL FM.	To make their own billeting arrangements.		
	520.COY./.S.C.		To make their own billeting arrangements.		
	1/12 L.N.L.	BOISBERGUES	To make their own billeting arrangements.		

"A" Form.
MESSAGES AND SIGNALS.

Army Form C. 2121.

TO	2/21 L.R.	2/24 L.R.	520 Coy ASC	
	2/22 L.R.	181 M.G Coy	ADMS	
	2/23 L.R.	181 T.M Batty	CRE	
		2/60 Field Amb	Bde Signals	
			11th L.N.L.	

Sender's Number: **BM 409**
Day of Month: **29th**
AAA

Reference my order No 28 of 5 days date AAA move of 520th Coy ASC cancelled Coy will remain as LE QUESNEL FARM AAA Refilling point from Monday 30th inst inclusive on the road between LE QUESNEL and BOIS BERGUES

From: **181 INF BDE**

SECRET.   Copy No. 15

181st INFANTRY BRIGADE ORDER No. 28.

Reference -- LENS II (1/100,000).   Headquarters,
                                                     29th October, 1916.

1. The following units billeted in the 181st Infantry Brigade area
   will move to fresh billets in the area during the 30th inst.
   as under:-

UNIT.	DESTINATION.	ROUTE.	REMARKS.
2/23 L.R.	CANDAS.	Le QUESNEL FARM - BOIS BERGUES - AUTHEUX - FIENVILLERS.	To be clear of Le QUESNEL FARM by 9.30 a.m.
520th Coy. A.S.C.	CANDAS.	do.	Not to leave Le QUESNEL FARM before 9.30 a.m.

2. Baggage wagons will accompany 2/23 Lond.R.

3. For Billeting Arrangements, see attached Table.

4. Refilling Point as shown in 181st Infantry Brigade Order No. 27
   of 28th inst.

5. Acknowledge.

                                        R. Macdonald
                                        Captain.
                                        Brigade Major.
                                        181st Infantry Brigade.

Issued at 4 p.m. 29.10.16.

Copy No. 1.   60th Divn.   10.   520th Coy. A.S.C.
        2.   2/21 L.R.   11.   A.D.M.S.
        3.   2/22 L.R.   12.   C.R.E.
        4.   2/23 L.R.   13.   Staff Captain.
        5.   2/24 L.R.   14.   Brigade Signal Officer.
        6.   181 M.G.Coy.   15.   War Diary.
        7.   181 T.M.Bty.   16.   File.
        8.   3/3rd Field Co. R.E.   17.   1/12 L.N.L.
        9.   2/6th Field Ambce.

TABLE "B"

Date	Unit	To be billeted at	Time for billeting party	To be at	To meet
30th	2/23 LOND.R.	CANDAS	9-30 a.m.	Town Major's Office CANDAS	To get all information re billets
	520 M.Y.A.S.C.	CANDAS near the station	9-30 a.m.	Town Major's Office CANDAS	To get all information re billets.

Units not mentioned above remain in billets of 29th.

SECRET.

181st INFANTRY BRIGADE.

WAR DIARY.

From 1st November, 1916.
To 30th November, 1916.

VOL. I. NO. 6.

-------------------oOo-------------------

WAR DIARY

INTELLIGENCE SUMMARY

of 181st INFANTRY BRIGADE

Army Form C. 2118.

(Erase heading not required.)

Instructions regarding War Diaries and Intelligence Summaries are contained in F.S. Regs., Part II. and the Staff Manual respectively. Title pages will be prepared in manuscript.

Hour, Date, Place	Summary of Events and Information	Remarks and references to Appendices
FIENVILLERS 1-11-16	A nice morning, very heavy shower about 4.30pm. Westwind. Units training in afternoon morning 2/22 2/23 2/24 L.R. Inspected by Commander-in-Chief Sir Douglas Haig between 2 and 4.30 p.m. Practice Alarms held by 2/21 2/24 L.R. 181 M.G. Coy, 181TH Batty. 2/6 Fd Amb. 525 Coy A.S.C. 1/1 L.M.L.(Pioneers) about 6 p.m. Orders received from Div G.O. to move to new area on 3rd inst.	APPENDIX I [initials]
FIENVILLERS 2-11-16	A cold damp morning with showers of rain. Beautiful afternoon. Wind West. All units training. Staff Captain goes to new area to see about Billets. 2/22 and 2/23 Lord R. have Practice Alarms both quite satisfactory. 50 minutes & 40 minutes respectively. Orders for move issued to Units.	[initials]
FIENVILLERS 3-11-16	Very raw, but sunny in morning, afternoon wind Easterly. Certain units move as shown in Appendix I. Remainder training. All Ammunition except that carried on the man or pack animals despatched by lorry to 5th Army at PUCHEVILLERS	[initials]

Army Form C. 2118.

WAR DIARY
of
INTELLIGENCE SUMMARY.
18/ INFANTRY BRIGADE
(Erase heading not required.)

Instructions regarding War Diaries and Intelligence Summaries are contained in F.S. Regs., Part II. and the Staff Manual respectively. Title pages will be prepared in manuscript.

Hour, Date, Place	Summary of Events and Information	Remarks and references to Appendices
FIENVILLERS BRUCAMPS 4-11-16	A nice day, fairly sunny in the morning. NE wind. About 1 a.m. information was received that 2 sections of 3/3 F.Coy RE were to proceed by lorry from ST HILAIRE to hut building for the 3rd & 14th RFC Wings near AMIENS. The move of the Brigade to the Irish Area as shown in APP. I. Orders received from DIV leaving the Brigade of the proposed move overseas of the DIV & leaving instructions as to change of establishment etc. Baggage wagons complete returned to them	APPENDIX I. [signature] [signature]
BRUCAMPS 5-11-16	A horrible day, blowing a southerly gale with attempts at rain. All units resting, cleaning equipment, ammo etc. Three inspections in a.m. disposal of transport etc.	[signature]
BRUCAMPS 6-11-16	A nasty day with showers of rain, strong South wind. Bn Carrying out Platoon & Coy Training, RWK marching, Interior digging etc. All limbered wagons with teams complete returned to trains and fresh limbers sent temporarily.	[signature]
BRUCAMPS 7-11-16	A terrible day, very heavy rain & strong SW wind, rain cleared & wind dropped towards evening. Very little training could be done owing to the weather. Lieut Gen DUCANE CDG 15th CORPS visited Brigade in the morning. Units busy outfitting. Orders as to leave come in. 6 otto 9 O.R. per Bn. 14 otto 6 O.R. per B.G.H.Q. M.G. Coy Ft Batty from 9th - 13th Nov.	[signature]

Army Form C. 2118.

WAR DIARY
INTELLIGENCE SUMMARY.
121st Infantry Brigade
(Erase heading not required.)

Instructions regarding War Diaries and Intelligence Summaries are contained in F.S. Regs., Part II. and the Staff Manual respectively. Title pages will be prepared in manuscript.

Hour, Date, Place	Summary of Events and Information	Remarks and references to Appendices
BRUCAMPS 8-11-16	A perfectly beastly day, heavy showers of rain. Wind strong S.W. Bn training greatly interfered with. M.G Coy held combined practice with 18 guns. BRIGADIER presented MILITARY MEDAL ribbons to H/Cpl HARRISON, PICCADILLY, Pte HOCKING 2/22 L.R for gallant conduct in a raid on the GERMAN trenches on 15th OCT, near ECURIE. Officer & O.R. Shown on 7th not proceed on leave of absence to ENGLAND)	[signature]
BRUCAMPS 9-11-16	A bright cold day with practically no rain. No Wind. Brig Gen G.C. deCota and Brigade Major proceeded on leave to England. Training programme of units carried on. Lecture to representatives of Units on Small Arm registers by Divn Gas Officer. Orders to leave come in:- 1 off 1 O.R. from H.Q. 4 off 7 O.R. per Bn.; 1 off 1 O.R. per M.G. Coy. from 11th to 14th. Notification from Divn that entrainment of Division will commence on 15th not earlier than probably on 16th inst.	[signature]
BRUCAMPS 10-11-16	A bright cold day. Units continuing outfitting and training. Officers & 20.R. detailed 9-11-16 proceeded on leave of absence to England	[signature]
BRUCAMPS 11-11-16	A dull day - Some rain. Bathing of the Brigade completed - units continuing training & outfitting -	[signature]

Army Form C. 2118.

WAR DIARY
of
INTELLIGENCE SUMMARY.
1st INFANTRY BRIGADE
(Erase heading not required.)

Instructions regarding War Diaries and Intelligence Summaries are contained in F.S. Regs., Part II. and the Staff Manual respectively. Title pages will be prepared in manuscript.

Hour, Date, Place	Summary of Events and Information	Remarks and references to Appendices
BRUCAMPS 12.11.16	dull day - no training - church parades as usual - reorganisation of Div. continuing.	BMd
BRUCAMPS 13.11.16	dull but fine - training as usual - no stores issued by DADOS as the other brigades are being completed first as they entrain before us. Training continued as usual. B. Major returns from leave.	BMd
BROCAMPS 14.11.16	Fine bright day, east wind. Training continued as usual	[sig]
BRUCAMPS 15.11.16	A very fine day, very cold, east wind. Divisional General visits Bde HQRS. Normal Training	[sig]
BRUCAMPS 16.11.16	Beautiful day. Autostring frost, east wind. Divisional General visits Brigade. Brigadier returns from leave. 1st TM Batty entrains for MARSEILLES. Training as usual	[sig]

Army Form C. 2118.

WAR DIARY
of 181 INFANTRY BRIGADE.
INTELLIGENCE SUMMARY.
(Erase heading not required.)

Instructions regarding War Diaries and Intelligence Summaries are contained in F.S. Regs., Part II. and the Staff Manual respectively. Title pages will be prepared in manuscript.

Hour, Date, Place	Summary of Events and Information	Remarks and references to Appendices
BRUCAMPS 17-11-16	Brilliant Day with very cold east wind & severe frost. Training continued as usual. Pangades watched the "B" attack carried out by the 9th L.R. All outlying units completed as far as possible.	[initials]
BRUCAMPS 18-11-16	Snow in the night. Thaw and rain during the day, everything fearfully horrible. South wind. Training much interfered with. "FODEN" disinfector doing good work. Necessary removals 22 in number drawn from the REMOUNTS, ABBEVILLE.	[initials]
BRUCAMPS 19-11-16	A raw dull day. East wind. DADVS struck down at noon. Sunday. Troops take a day off. Divine Service.	[initials]
BRUCAMPS 20-11-16	Dull morning, fine afternoon, much warmer. Light S. wind. Training as usual. Orders for entrainment of portions of Bde on the 28th not received.	[initials] APPENDIX II
BRUCAMPS 21-11-16	Very cold, severe frost, foggy in the morning. Training as usual. BRIGADIER sees CAPT OWEN 2/23rd L.R. re allegations against him. Further orders for move on 28th not received.	[initials] APPENDIX II

Army Form C. 2118.

WAR DIARY

of 161st INFANTRY BRIGADE.

INTELLIGENCE SUMMARY.

(Erase heading not required.)

Instructions regarding War Diaries and Intelligence Summaries are contained in F.S. Regs., Part II. and the Staff Manual respectively. Title pages will be prepared in manuscript.

Hour, Date, Place		Summary of Events and Information	Remarks and references to Appendices
BRUCAMPS	22-11-16	A fine day though very misty in the morning, bright sun in afternoon. Units carrying out a certain amount of training mainly employed however in preparing for the move. B/G DIV GEN 2nd CAPT OWEN 2/23 LR.	*initials*
BRUCAMPS LONGPRÉ	23-11-16	A beautiful day. B'de HQ entrains at LONGPRÉ accompanied by 2/23 LR for MARSEILLES. Train leaves LONGPRÉ at 1.35 P.M. 2/21 LR leave in afternoon.	*initials*
EN ROUTE	24-11-16	Fine but foggy. Halt of 1 hour at MONTEREAU & MÂCON at 6 am & 11 PM respectively. 2/22 LR entrain at LONGPRÉ.	*initials*
EN ROUTE MARSEILLES	25-11-16	Beautiful. Halt for one hour at PIERRELATTE 11.30 am. Arrive at ARE No 1 STATION MARSEILLES at 4.35 PM. Thence 2 miles to CARCASSONE rest Camp. Horses to FOURNIER Camp 2/24 LR, 181 MG Coy 3/1/3 RE field Coy leave LONGPRÉ.	*initials*
MARSEILLES	26-11-16	Dull day. 2/21 LR arrive MARSEILLES. Troops in Camp. Both B'ns at CARCASSONE with horses at FOURNIER. 2/22 LR arrive at 6 pm march to MOUSSOT Camp. Horses to VALENTINE.	*initials*
MARSEILLES	27-11-16	Beautiful Day. 1st half 2/24 LR under MAJOR MCANALLY arrive go to MOUSSOT camp.	*initials*
MARSEILLES	28-11-16	Beautiful day. Remainder of 2/24 LR arrive at 6 pm very late go to billets in distillery near FOURNIER. 181 MG Coy to CARCASSONE B/3°Co/RE to distillery. Their train had an accident advices consequently delayed 15hours.	*initials*

Army Form C. 2118.

WAR DIARY
of 181 INFANTRY BRIGADE
INTELLIGENCE SUMMARY.
(Erase heading not required.)

Instructions regarding War Diaries and Intelligence Summaries are contained in F.S. Regs., Part II. and the Staff Manual respectively. Title pages will be prepared in manuscript.

Hour, Date, Place	Summary of Events and Information	Remarks and references to Appendices
MARSEILLES 29-11-16	Fine day. Units in camp. All orders re. embarkation received direct from BASE OFFICE by units. 9/24 L.R. 2000.	[initials]
" 30-11-16	Fine day. 9/24 L.R. embark on board S.S. IVERNIA. 3/24 L.R. at a U concentrated at No. 5 SOT Camp	[initials] APPENDIX III reference to Training Programme [initials]

[signature]
Brigadier General
C.O.G 181st Infantry Brigade

SECRET. APPENDIX I.

181st INFANTRY BRIGADE.

APPENDIX TO

W A R D I A R Y

for

NOVEMBER, 1916.

ORDERS FOR MOVE TO NEW AREA.

VOL. I. NO. 6.

----------------oOo--------------

SECRET. Copy No. 15

181st INFANTRY BRIGADE ORDER No. 29.

Reference - LENS II (1/100,000). Headquarters,
 2nd November, 1916.

1. The 60th (London) Divn. is to move westward on the 3rd inst.

2. The following units, billeted in the 181st Infantry Brigade Area, will move into fresh billets south of the BERNAVILLE - CANDAS road on that date, as under :-

Unit.	Starting Point.	Time.	Destination.	Route.
2/21 L.R.	Cross roads just W. of A in AUTHEUX.	10 a.m.	BERNEUIL.	FIENVILLERS
181 M.G.Coy.) 181 T.M.Bty.)	do.	10.10a.m.	BERNEUIL.	FIENVILLERS
3/3 Fld.Co.R.E.	do.	10.20a.m.	ST. HILAIRE.	FIENVILLERS - BERNEUIL.
2/6 Fld.Ambce.	do.	10.25a.m.	GORGES.	FIENVILLER
520 Coy.A.S.C.	Junc. of BOIS BERGUES - AUTHEUX Road.	10 a.m.	BERNAVILLE.	BOIS BERGUES direct to BERNAVILLE.

All above units, except 520 Coy.A.S.C., will move to starting point via AUTHEUX.

3. A distance of 100 yards is to be maintained between units.

4. Baggage wagons will accompany their units.

5. Billeting arrangements as shown in attached Table.

6. Troops not mentioned in above will remain in their present billets.

7. Refilling point for all units about 1 mile W. of FIENVILLERS on BERNAVILLE-FIENVILLERS Road.

8. Brigade H.Q. will remain at FIENVILLERS on 3rd inst.

9. Acknowledge.

 Captain,
 Brigade Major,
 181st Infantry Brigade.

Issued at 5 p.m. 2.11.16.

Copy No. 1. 60th Divn.
  2. 2/21 L.R.
  3. 2/22 "
  4. 2/23 "
  5. 2/24 "
  6. 181 M.G.Coy.
  7. 181 T.M.Battery.
  8. 3/3rd Field Coy.R.E.
  9. 2/6th Field Amb.
 10. 520th Coy. A.S.C.
 11. A.D.M.S.
 12. C.R.E.
 13. Staff Captain.
 14. Brigade Signal Officer.
 15. War Diary.
 16. File.

BILLETING LIST.

Date.	UNIT.	To be billeted at.	Time for billeting party.	To be at.	Remarks.
Nov. 3rd.	2/21 Lond.R.	BERNEUIL.	8 a.m.	M., 2/19 L.R. at BERNEUIL.	To get all details re billets.
	181 T.M.Battery.	BERNEUIL.	8 a.m.	do.	do.
	181 M.G.Company.	BERNEUIL.	8 a.m.	H.Q. 180 M.G.Coy. at BERNEUIL.	do.
	3/3rd Fld.Co.R.E.	ST. HILAIRE.	9 a.m.	House opposite Church.	To get all information from A/Town Major.
	Det. Divnl.Train.	BERNAVILLE.	To make their own billeting arrangements.	do.	
	2/6th Fld.Amb.	GORGES.			

SECRET.   Copy No...... 00530

181st INFANTRY BRIGADE ORDER No. 30.

Reference – LENS II   ) 1/100,000.   Headquarters,
            ABBEVILLE 14)   2nd November, 1916.

1. The 181st Infantry Brigade and attached troops will move westward on the 4th Nov. and halt for the night 4/5th Nov. as under :-

Group	Unit	Starting Pt.	Time	Destination	Route
A	2/21 L.R.	Rd. junc. ¼-mile S. of ST. HILAIRE CH.	10 a.m.	VILLERS-SOUS-AILLY.	DOMART-en-PONTHIEU - VAUCHELLES-LES-DOMART.
	181 M.G.Co) 181 T.M.By)	do.	10.10a.m.	BRUCAMPS.	DOMART-en-PONTHIEU - SURCAMPS.
	3/3rd Fld. Co. R.E.	do.	10.40a.m.	BRUCAMPS.	do.
B	181 Bde. Hd.Qrs.	Rd. junc. W. end of FIENVILLERS.	8.30a.m.	BRUCAMPS.	BERNEUIL - DOMART-en-PONTHIEU - SURCAMPS.
	2/24 L.R.	do.	8.30a.m.	MOUFLERS & VAUCHELLES-les-DOMART.	BERNEUIL - DOMART-en-PONTHIEU.
	2/22 L.R.	do.	8.38a.m.	BRUCAMPS.	BERNEUIL - DOMART-en-PONTHIEU - SURCAMPS.
	2/23 L.R.	do.	8.46a.m.	ERGNIES.	BERNEUIL - DOMART-en-PONTHIEU - GORENFLOS.
C	2/6 Fld. Ambce.	Rd. junc. at E. end of BERNEUIL.	10.10a.m.	VAUCHELLES-les-DOMART.	BERNEUIL - DOMART-en-PONTHIEU.
D	520 Coy. A.S.C.	X Rds. about 1 mile N.E. of BERNEUIL.	10 a.m.	Destination and route will be notified later.	

2. Baggage wagons will accompany their units.
3. A distance of 100 yards will be maintained between units.
4. Billeting arrangements as shown in attached Table.
5. Refilling Point – ABBEVILLE - FLIXECOURT Road, just south-east of AILLY-LE-HAUT-CLOCHER.
6. Brigade Hd.Qrs. will close at 10 a.m. at FIENVILLERS and reopen at the same hour at BRUCAMPS.
7. Acknowledge.

                                                    Captain.
                                                    Brigade Major.
Issued at 8 p.m.   181st Infantry Brigade.
Copy No. 1. 60th Divn.   9. 2/6th Field Amb.
         2. 2/21 L.R.   10. 520th Coy. A.S.C.
         3. 2/22 L.R.   11. A.D.M.S.
         4. 2/23 L.R.   12. C.R.E.
         5. 2/24 L.R.   13. Staff Captain.
         6. 181 M.G.Coy.   14. Brigade Signal Officer.
         7. 181 T.M.Battery.   15. War Diary.
         8. 3/3rd Field Coy.R.E. 16. File.

BILLETING TABLE.

Date.	Unit.	To be billeted at.	Time for billeting party.	To be at.	Remarks.
4th Nov. Oct.	Brigade H.Q.	BRUCAMPS.	9 a.m.	Church.	To meet Staff Captain or representative.
	2/21 L.R.	VILLERS-SOUS-AILLY.	9.30 a.m.	School.	do.
	2/22 L.R.	BRUCAMPS.	9 a.m.	Church.	do.
	2/23 L.R.	ERGNIES.	To make their own billeting arrangements.		
	2/24 L.R.	MOUFLERS (H.Q. & 2 Coys.) and VAUCHELLES-LES-DOMART (2 Coys.)	8.30 a.m.	Church at MOUFLERS.	To meet Staff Captain or representative.
	181 M.G.Coy.	BRUCAMPS.	9 a.m.	Church.	do.
	181 T.M.Bty.	BRUCAMPS.	9 a.m.	Church.	do.
	3/3rd Fld.Co. R.E.	BRUCAMPS.	9 a.m.	Church.	do.
	Det. Divnl. Train.	Details as to billeting arrangements will be issued later.			do.
	2/6th Fld. Ambce.	VAUCHELLES-LES-DOMART.	8.30 a.m.	Church at MOUFLERS.	do.

Water for troops and horses at VILLERS-SOUS-AILLY must be obtained from LONG.

For information

SECRET.	Copy No. 15

ADDENDA A TO
181st INFANTRY BRIGADE ORDER No. 30.

BERNEUIL and
The 520th Coy. A.S.C. on the 4th Nov. will march into billets at HOUFLERS from BERNAVILLE via DOMART-en-PONTHIEU, passing the cross roads about 1 mile N.E. of BERNEUIL at 10 a.m.

Billeting party will meet the Staff Captain or his representative at HOUFLERS CHURCH at 8.30 a.m. on 4th inst.

[signature]
Captain.
Brigade Major.

H.Q. 181 Inf.Bde.
3.11.16.

Copy No. 1. 60th Divn.	10. 520th Coy.A.S.C.
2. 2/21 L.R.	11. A.D.M.S.
3. 2/22 L.R.	12. C.R.E.
4. 2/23 L.R.	13. Staff Captain.
5. 2/24 L.R.	14. Brigade Signal Officer.
6. 181 M.G.Coy.	15. War Diary.
7. 181 T.M.Bty.	16. File.
8. 3/3rd Field Coy.R.E.	17. 60th Divnl.Train.
9. 2/6th Field Ambulance.

SECRET.

ADDENDA B TO
181st INFANTRY BRIGADE ORDER No. 30.

The order of march of Units marching under the orders of 181st Infantry Brigade on the 4th Nov. is as under:-

    2/21 Lond.R.
    181 M.G.Coy.
    181 T.M.Battery.
    H.Q. 181 Inf.Bde.
    2/24 Lond.R.
    2/22 Lond.R.
    2/23 Lond.R.
    3/3rd Field Coy., R.E.
    2/6th Field Amb.
    520th Coy. A.S.C.

[signature]

Captain.
Brigade Major.

H.Q. 181 Inf.Bde.
3.11.18.

S E C R E T.   APPENDIX II.
———————   ———————————

                        181st   INFANTRY BRIGADE.
                        ———————————————————————————

                           APPENDIX II TO

                        W A R   D I A R Y
                               for
                           NOVEMBER, 1916.
                        ————————————————————

                   ORDERS FOR ENTRAINMENT FOR MARSEILLES.
                        ON 23rd & 24th Nov/16.

                        ————————————

                           VOL. I.   NO. 6.

                  ---------------------oOo-------------------

SECRET.

G.S.104.

O.C. 2/21 Lond.R.   2/6th Field Amb.
    2/22   "   "   No.4 Sec. Div.Sig.Co.
    2/23   "   "   Staff Captain.
    2/24   "   "   War Diary.
    181 M.G.Coy.   File.
    2/3rd Field Co.R.E.   Divn.

  Units of the Brigade will entrain on the 23rd November, 1916 in accordance with attached Schedule "A" and Programme of Entrainment.

  Acknowledge.

                 Captain.
                Brigade Major.

H.Q. 181 Inf.Bde.
21.11.16.

SECRET.

O.C. 2/21 Lond.R.	2/6th Field Amb.
2/22 " "	No.4 Sec.Div.Sig.Coy.
2/23 " "	Staff Captain.
2/24 " "	War Diary.
181 M.G.Coy.	File.
3/3rd Field Coy.R.E.	

C.B.104/1.

The following is the forecast of moves on the 24th and 25th November, 1916:-

24th November.

No. 1 and 3 S.A.A. Sec. Amn.Col.
2/6 Field Ambulance.
H.Q. Div.R.A.
60th San. Sect.
Div.H.Q. (less det.)
Det. Div.Train.
2/22 Lond.R.
No. 4 Sec. Div. Sig. Co.

25th November.

3/3 Field Coy.R.E.
181 M.G.Coy.
2/24 Lond.R.
Rem. Divnl. Train.
Div. H.Q.
Rem. Div. Sig. Co. (det).

H.Q. 181 Inf.Bde.
21.11.16.

Captain.
Brigade Major.

SECRET.

Copy No.........

Ref.Map: LENS, Sheet 11.
AMIENS, Sheet 17.
ABBEVILLE, Sheet 14. 1/100,000.

PROGRAMME OF ENTRAINING.

23rd November, 1916.

UNIT.	STARTING POINT.	TIME OF STARTING.	ROUTE TO ENTRAINING STATION.	ENTRAINING STATION.	TIME DUE AT STATION.	TIME OF DEPARTURE OF TRAIN.
H.Q. 181 Inf.Bde.	Cross Roads, BRUCAMPS.	5.20 a.m.	VAUCHELLES les DOMART - LA FOLIE - L'ETOILE - CONDE.	LONGPRE	7.27 a.m.	10.27 a.m.
2/23 Lond.R.	Cross Roads, ERGNIES.	5.30 a.m.	AILLY-ONC-LE CARDIOT.	"	"	"
Y.60 & Z.60 T.M.Batteries.	Cross Roads just W. of E of PONT REMY.	5.30 a.m.	LIERCOURT - FONTAINE.	"	"	"
2/21 Lond.R.	Cross Roads, VILLERS-SOUS-AILLY.	12.40 p.m.	LONG-LE CARDIOT.	"	2.27 p.m.	5.27 p.m.
1st.Mob.Vet.Sec.	Cross Roads, AILLY LE HAUT CLOCHER.	12.30 p.m.	"	"	"	"

SECRET.

Copy No........

Schedule "A".

TABLE OF PERSONNEL, ANIMALS and VEHICLES
proceeding on 23rd November, 1916.

No. of Train.	Type of Train.	Time of Departure.	UNIT.	Officers.	Other Ranks.	Animals.	Vehicles. 4.W.	Vehicles. 2.W.
29.	Special X	10.27 a.m.	H.Q. 181 Inf.Bde. 2/23 Lond.R. Y.60 & 2.60 T.M.Btys.	8 39 .	40 958 46	21 24	– – –	– – –
30.	T.C.	2.17 p.m.	One Bty. 303 R..... Bde. Det.Div.Train.	5 4	140 100	155 49	1 –	26 15
31.	Special ∅	5.27 p.m.	2/21 Lond.R. 60 Mob.Vet.Sec.	39.	958 15	24 20	– –	– –

Types of Trains.   T.C.   = Type Combatent, composed of
                   Special X = composed of
                   Special ∅ = composed of

	1st Class.	Covered Trucks.	Flat Trucks.
	1	33	14
	2	44	2 Brake Vans.
	2	42	2 Brake Vans.

SECRET.

G.S.104/2.

O.C. 2/22 Lond.R.   2/6th Field Amb.
    2/24   "   "   Staff Captain.
    181 M.G.Coy.   War Diary.
    2/3rd Field Co.R.E.   File.
    No. 4 Sec. Div. Sig. Coy.

    Units of the Brigade will entrain on the 24th November, 1916 in accordance with attached Schedule "A" and Programme of Entrainment.

    Acknowledge.

                                        Captain.
                                  Brigade Major.

H.Q. 181 Inf.Bde.
    22.11.16.

SECRET.

SECRET.

PROGRAMME OF ENTRAINMENT

24th November, 1916.

Ref.Map: IMS, Sheet 11.
AMIENS, Sheet 17.
ABBEVILLE Sheet 14. 1/100,000.

UNIT.	Starting Point.	Time of Starting.	Route to Entraining Station.	Entraining Station.	Time due at Station.	Time of Departure of train.
2/22 Lond.R.	Crossroads BRUCAMPS.	5.20 a.m.	VAUCHELLES-les-DOMART - LA FOLIE - L'ETOILE - CONDÉ.	LONGPRE	7.27 a.m.	10.27 a.m.
No.4 Sec.Div. Sig.Coy.	"	5.25 a.m.	"	"	"	"
Div.H.Q.	Crossroads AILLY-EN-HAUT-CLOCHER.	9.20 a.m.	LONG - IN CAMELS.	"	11.17 a.m.	2.17 p.m.
60 San.Sect.	"	9.20 a.m.	"	"	"	"
Det.2/6 Fld.Amb.	LA FOLIE Crossroads.	10.15 a.m.	L'ETOILE - CONDÉ.	"	"	"
Det.Div.Train.	(To be arranged by O.C. Divnl. Train).					"
No.1 S.A.A. Sec. Amm. Column.	Crossroads S.W. of BUCHENCOURT.	12 noon.	WIRYCOURT - CONDÉ.	"	2.27 p.m.	5.27 p.m.
No.3 S.A.A. Sec. Amm. Column.	Road junction just W. of BEHEN sur SOMME.	11.40 a.m.	BOUDON - HANGEST - CONDÉ.	"	"	"
Det.2/6 Fld.Amb.	LA FOLIE Crossroads.	1.0 p.m.	L'ETOILE - CONDÉ.	"	"	"
D.Q. Div.A...	Road junction S. of AILLY-LE-HAUT-CLO-CHER.	12.40 p.m.	LONG - IN CAMELS.	"	"	"

SCHEDULE "A".

TABLE OF PERSONNEL, ANIMALS and VEHICLES.

Proceeding on the 24th November, 1916.

No. of Train.	Type of Train.	Time of departure.	Unit.	Officers.	Other Ranks.	Animals.	Vehicles 4 W.	Vehicles 2 W.
32	Special	10.27 a.m.	2/22 Bond.I.T.	39	958	24	-	-
			No. 4 Sec.Div.Sig.Co.	1	27	10	-	1
33	T.C.	2.17 p.m.	60 San. Sect.	1	29	9	-	4
			Div.H.Q.	7	137	77	1	8
			Det. 2/6 Field Ambce.	2	40	25	-	-
			Det. Div. Train.	4	200	40	8	12
34	Special	5.27 p.m.	No. 1 S.A.A. Sec.Am.	3	255	25	-	-
			Column.					
			No. 3 S.A.A. Sec.Am.	5	255	25	-	-
			Column.					
			Det. 2/6 Field Ambce.	9	369	42	-	-
			H.Q., Div. F.A.	2	4	-	-	-

Types of Trains. T.C. = Type Combatant, composed of   1st Class. Covered Trucks. Flat Trucks.
                                                           1   35   14
                  Special = Composed of   1   47   -

SECRET.   APPENDIX III

181st INFANTRY BRIGADE.

APPENDIX III TO
W A R   D I A R Y
For
NOVEMBER, 1916.

PROGRAMMES OF TRAINING.

VOL. I.   NO. 6.

---------------oOo---------------

O.C. 2/21 Lond.R.
     2/22 " "
     2/23 " "
     2/24 " "

INSTRUCTIONS REGARDING TRAINING.
Issued in connection with 60th Divn.
No. S.G./391 dated 21.10.16.

1.   The uncertainty as regards the time and facilities available make it impossible to lay down a definite programme.
    Commanding Officers must make the best use of the facilities existing near their Billets in drawing up their daily programme. It is often possible to find old trenches etc. near Billets which can be utilised.

2.   The following are the principal objects to which training should be directed; special attention being paid to the developement of the platoon system:-

(a) <u>MAKING THE MEN FIT</u>. Physical exercises and running drill.
    ($\frac{1}{2}$-hour immediately after reveille.)
    Route marching. 4 to 5 miles daily, the best hour probably being immediately before dinner.
    Games, as taught in the Gymnastic Schools, for a $\frac{1}{4}$-hour at the commencement of the afternoon parade are useful to warm them up and induce cheerfulness.

(b) <u>STIFFENING UP DISCIPLINE</u>.
    Close Order Drill - One Drill at least to be carried out daily.
    Arms Drill.
    Saluting.
    Attention to minutiae of Dress and Routine.

(c) <u>CULTIVATION OF OFFENSIVE SPIRIT</u>.
    Bayonet Fighting.
    Attack Practice.
    Lectures.

    All the above can be carried out near billets without any special arrangements for ground or paraphernalia.
    Digging, Rapid wiring, practice with live bombs and Rapid Loading with dummy cartridges will be carried out as facilities are available.

3.   A Programme for the following day should be issued by Commanding Officers in sufficient time to allow Company Officers and N.C.Os. to prepare for the next day's work.
    A suggested time-table is attached, but this should be varied according to circumstances. The following principles should, however, be followed.

(a) Drills should not be of more than $\frac{3}{4}$-hour duration.
(b) The Programme should be varied.
(c) Men should <u>NOT</u> be inspected before the early morning (Physical Training) Parade, and should turn out without coats or puttees. A clear two hours should be allowed before the main Morning Parade for Breakfast, clearing up &c.

4.   The technical training of specialists will be carried out under special arrangements; but the need for their tactical training with their Companies must not be lost sight of.

5.   Every officer and, if possible, every N.C.O. should secure sufficient instruction in the Lewis Gun to enable him to fire it on emergency.

(signed) J.N.HORWICK.
Captain.
Brigade Major.

H.Q. 181 Inf.Bde.
22.10.16.

SUGGESTED DAILY TIME TABLE.

6.15 a.m.	-	Reveille.
6.30 to 7.0.	-	Physical Training and Running Drill.
7 a.m.	-	Breakfast.
7.0 to 9.0 a.m.	-	Cleaning up, Sick Parade, Orderly Room, etc.
9.0 to 10.30 a.m.	-	Parades. (2 parades of ¾-hour each).
10.30 to 11.0 a.m.	-	Stand Easy.
11.0 to 12.30 p.m.	-	Parades.
12.45 p.m.	-	Dinners.
2.0 p.m. to 3.30 p.m.	-	Parades.
4.15 p.m.	-	Teas.
5.30 p.m. to 6.15 p.m.	-	Lectures.
9.0 p.m.	-	Lights out.

-----------oOo-----------

O.C. 2/21 Lond.R.
    2/22 " "
    2/23 " "
    2/24 " "
    181 M.G.Coy.
    181 T.M.Bty.
H.Q. 60th Divn. "G". on 10.11.16.

    Platoon and Company Training will be continued during the ensuing week on the lines indicated in this office No. G.346 and 346/1.

    Special attention will be paid to the development of the habit of command in Section Leaders.

    In addition to the above, the following will be arranged:-

    1. One Parade (1½ hours) will be devoted by Companies to Outpost Drill.

    The organisation of an Outpost Company, Piequets, Sentry Groups etc. will be practiced in detail. The importance of economy of energy, based on a sound system, will be emphasised.

    2. Battalions will carry out a Practice Attack from Trenches on the days allotted below.

    The Schemes should be explained to Company Officers on the ground on the day preceding the practice.

Thursday morning (16th)	-	2/23 London R.
Thursday afternoon "	-	2/22 " "
Friday morning (17th)	-	2/24 " "
Saturday morning (18th)	-	2/21 " "

                                          Captain.
                                      Brigade Major.

H.Q. 181 Inf.Bde.
8.11.16.

Headquarters,
   60th (London) Divn. "G".

　　　　Reference your S.G.421 of the 4th inst.

　　　　The proposed training for the week commencing Sunday 5th Nov. will consist of platoon and Company training on the lines indicated in the attached instructions issued to units from this office. The Time-Table contained therein is not intended to be strictly observed but is merely for the guidance of Commanding Officers.

　　　　A great point has been made of the developement of the powers of command of subordinate leaders, especially section commanders, and for the necessity of steady drill.

　　　　　　　　　　　　　　　　Brig.-General.
　　　　　　　　　　　　Cmdng. 181st Infantry Brigade.

4.11.16.

NOTE:- Physical Training will, in future, be carried out after breakfast instead of as shown in the Time-Table. Troops will be taken for a sharp walk before breakfast.

www.ingramcontent.com/pod-product-compliance
Lightning Source LLC
Chambersburg PA
CBHW080914230426
43667CB00015B/2681